STUDIES IN ENGLISH LITERATURE

Volume LV

THE ASSOCIATION OF IDEAS AND CRITICAL THEORY IN EIGHTEENTH-CENTURY ENGLAND

A History of a Psychological Method in English Criticism

by

MARTIN KALLICH
Northern Illinois University, DeKalb

1970

MOUTON
THE HAGUE · PARIS

LIBRARY OF CONGRESS CATALOG CARD NUMBER: 79-110951

Printed in The Netherlands by Mouton & Co., Printers, The Hague.

PREFACE

The psychology known as "the association of ideas" has often been mentioned in studies in the history of ideas, taste, and criticism in eighteenth-century English literature. It has been dealt with in discussions of several important focal concepts in critical thought: genius and the imagination, the sublime and the picturesque, the idea of progress, and standards of taste. It has also been considered of some moment in the criticism of Shakespeare, and in specialized studies of such figures as Hobbes, Locke, Addison, Kames, Gerard, and Erasmus Darwin; and, of course, its influence on Wordsworth and Coleridge has been assayed more than once.

The significance of this psychology with respect to criticism is clearly acknowledged. But because emphasis is placed elsewhere, the association of ideas has always been treated as incidental to some other purpose and its real significance effectually minimized. As a result, there has never been a comprehensive overview of the relationship between this psychology and criticism and neoclassic and romantic modes of thought; it has not been clearly understood, nor has a genuine estimate of its impact on critical theory been carefully made. The following essay, an attempt to fill this gap in scholarship, has the sole purpose of describing and synthesizing the details of associationist criticism in eighteenth-century England from its beginnings with Hobbes and Locke to the peak of its development with Alison and Wordsworth.

Portions of this work have been published in several journals: on Hobbes, Locke, and Addison in *English Literary*

History, XII (1945), 290-315; on Hutcheson and Hume in *Studies in Philology*, XLIII (1946), 644-67; on Akenside in *Modern Language Notes*, LXII (1947), 166-73; on Alison in *Philological Quarterly*, XXVII (1948), 314-24; on Burke and Reid in *Modern Language Quarterly*, XV (1954), 125-36. I am grateful to the editors of these journals for granting me permission to reprint these sections and to incorporate them in the text. A related study of Samuel Johnson, not included in this essay, may be seen in *Modern Language Notes*, LXIX (1954), 170-76.

This history was undertaken and completed many years ago – many more than I care to remember – under the guidance of Raymond D. Havens at Johns Hopkins University. Nothing that I can now do can ever repay my debt to the late Professor Havens, for at a critical time in my life he gave me the opportunity to demonstrate my ability and thereby to initiate my career as a teacher and scholar. All that I can do at present is to indicate that I remember RDH and my debt to him, and to hope that this work will in some small way suggest my gratitude. Finally, I must mention my wife who loyally and unstintingly helped with moral support in the trying early years of marriage and career-making when this book was being written.

M. K. Northern Illinois University

CONTENTS

I

DEFINITION

To the intelligent lay mind of the mid-eighteenth century, the term *association of ideas* usually meant *connection of ideas.* Such a definition, probably acceptable to almost everyone at the time, is found in Johnson's *Dictionary* (1755) together with an illustrative sentence by Watts: "Association of ideas is of great importance, and may be of excellent use." [1] Although the illustration is unhappily chosen, yet indirectly it suggests the respectable position of the association psychology in Johnson's estimation. This definition, however, fails to indicate the nature of complex behavior of ideas in the mind and suggests nothing about the existence of principles of association, nothing, that is to say, about the ways in which these ideas may be connected or associated in the mind. Hence a sounder and more adequate description is that in Ephraim Chambers' *Cyclopaedia* (1727), since here the nature of the connection in the mind and the controlling principles are both defined: "Association *of Ideas*, is where two or more ideas, constantly and immediately follow or succeed one another in the mind, so that the one shall almost infallibly produce the other; whether there be any natural relation between them, or not." [2] It is significant that Chambers describes two types of association, the one that is based on a "natural relation" or "real affinity",

[1] Cf. Hume, *A Treatise of Human Nature* (1739), Pt. I, Sec. iv, "Of the Connexion or Association of Ideas". – *An Enquiry Concerning Human Understanding* (1748), Sec. iii, "Of the Connexions of Ideas". In the 1750 edition "connexions" becomes singular; thereafter it becomes "association".

[2] I use the fourth edition, London, 1741.

and the other that is based on an unnatural relation, so to speak, or on a chance or accidental association. He recognizes, thus, the rational as well as the irrational effects of association upon the mind, although he devotes much space in the article to a repetition of Locke's views on the psychopathic effects of "unnatural" and irrational associations.

Where there is a real affinity or connection in ideas, it is the excellency of the mind, to be able to collect, compare, and range them in order, in its enquiries: but where there is none, nor any cause to be assigned for their accompanying each other, but what is owing to mere accident or habit; this unnatural *association* becomes a great imperfection, and is, generally speaking, a main cause of error, or wrong deductions in reasoning. . . . [B]ut some loose and independent ideas are by education, custom, and the constant din of their party, so coupled in their minds, that they always appear there together: these they can no more separate in their thoughts, than if they were but one idea, and they operate as if they were so.

This description was acceptable to the Scottish philosophers at Edinburgh and was borrowed almost without verbal change for the brief definition in their *Encyclopaedia Britannica* (1771). [3]

To the intelligent reader of the eighteenth century, then, association was synonymous with connection, and the special type of mental activity known as the association or connection of ideas was understood to occur when ideas are so joined in the mind that one idea almost invariably is succeeded by those which in some way are attracted to it. Furthermore, the attraction (to use Hume's word) between ideas is of two sorts, natural or unnatural. Ideas may naturally associate in the sense that they have an objective or "real affinity": they must have, we may infer, one or more qualities in common; they may be *like* (ferocity of lion and tiger) or *unlike* (lion and lamb), or they may be related as *cause* is to *effect* (sword and blood). On the other hand, ideas unnaturally associate in the sense that they have logically nothing in

[3] The reader is also referred to an article on "Metaphysics", which, being merely an abridged reprint of *The Essay Concerning Human Understanding,* repeats Locke's analysis of the corrupting influences of association.

common and have been thrown together by accident or chance (lion and zoo). They are, we may say, merely *contiguous* to each other. In either case, natural or unnatural, rational or irrational, the underlying subjective characteristic of an association of ideas remains constant: when one idea or quality is perceived or experienced, it immediately calls to mind or suggests others to which it is in some manner related.

The philosophers and critics in the eighteenth century consistently employ these two types of the association of ideas in the mind in order to explain the way in which the mind or human nature is prone to act.

Locke uses only one principle of association, contiguity, and has emphasized only its irrational effects on the mind; Hartley, however, uses the same principle as the basis of all habits and customs, good as well as bad, and of the rational processes. It is Hartley's interpretation that is accepted today as representative of the "Principle (or the Doctrine) of the Association of Ideas". In the first half of the century, Hutcheson clearly uses this interpretation:

> We may observe a natural involuntary determination to associate or bind together all such perceptions as have often occurred together, or have made at once a strong impression on the mind, so that they shall still attend each other, when any object afterwards excites any one or more of them.[4]

And in 1794 Walter Whiter expresses the same and what may now be called the modern opinion. He specifically rejects an interpretation of the association of ideas that was given by the Scottish critics and metaphysicians from Hume to Alison.

> By the *associating principle* I do not mean (as it appears to be understood by some metaphysicians) that faculty of the understanding, by which, on all occasions, the chain of our ideas is generated and preserved; nor, as referred to the genius of the poet, do I mean that active power, which passes rapidly through a variety of successive images, which discovers with so wonderful an acuteness their relation

[4] *A System of Moral Philosophy* (London, 1755), I, 30. This book was written between 1733 and 1737.

and dependencies; and which combines them with such exquisite effect in all the pleasing forms of fiction and invention. In this indefinite and unlimited sense, the *association of Ideas,* when applied to the general operations of the mind, expresses little less than the whole arrangement of the reasoning principle, and as referred to the workings of imagination must signify all the embellishments of eloquence, and all the graces of poetry.

He selects Locke as the source of his definition; and it is this definition that he so cleverly uses in studying Shakespeare's unconscious imaginative processes.

In the theory of Mr. Locke, by the term *association* is *not* understood the combination of ideas *naturally* connected with each other; for these (as he observes) "it is the office and the excellency of our reason to form and preserve in that union and correspondence, which is founded on their peculiar beings." On the contrary, it is understood to express the combination of those ideas, which have *no* natural alliance or relation to each other, but which have been united only by chance, or by custom. Now it is observable that no task can be imposed on the understanding, of greater difficulty than to separate ideas thus accidentally combined; as the mind is commonly passive in admitting their original formation, and often totally unconscious of the force and principle of their union. . . . I define therefore the power of this *association* over the genius of the poet, to consist in supplying him with words and with ideas, which have been suggested to the mind by a principle of union unperceived by himself, and independent of the subject, to which they are applied.[5]

The total eighteenth-century picture, however, must not be distorted by an unhistorical application of modern standards or by a deliberate neglect of another interpretation. It should be remembered that in the eighteenth century "natural" principles of association other than the principle of casual contiguity were equally acceptable to many critics and philosophers. For explanations and analyses of these natural associations of ideas, Hobbes and Hume are responsible, although both, it must be admitted, also write about the influence of contiguity upon the mind. Because Hume's influence upon associationist critics was of paramount importance, it will be useful to present his account

[5] *A Specimen of A Commentary on Shakespeare* (London, 1794), pp. 64-5, 68.

of these natural laws of association controlling the movement of ideas in our minds.[6]

Hume regards association as "a gentle force" which automatically unites simple ideas separately perceived and which also regulates the ideas in the imagination. "Were ideas entirely loose and unconnected, chance alone wou'd join them"; consequently, as there cannot be order when things are controlled by chance, the result is chaos. To avert confusion, nature provides that the proper simple ideas will be united in a complex one; and this it does through several associative laws:

The qualities, from which this association arises, and by which the mind is after this manner convey'd from one idea to another, are three, *viz.* Resemblance, Contiguity in time or place, and Cause and Effect. I believe it will not be very necessary to prove, that these qualities produce an association among ideas, and upon the appearance of one idea naturally introduce another. 'Tis plain, that in the course of our thinking, and in the constant revolution of our ideas, our imagination runs easily from one idea to any other that *resembles* it, and that this quality alone is to the fancy a sufficient bond and association. 'Tis likewise evident, that as the senses, in changing their objects, are necessitated to change them regularly, and take them as they lie *contiguous* to each other, the imagination must by long custom acquire the same method of thinking, and run along the parts of space and time in conceiving its objects. . . .
Of the three relations above-mention'd this of causation is the most extensive. Two objects may be consider'd as plac'd in this relation, as well when one is the cause of any of the actions or motions of the other, as when the former is the cause of the existence of the latter. For as that action or motion is nothing but the object itself, consider'd in a certain light, and as the object continues the same in all its different situations, 'tis easy to imagine how such an influence of objects upon one another may connect them in the imagination.[7]

This discussion is to be found in *A Treatise of Human Nature* (1739); but in the later *Enquiry Concerning Human Understanding* (1748) Hume briefly illustrates each of the laws:

[6] A discussion of Hume's views appears below, pp. 73-95.

[7] *The Philosophical Works of David Hume,* ed. Green and Grose (London, 1874), I, 319-20.

A picture naturally leads our thoughts to the original (resemblance): The mention of one apartment in a building naturally introduces an enquiry or discourse concerning the others (contiguity): And if we think of a wound, we can scarcely forbear reflecting on the pain which follows it (cause and effect).

In a footnote he also adds another general law of association, contrast or contrariety, which "may, perhaps, be considered as a mixture of Causation and Resemblance".[8]

By and large, therefore, two types of movement descriptive of the ways in which ideas are related to or succeed each other in the mind were agreed upon by the eighteenth-century philosophers and critics in the associationist tradition: (1) casual, or chance, or unnatural associations, according to contiguity in time and place; and (2) more regular, or natural associations, according to resemblance, contrariety, and causality. Locke, Gay, Hartley, Priestley, Whiter, and Wordsworth, Coleridge, and, no doubt, every critic in the nineteenth century accepted (or rejected) only the first. But, on the other hand, Hobbes, Hume, Kames, Gerard, Beattie, and Alison accept not only the first but also the second. Locke presumes that the process by which ideas, formerly dormant in the memory, are awakened into novel, unnatural, and irrational connections, is a cause of error. His view influenced Hutcheson and persisted until it was modified by the Reverend John Gay and David Hartley. With Gay and Hartley this type of association became the basis of all mental activity, of morality and of taste. But Hobbes and Hume believe that the mind functions normally and naturally by means of other principles of associations as well. Observing that ideas fall into association in regular and consistent order in addition to chance order, they thereby are able to deduce such governing laws as resemblance, contrariety, and causality. Thus were "discovered", as Hume boasted, the "natural" laws of association regulating the flow of linked ideas in the imagination. Since these laws are expressive of order and unity, they become highly significant, as will be seen, for

[8] *Ibid.*, IV, 18 and 18n.

the associationist reinterpretation by Kames, Beattie, and Alison, of neoclassic criticism and taste.

Even Aristotle, as Coleridge has noticed, has isolated three or four laws of association, contiguity in time and proximity in place, resemblance, and contrast. [9] But of this source the eighteenth-century writers were generally unaware. Nor did they refer to Hobbes for their associationism. They preferred to trace the beginnings of association to Locke, who is unconcerned about the natural and orderly type of subjective associations, and to Hume. [10]

From Hobbes and Locke to Alison and Wordsworth, there were thinkers and critics who believed that principles of art must be founded on principles of human nature, or, to be more precise, that critical doctrines and standards of taste must be interpreted according to the accepted mental science of the period – the operations of the mind known as the association

[9] Sir William Hamilton, *The Works of Thomas Reid* (Edinburgh, 1872), II, 890: "In England, indeed, we have a chapter in Mr. Coleridge's 'Biographia Literaria' entitled, *On the Law of Association – its history traced from Aristotle to Hartley*; but this, in so far as it is of any value, is a plagiarism, and a blundering plagiarism, from Maass."

[10] I know of only two exceptions. The learned and scholarly James Harris distinguishes between memory, recollection, and imagination and refers to the source *Parva Naturalia* ("On Memory and Recollection"), where Aristotle analyzes the association of ideas. See *Hermes, or a Philosophical Inquiry concerning Universal Grammar* [1751] in *The Works of James Harris* (London, 1803), II, 355-7n. Beattie also observes [*Dissertations Moral and Critical* (Dublin, 1783), I, 11, 175] that the theory of association is not peculiar to "modern" philosophy: "The doctrine is not peculiar to modern philosophy. Aristotle, speaking of Recollection, or active remembrance, insinuates, with his usual brevity, that the relations, by which we are led from one thought to another, in tracing out, or *hunting out* (as he calls it) any particular thought which does not immediately occur, are chiefly three, *Resemblance, Contrariety,* and *Contiguity*. And this enumeration of the associating principles does not differ, in any thing material, from what is here given. I reduced them to five, *Resemblance, Contrariety, Nearness of Situation, the relation of Cause and Effect, and Custom or Habit*. Now the three last may very well be referred to that one which Aristotle calls *Contiguity*." For Aristotle's remarks see W. A. Hammond, *Aristotle's Psychology* (London, 1902), pp. 203-8. References to Hobbes's psychology in the eighteenth century are noted below, p. 17, fn. 1. It may be said that Aristotle first described the association of ideas but that Locke first used the term in English.

of ideas. The meaning of this term is here outlined at the expense of details. These details are now in order: they are conclusive proof of the extent to which the theory of association, beginning with Hobbes and Locke, affected the literary mind and permeated theories of criticism and taste in England during the eighteenth century.

II

THE BEGINNINGS: HOBBES AND LOCKE

In England the first important speculation upon the theory of the association of ideas can be traced to Hobbes and Locke. In 1783 a reviewer of Beattie's *Dissertations Moral and Critical* needed no acumen to remark that the association of ideas served as the basis of many contemporary theories of criticism; but he showed some originality in correcting a fallacy which credited only Locke with fathering the psychology:

> It is but justice to the memory of a great philosopher and very original thinker of the last age to observe, that this doctrine, which is commonly considered as having been proposed by Mr. Locke, is to be found illustrated with great ingenuity in the philosophical writings of Hobbes.[1]

To Hobbes we must therefore turn for the first important English statement on association and for its first important application to criticism.

[1] *Monthly Review,* LXIX (1783), 32. Thomas Reid also notes that the theory of association is suggested in Hobbes's works [*Essays on the Intellectual Powers of Man* (1785) in *The Works of Thomas Reid,* ed. Sir William Hamilton (Edinburgh, 1872), I, 386a]: "I shall now make a few reflections upon a theory which has been applied to account for this successive train of thought in the mind. It was hinted by Mr. Hobbes, but has drawn more attention since it was distinctly explained by Mr. Hume." Priestley has the common notion and assigns to Locke the honor of having first observed the fact of association. See, for example, his *Hartley's Theory of the Human Mind, on the Principle of the Association of Ideas* [1775] (London, 1790), p. xxv: "The mechanical association of ideas that have been frequently presented to the mind at the same time was, I believe, first noticed by Mr. Locke."

At the base of Hobbes's theory of association is the premise that motion determines all mental activity. Single images are formed by the outward motion of the senses counteracting the pressure of external objects moving towards the brain. This outward motion causes the apparent effect of fancying or imaging. "The nature of sense consists in motion", writes Hobbes in the *Elements of Philosophy.* [2] And when the object is removed from the senses, its image is retained in the imagination, which, Hobbes maintains, is only another name for memory. [3] This image is but the "relic" of motion outwards; it is "decaying sense". Now, it is these decaying or weak images of sense, retained in the imagination, that move together in connected trains or sequences of thought. There are, thus, but two motions in Hobbes's philosophy: the first produces independent or separate ideas of sense; the second produces thought sequences in which the formerly separate ideas become dependent upon one another. "For besides sense, and thoughts, and the train of thoughts, the mind of man has no other motion." [4]

The connections between the dependent ideas in a train are not casual; they are determined by relations established by the original sensation. Or, as Hobbes says, the train of imaginations is governed by connections or "transitions" already in the imagination, which (acting as memory) retains the order of the sense perceptions: "But as we have no imagination, whereof we have not formerly had sense, in whole, or in part; so we have no transition from one imagination to another, whereof we never had the like before in our senses." [5] This is nothing but the law of contiguity in space or time. In *Human*

[2] IV, xxv (I, 394), "Sense is a phantasm, made by the reaction and endeavour outwards in the organ of sense, caused by an endeavour inwards from the object, remaining for some time more or less". *Ibid.,* (I, 391). See also *Leviathan,* I, i (III,1-2). All references in parentheses are to volume and page and all references before the parentheses are to the special divisions of that volume in *The English Works of Thomas Hobbes of Malmesbury,* ed. Molesworth (London, 1839-45). The works used are *Human Nature* (1640), *Leviathan* (1651), and *Elements of Philosophy* (1655).

[3] *Lev.,* I, ii (III, 4-6); *Hum. Nat.,* iii (IV, 9); *Ele. of Philo.,* IV, xxxv (I, 396).

[4] *Lev.,* I, iii (III, 16).

[5] *Ibid.,* (III, 11).

Nature, the train of ideas in accordance with the principle of contiguity is more obvious:

The cause of the coherence or consequence of one conception to another, is their first coherence or consequence at that time when they are produced by sense: as for example, from St. Andrews the mind runneth to St. Peter, because their names are read together. . . and according to this example, the mind may run almost from anything to anything.[6]

Hobbes, however, also admits that associations occur in dreams, where ideas freely succeed one another with no apparent law. This train of ideas in dreams is unguided; the imagination wanders:

The. . . [train] is unguided, without design, and inconstant; wherein there is no passionate thought, to govern and direct those that follow, to itself, as the end and scope of some desire or other passion: in which case the thoughts are said to wander, and seem impertinent one to another, as in a dream. . . . And yet in this wild ranging of the mind, a man may oft-times perceive the way of it, and the dependence of one thought upon another.[7]

Hobbes describes an additional principle or bond of association that is favorable to coherence. A guided train of ideas, he declares, is directed by passion to some end; and the imagination is apparently guided towards this end by logical transitions of cause and effect. This order of ideas is obviously unlike that in dreams, where there is "disorder and casual consequence of one conception or image to another". On the contrary, "when we are waking, the antecendent thought or conception introduceth, and is cause of the consequent, as the water followeth a man's finger upon a dry and level table; but in dreams there is commonly no coherence." Again, this causal chain of ideas is explicit in *Human Nature:*

But as in the sense the conception of cause and effect may succeed one another; so may they after sense in the imagination. . . the cause whereof is the appetite of them, who, having a conception of the end,

[6] *Hum. Nat.,* ch. iv (IV, 15).
[7] *Lev.,* I, iii (III, 12).

have next unto it a conception of the next means to that end: as, when a man, from a thought of honour to which he hath an appetite, cometh to the thought of wisdom, which is the next means thereunto; and from thence to the thought of study, which is the next means to wisdom.[8]

Moreover, after summing up the discussion of unregulated and regulated trains of thought in *Human Nature,* Hobbes also calls the coherent succession of ideas *discursion.*

The succession of conceptions in the mind, series or consequence of one after another, may be casual and incoherent, as in dreams for the most part; and it may be orderly, as when the former thought introduceth the latter; and this is discourse of the mind. But because the word discourse is commonly taken for the coherence and consequence of words, I will, to avoid equivocation, call it discursion.[9]

There are, then, two general types of movement among the ideas in the imagination. These are the casual or random trains of ideas in dreams and the guided and regulated trains of ideas in discursion and coherent thought. Now, as Hobbes continues making his categories, there are two types of regulated trains of thought: remembrance and invention, each corresponding to a principle of association. Remembrance depends solely upon contiguity or the place and the time in which objects are perceived. That is to say, it is an act of memory by which stored ideas are recalled according to associative transitions, identifiable as contiguity but called simply place and time by Hobbes.

Sometimes a man seeks what he hath lost; and from that place, and time, wherein he misses it, his mind runs back, from place to place, and time to time, to find where, and when he had it; that is to say, to find some certain, and limited time and place, in which to begin a method of seeking. Again, from thence, his thoughts run over the same places and times, to find what action, or other occasion might make him lose it. This we call remembrance, or calling to mind: the Latins call it *reminiscentia,* as it were a *re-conning* of our former actions.[10]

[8] *Hum. Nat.,* iii, iv (IV, 10-11, 15). The description of random succession of ideas in dreams is also found in *Elements of Philosophy,* IV, xxv (I, 399-400).

[9] *Hum. Nat.,* iv (IV, 14f.).

[10] *Lev.,* I, iii (III, 14).

This activity is compared to that of "a spaniel [that] ranges the field, till he find a scent; or [to that of] a man [who] should run over the alphabet, to start a rhyme".[11]

Invention, however, is not controlled by the spatial or temporal relations of the original perception; it arranges ideas itself in accordance with cause and effect transitions. To be more explicit, this "train of regulated thoughts" operates by arranging causes for imagined effects, or vice versa, by studying effects in order to ascertain causes: "when of an effect imagined we seek the causes, or means that produce it . . . . [and] when imagining any thing whatsoever, we seek all the possible effects, that can by it be produced; that is to say, we imagine what we can do with it, when we have it." In both cases, the mind *seeks* or *invents* an orderly succession of ideas.

In sum, the discourse of the mind, when it is governed by design, is nothing but seeking, or the faculty of invention, which the Latins call *sagacitas,* and *solertia*; a hunting out of the causes, of some effect, present or past; or of the effects, of some present or past cause.[12]

Another class of guided, coherent thought is listed in *Human Nature*. This is ranging, which, in the *Leviathan,* had been subordinated to remembrance: Hobbes there likened it to "a spaniel [that] ranges the field". But in the earlier-composed *Human Nature*, ranging apparently describes the activity of mind midway between direction forwards and direction backwards to some definite end. Ranging can begin anywhere within a series of ideas; its activity, almost haphazard, almost unguided, lacks the direction of emotion. Examples of ranging occur when "a man casteth his eye upon the ground, to look about for some small thing lost; the hounds casting about a fault in hunting; and the ranging of spaniels". The transitions in this type of train are apparently neither governed by any clear law nor directed to any specific end. If for nothing else, this train of ideas is important in that it provided Dryden with a splendid figure, used to such excellent effect in the Preface to *Annus*

11 *Ibid.*

12 *Lev.*, I, iii (III, 13-4).

Mirabilis (1667).[13] In *Human Nature,* furthermore, Hobbes also expresses more clearly than in *Leviathan* the emotional direction of invention and remembrance. Invention is said to occur "when the appetite giveth a man his beginning . . . where honour to which a man hath appetite, maketh him think upon the next means of attaining it, and that again of the next, etc." Remembrance, however, is the succession "beginning with the appetite to recover something lost, proceeding from the present backward, from thought of the place where we miss at, to the thought of the place from whence we came last." [14]

There are, we have noticed, three possible ways in which the ideas in the imagination can be regulated: these are the order of original perception or contiguity in time and in place, and the dependent relations of cause and effect or means to ends. In addition to these connections between thoughts in a train, Hobbes now suggests a fourth, resemblance, which describes the ease and speed that ideas are connected in the mind and, as we shall see, is the source of the "wild" imagination. In the *Leviathan,* for example, Hobbes notes four ways of examining ideas in succession: these are "like one another, or in what they be unlike, or what they serve for, or how they serve to such a purpose". The first, resemblance, produces fancy; the second, perhaps contrast, produces judgment. The third and the fourth, although unelaborated, are no doubt means to ends or fitness, which has already been mentioned. [15]

[13] This figure occurs twice in Dryden's criticism. Ker, *Essays of John Dryden* (Oxford, 1900), I, 8, 14: – *Epistle Dedicatory of the Rival Ladies* (1664): "For imagination in a poet is a faculty so wild and lawless, that like an high-ranging spaniel, it must have clogs [rhymes] tied to it, lest it outrun the judgment." Preface to *Annus Mirabilis:* "The composition of all poems is, or ought to be, of wit; and wit in the poet, or *Wit writing,* (if you will give me leave to use a school distinction), is no other than the faculty of imagination in the writer, which, like a nimble spaniel, beats over and ranges through the field of memory till it springs the quarry it hunted after; or, without metaphor, which searches over all the memory for the species or ideas of those things which it designs to represent."

[14] *Hum. Nat.,* iv (IV, 15-6).

[15] *Lev.,* I, viii (III, 57). Only this sentence appears on fitness: "There is required also an often application of his thoughts to their end; that is to say, to some use to be made of them."

A good fancy is one that produces original resemblances or similitudes. "Those that observe their similitudes, in case they be such as are but rarely observed by others, are said to have a *good wit*; by which, in this occasion, is meant a *good fancy*."[16] "He that observes readily the likenesses of things of different natures, or that are very remote from one another, is said to have a good fancy."[17] In *Human Nature* this original fancy accounts for figures of speech and is clearly connected with the processes of art:

> The contrary hereunto [of dulness], is that quick ranging of mind described in Chapter iv, section 3, which is joined with curiosity of comparing the things that come into the mind, one with another: in which comparison, a man delighteth himself . . . with finding unexpected *similitude* of things, otherwise much unlike, in which men place the excellency of *fancy*, and from whence proceed those grateful similies, metaphors, and other tropes, by which both poets and orators have it in their power to make things please or displease, and shew well or ill to others, as they like themselves. . . .[18]

Wit also means judgment, however, when it dissociates and discerns differences or "dissimilitude in things" apparently alike. It is exactly the opposite faculty from that of the fancy, which associates by means of resemblances. "But they that observe differences, and dissimilitudes; which is called *distinguishing*, and *discerning*, and *judging* between thing and thing; in case such discerning be not easy, are said to have a good judgment."[19] Because fancy is not commended for itself, it must be constantly watched and checked by judgment: "The former, that is, fancy, without the help of judgment, is not commended as a virtue: but the latter, which is judgment, and discretion, is commended for itself, without the help of fancy."[20]

16 *Ibid.*

17 *Ele. of Philo.*, IV, xxv (I, 399).

18 *Hum. Nat.*, x (IV, 55).

19 *Lev.*, I, viii (III, 57). Cf. *Ele. of Philo.*, IV, xxv (I, 399): "So he is said to have a good judgment, that finds out the unlikenesses or differences of things that are like one another." *Human Nature,* x, (IV, 55-6), does not add much that is different.

20 *Lev., loc. cit.*

And so, he who has the ability to use his fancy can adorn his discourse with "apt metaphors" and rare inventions. A danger constantly present, however, is that the exuberant fancy will approach madness and run amok with countless resemblances and digressions. Thus Hobbes must needs use the judgment in order to see that only the proper images are associated by the fancy. Judgment and fancy are therefore equally necessary for art: the one checks on the unity and propriety of the other's resemblances or figures.

In a good poem, whether it be epic, or dramatic, as also in sonnets, epigrams, and other pieces, both judgment and fancy are required: but the fancy must be more eminent; because they please for the extravagancy; but ought not to displease by indiscretion.[21]

Thus, according to Hobbes's psychology, the total man is supposed to function when "inventing" an orderly work of art, which is, in substance, only an orderly succession of ideas. Appetite (passion), judgment, and fancy must all contribute their share, Hobbes implies in *Elements of Philosophy*, to the assembling of coherent and controlled associations that are taken from the large store of fading ideas in the memory:

For the thought or phantasm of the desired end *brings in* all the phantasms, that are means conducing to that end, and that in order backwards from the last to the first, and again forwards from the beginning to the end. But this supposeth both appetite and judgment to discern what means conduce to the end, which is gotten by experience; and experience is store of phantasms, arising from the sense of very many things.[22]

[21] *Lev.*, I, viii, (III, 58).

[22] *Ele. of Philo.*, IV, xxv (I, 398). Cf. *Lev.*, I, ii (III, 6): "Much memory, or memory of many things, is called experience"; and *Answer to Davenant, post,* p. 28: "Experience begets memory." Bolingbroke seems to have borrowed a leaf from Hobbes in his *Essay Concerning the Extent and Reality of Human Knowledge* (1754) [*The Works of Henry St. John* (Dublin, 1793), III, 447]: "What is the juxta-position of ideas? What is that chain which connects, by intermediate ideas, that are links of it, ideas that are remote, but figurative stile? What else are those dormant, that is, sleeping pictures, which are wakened as it were, and brought into appearance by an act of the mind? what else are the pictures drawn there, but laid in fading colors?"

It is important to remember the close resemblance of this statement to Hobbes's critical testament in the *Answer to Davenant,* where judgment assembles and controls the associations of the poet's fancy – fancy, that is to say, is "guided by the Precepts of true Philosophy".

In the course of his examination of natural wit, Hobbes emphasizes the importance of speed in making and arranging associations. Wit is judged by the rapidity in which associations are made. Natural wit consists in "celerity of imagining" and "steady direction to some approved end", [23] while dullness or stupidity signifies "slowness of motion", or "a slow imagination". This difference in the rate in which images succeed each other in the imagination is caused, Hobbes suggests, by differences in emotions:

And this difference of quickness, is caused by the difference of men's passions; that love and dislike, some one thing, some another: and therefore some men's thoughts run one way, some another; and are held to, and observe differently the things that pass through their imagination.[24]

And these differences proceed from differences in custom or education and the physical condition of the body.

The causes of this difference of wits, are in the passions; and the difference of passions proceedeth, partly from the different constitution of the body, and partly from different education. . . . It proceeds therefore from the passions, which are different, not only from the difference of men's complexions; but also from their difference of customs, and education.[25]

[23] *Lev.,* I, viii (III, 56); *Hum. Nat.,* x (IV, 56). Previously he defines wit, which is of two sorts, natural and acquired *(Lev., loc. cit.)*: "By natural, I mean not, that which a man hath from his birth; for that is nothing else but sense; wherein men differ so little one from another, and from brute beasts, as it is not to be reckoned amongst virtues. But I mean that wit which is gotten by use only, and experience; without method, culture, or instruction."

[24] *Lev.,* I, viii (III, 57).

[25] *Lev.,* I, viii (III, 61). There are four driving emotions or passions – power, riches, knowledge, honor – which direct the thoughts to different goals or objectives. With his customary realism, Hobbes would reduce all these to the first, "desire of power". Cf. also *Hum. Nat.,* x (IV, 54).

Here, diversity, arising first from custom and education and the several passions, is immediately caused by the relative ease and speed with which the imagination associates images. As a uniformitarian and neoclassicist, Hobbes tries to limit the extremes of this subjective diversity. As we noted before, the fancy cannot be too quickly associative for it may run wild; therefore, it must constantly be curbed by the judgment. Such a conservative and neoclassic writer in the associationist tradition as Gerard follows Hobbes in this respect; but other associationists like Alison late in the eighteenth century cultivated a freely rambling imagination and emphasized those diversitarian aspects that helped undermine the rules and the methods of the ancients.

Up to this point in our analysis of Hobbes's use and explanation of the theory of association, we notice that the laws of association are already clearly defined. The terminology is not always the same, but obviously the meaning is in agreement with the usage of later writers. For association of ideas, Hobbes uses succession of ideas, train of imaginations, or discursion. Coherent, regular successions of ideas are primarily directed by passion; also, several connections or links, of which some will be translated later into laws of association, unite separate ideas in the mind, and are known as time and place, cause and effect (antecedent and consequent, means to ends), and lastly, resemblance.[26] Finally, Hobbes be-

[26] Thorpe correctly makes *cohesion* the equivalent of contiguity in time and place; see *The Aesthetic Theory of Thomas Hobbes* (Ann Arbor, 1940), p. 91. *Elements of Philosophy,* IV, xxv (I, 397-8): "Now it is not without cause, nor so casual a thing as many perhaps think it, that phantasms in this their great variety proceed from one another; and that the same phantasms sometimes bring into the mind other phantasms like themselves, and at other times extremely unlike. *For in the motion of any continued body, one part follows another by cohesion*; and therefore, whilst we turn our eyes and other organs successively to many objects, the motion which was made by every one of them remaining, the phantasms are renewed as often as any one of those motions comes to be predominant above the rest; and they become predominant in the same order in which at any time formerly they were generated by sense. So that when by length of time very many phantasms have been generated within us by sense, then almost any thought may arise from any other thought; inso-

lieves that the regulated train of ideas with definite design in view is the product of invention. And as invention uses ideas long in the memory and is unaffected by original contiguity, it connects ideas by the principle of cause and effect or means to ends.

Furthermore, we have seen that Hobbes's philosophy admits the need in art for fancy's similitudes or associated ideas in conjunction with judgment's correcting discretion. This resembling fancy is an active power and must be distinguished from the passive fancy (memory) which merely stores up the ideas of the senses; but both memory and fancy nevertheless function in accordance with the laws of association. Therefore, only in relation to the theory of association of ideas can their use in the notable passage on judgment and fancy in the *Answer to Davenant* (1650) be correctly evaluated. As applied to thoughts, ideas, and images, dependent upon or united with one another, and moving in the mind according to certain and clearly defined types of association, Hobbes's theory of motion supplies the philosophic gloss for the text. This passage, so rich in meaning, sums up every important idea in his associative system.[27]

The quotation that describes fancy's manner of functioning is long; but because it illustrates Hobbes's exceptional awareness of the literary uses of his theory of associated ideas, it can be quoted without distortion only in its entirety.

In the text, it will be observed that judgment examines and registers the images in memory's storehouse according to several types of connections, "order [logical order of reason?], causes, uses, differences [contrasts], and resemblances". The motion of the good fancy is determined, for it travels quickly and widely in the memory and among the copious materials or images already pre-arranged there by the judgment, that is (as he writes

---

much that it may seem to be a thing indifferent and casual, which thought shall follow which."

[27] It is surprising to find that in his accurate analysis of this passage Thorpe overlooks the patterns of association. (*Op. cit.*, pp. 107-8.) Hobbes's use of the "laws of association" is noted by R. L. Brett, "The Third Earl of Shaftesbury as a Literary Critic", *MLR*, XXXVII (1942), 134.

in the next sentence), "discreetly ordered & perfectly registered in the memory".

Time and Education beget experience; Experience begets memory; Memory begets Judgement and Fancy: Judgement begets the strength and structure, and Fancy begets the ornaments of a Poem. The Ancients therefore fabled not absurdly in making memory the Mother of the Muses. For memory is the World (though not really, yet so as in a looking glass) in which the Judgement, the severer Sister, busieth her self in a grave and rigid examination of all the parts of Nature, and in registering by Letters their order, causes, uses, differences, and resemblances; Whereby the Fancy, when any work of art is to be performed, findes her materials at hand and prepared for use, and needs no more than a swift motion over them, that what she wants, and is there to be had, may not lie too long unespied.

In this mechanical way, the quick fancy is enabled, without much trouble and without going wild, to beget the necessary ornaments of a poem from the memory. Furthermore, the "philosophy" mentioned by Hobbes may be only the mechanist system of rational and orderly motion and connection, so thoroughly explained in his philosophical treatises, *Human Nature, Leviathan*, and *Elements of Philosophy*. Fancy thus follows the ways of this philosophy, the paths of reason and judgment, or, as Hobbes writes, fancy "has traced the ways of true Philosophy".

So that when she seemeth to fly from one Indies to the other, and from Heaven to Earth, and to penetrate into the hardest matter and obscurest places, into the future and into her self, and all this in a point of time, the voyage is not very great, her self being all she seeks; and her wonderful celerity consisteth not so much in motion as in copious Imagery discreetly ordered & perfectly registered in the memory, which most men under the name of Philosophy have a glimpse of, and is pretended to by many that, grosly mistaking her, embrace contention in her place. But so far forth as the Fancy of man has traced the ways of true Philosophy, so far it hath produced very marvellous effects to the benefit of mankinde. All that is beautiful or defensible in building, or marvellous in Engines and Instruments of motion, whatsoever commodity men receive from the observations of the Heavens, from the description of the Earth, from the account of Time, from walking on the Seas, and whatsoever distinguisheth the civility of Europe from the Barbarity of the American savages, is the workmanship of Fancy but guided by the Precepts of true Philosophy.

According to Hobbes, fancy not only uses resemblance (as he had before explained), but other principles of association or connection as well. Thus it is capable of invention (anticipating Gerard's discussion of the associative and inventive imagination), previously described by Hobbes as regulated and coherent trains of thoughts governed by unifying design and cause and effect. And so the creative artist is an inventor and may be considered as one who is both the fanciful poet and the rational philosopher, for he exhibits two powers while he invents a regular sequence of imaginations, in this case, a heroic poem: the poetic power or fancy enables him "to place & connect" the ornaments, which is half of the "matter"; while the philosophic power or judgment enables him "to furnish and square" these images or ornaments in terms of the moral end desired, the other half of the "matter". The "matter" of the poem consists, therefore, in the "body and Soul" [design, end, structure], and "colour and shadow" [ornament, expression, figures, tropes, etc.]. And, finally, to round out the idea, the "matter", or design and ornaments, is ultimately dependent upon memory's "Store" of ideas.

But where these precepts fail, as they have hitherto failed in the doctrine of Moral vertue, there the architect, Fancy, must take the Philosophers part upon her self. He therefore that undertakes an Heroick Poem, which is to exhibite a venerable & amiable Image of Heroick vertue, must not only be the Poet, to place & connect, but also the Philosopher, to furnish and square his matter, that is, to make both Body and Soul, colour and shadow of his Poem out of his own Store: Which how well you have performed I am now considering.[28]

[28] J. E. Spingarn, *Critical Essays of the Seventeenth Century* (Oxford, 1908), II, 59-60. In the later *Vertues of an Heroique Poem* (1675) Hobbes's account of fancy is not so complex. Although it gives the superficial explanation of the imagination flying "abroad swiftly to fetch in both Matter and Words" under the control of judgment, this account is not inconsistent with his previous analyses. See Spingarn, II, 67, 70.

Hobbes is the first important writer to apply the association psychology to English critical theory. The importance of understanding this psychology has been demonstrated by Bond and Thorpe. But neither has tried to indicate exactly how Hobbes's theory of the imagination and of the creative processes becomes so closely related to the theory of association.[29] Indeed, as we have tried to prove, the association of ideas provides the psychological basis for the collaboration of fancy and judgment. According to Hobbes, the judgment has two functions: it checks the overly hasty activity of the fancy when it operates in the memory only in accordance with the principle of resemblance; and it also provides in the rational principle of cause and effect a path in the materials of memory for coherent imaginative invention. Hobbes, unlike Hume, does not discard the memory; on the contrary, the memory is the source of ideas and the place where the fancy fishes for them – but not without license, for, as we have said, it must heed the laws by which ideas in the memory are associated. And these laws are pointed out by the policing judgment. This, in sum, is how Hobbes's psychology of association is applied to critical theory. Without un-

[29] D. F. Bond, "Neoclassical Psychology of the Imagination", *ELH*, IV (1937), 245-64; C. D. Thorpe, *The Aesthetic Theory of Thomas Hobbes* (Ann Arbor, 1940), pp. 90-6. Two comments on association are made by Bond (p. 258): "Of even greater importance for literary criticism is Hobbes's interest in the combinatory powers of the imagination – not merely so much its ability to form compound images (the centaur, the golden mountain, etc.) but to function freely in what was later to be called the association of ideas. Hobbes displays a lively interest in the freedom of the imagination to associate ideas in a 'Trayne of Thoughts' and to supply wit with its quickness in tracing resemblances." Neither Hobbes nor Locke thought that association helped the imagination compound images; this is Hume's contribution. Bond is therefore guilty of anachronism. Furthermore, as we have tried to show, the train of ideas not only is composed of free or purposeless or contiguous associations, as in dreams and recollection, but is also under the control of other laws of association, such as resemblance and causality; and the function of judgment is to see that the fancy employs ideas in accordance with these laws. Bond adds nothing to this comment by way of further illustration or exegesis, except for the concluding remark (p. 264): "Thanks to both Hobbes and Locke its associative powers were to be studied more intently and sympathetically."

derstanding this psychology first, Hobbes's theory of the imagination cannot be properly understood.

In the eighteenth century, Locke's *Essay Concerning Human Understanding* (1690) received far more careful study than any of Hobbes's works. And insofar as the history of the association of ideas in criticism during the eighteenth century is concerned, Locke's influence was of supreme importance up to the time of Hume's *Treatise* (1739) and *Enquiry* (1748) and persisted, in modified form, throughout the course of the century in Burke and the Scottish critics.

It was almost as an afterthought that Locke added the chapter "Of the Association of Ideas" to the fourth edition of his *Essay* (1700).[30] In this chapter, association is analyzed as an unusual activity of the mind prejudicial to understanding and akin to madness. Locke seems to have been ignorant of Hobbes's favorable analysis. On the face of it, such is the inference to be derived from Locke's letter to Molyneux (April 26, 1695), in which he informs his friend of the addition "on the connection of ideas, which has not that I know been hitherto considered, and has, I guess, a greater influence upon our minds than is usually taken notice of". But Locke may be considered original, for perhaps no one from Aristotle to Hobbes had examined association only as a weakness of the mind and as a hindrance to right thinking.

As Locke writes, the association of ideas "hinders men from seeing and examining".[31] All his examples illustrate how association mars the quality of our ideas and makes them unfit for the determination of knowledge. Madness is also traced to these wrong connections of ideas. It must be noted, however, that Locke appears to recognize the existence of valid connections, which he calls *natural*; that is to say, natural associations of ideas agree with rational relations of things, and unnatural associations with irrational and accidental relations. "Some of our ideas have a natural correspondence and connexion one

[30] The edition of A. C. Fraser (Oxford, 1894) is used.
[31] *Essay*, II, xxxiii, 18.

with another: it is the office and excellency of our reason to trace these, and hold them together in that union and correspondence which is founded in their peculiar beings." [32] However, no more is said here of these natural associations. [33] Locke prefers to expatiate upon the irrational, unnatural trains of ideas, "ideas in themselves loose and independent of one another".

Besides this, there is another connexion of ideas wholly owing to *chance* or *custom*: Ideas that in themselves are not all of kin, come to be so united in some men's minds, that it is very hard to separate them; they always keep in company, and the one no sooner at any time comes into the understanding, but its associate appears with it; and if they are more than two which are thus united, the whole gang, always inseparable, show themselves together.[34]

Custom, which is only the continued succession of associated ideas, produces habits. Habits maintain the erroneous association; they are "but trains of motion in the animal spirits, which, once set a going, continue in the same steps they have been used to; which, by often treading, are worn into a smooth path, and the motion in it becomes easy, and as it were natural."[35] This habitual "tying together of ideas" is, however, contrary to nature and reason. The connections come in time to be accepted as natural (or, as we now say, "second-nature") only after long and repeated use, so that their erroneous and accidental origin escapes analysis. Most of our sympathies and antipathies are thought to be natural while they are really attributable to false associations. Sometimes, Locke qualifies without illustrating, our antipathies "are truly natural, depend upon our original constitution, and are born with us." [36] Here, Locke has made the distinction between original, natural physical condition – the senses are meant – and later acquired and accidental as-

[32] II, xxxiii, 5.
[33] But Locke does, of course, write of these rational and natural relations or modes (as contrasted with gradually generated irrational connections) in parts of Book II and Book IV. He does not, however, consider them as the subjective mental phenomenon known as the "association of ideas".
[34] II, xxxiii, 5, 9.
[35] II, xxxiii, 6.
[36] II, xxxiii, 7.

sociation. It is just this distinction that Burke later borrows in his argument against association. Burke even follows Locke in suggesting that natural (sensuous) sources of taste are very often confused with acquired sources, because when the associations occur very early in life, they appear to be the natural outgrowth of fundamental likes and dislikes.[37] But Burke adds to his sources in Locke the thought that associations differ while the senses remain the same in all men. Locke suggests only the thought that diversity is the result of varying associations among men with varying tempers, educations, and interests; he says nothing of the uniformity of the senses: "This strong combination of ideas, not allied by nature, the mind makes in itself either voluntarily or by chance; and hence it comes in different men to be very different, according to their different inclinations, education, interests, etc." [38] Each of us may have different associations in our minds with the same thing: this is the subjective and relativist aspect of associationism. And if this aspect of associationism were stressed, the widest diversity could be allowed in the standards of taste.

The support given by the subjectivism implicit in the theory of association to the diversitarian or relativist point of view was recognized and disapproved by those writers who followed Locke closely, Hutcheson and Burke. But upon the modification of Locke's associationist opinions by Gay and Hartley and Hume, associationist diversity began to be approved by many other writers, among whom may be mentioned Shenstone,

[37] *Ibid.*; see *post,* pp. 141-2. for Burke's remarks. In his analysis of the terror and sublimity of darkness, Burke takes issue with Locke by noting that Locke's association of sprites and goblins with darkness at an early age does not adequately explain why darkness is terrible. Burke would rather explain the terrible nature of darkness through the associated idea of danger. See Burke, *Enquiry* (London, 1780), IV, xiv, 273-4. Locke's words on this association are as follows [*Essay,* II, xxxiii, 10]: "The ideas of goblins and sprites have really no more to do with darkness than light: yet let but a foolish maid inculcate these often on the mind of a child, and raise them there together, possibly he shall never be able to separate them again so long as he lives, but darkness shall ever afterwards bring with it those frightful ideas, and they shall be so joined, that he can no more bear the one than the other."

[38] *Essay,* II, xxxiii, 6.

Hartley himself, Priestley, Beattie, and Alison. Although Hobbes also explains how diverse standards are produced by the diversity of associational effects and principles, Locke's views may be considered as the chief source of the associationist arguments pressed in favor of this romantic tendency. But in neither of these early philosophers is there any recognition of the effect of differing associations upon taste or criticism. They supply only the germ of an idea which was, throughout the eighteenth century, constantly to undermine the belief in static, objective, and uniform standards of criticism.

While Hobbes regarded the association of ideas as a natural phenomenon of the mind and as a requisite for coherent expression, invention, and imagining, Locke, on the other hand, regarded it as an irrational source of error. While Hobbes believed that fancy operates through well-defined transitions and connections between ideas moving in the mind, Locke merely made the conventional assertion that fancy and wit are extravagant without relating the association of ideas to their operation.[39] Thus Hobbes's analysis of the regular and guided movement of associated ideas looks forward to the further development of the concept by Hume, Kames, Gerard, Beattie, and Alison during and after the middle of the eighteenth century. In all these Scottish writers the association psychology superseded the methods of the Stagirite, although, it must be admitted, the psychology only reinforced neoclassic rules of criticism and standards of taste. Locke's distrust and disparagement of association influenced Hutcheson and Burke; but his analysis of the associational processes had a great positive influence upon Berkeley and Hartley, and innumerable others. We shall now proceed to trace the use of this concept in the critical theory of the eighteenth century.

[39] That Locke has nowhere analyzed fancy and judgment in accordance with association of ideas is also noted by Bond, "Neoclassical Psychology of the Imagination", *ELH*, IV (1937), 263.

III

FROM DENNIS TO HUTCHESON

It was not long after the theory of associated ideas was promulgated in the philosophic works of Hobbes and Locke that it found a place in the works of literary critics. Dryden vaguely and perhaps playfully mentions Hobbes's version, but of its potentialities for criticism he is generally unaware. Dennis, on the other hand, seriously exploits the concept of association for his theory of the sublime and poetic emotions, and far more completely than other writers of the first decade realizes the significance of the modern mental science for esthetic responses. Dennis, however, does not include the term in his vocabulary. Berkeley, concerned with the psychological problem of vision, resorts to the association of two senses, sight and touch, for its solution, and as we shall see in the next chapter, anticipates Hume in the extension of the association principle. Berkeley is also important for supplying Burke with a few associationist ideas. It is not until Addison and Hutcheson discuss differences in taste in accordance with the association of ideas that the doctrine really comes into its own as a focal concept in critical theory. The opinions of these two influential men and their application of the contemporary Lockian version of associationist psychology to taste, in conjunction with the sympathetic accounts by popular Isaac Watts, defined associationism for readers of the first quarter of the century and also set forth the pattern of associationist conceptions of art which many critics were later to follow.

It should be remembered that two analyses, by Hobbes and Locke, of the principle of association were available to writers after 1700. Hobbes thought of ideas in associated or linked chains which were regulated by the laws of original perception in time and place (contiguity), cause and effect, and resemblance. But Locke believed that connections between ideas in the mind are often made by chance, and that constant repetition makes these chance connections or associations habitual. Judgment, he added, must separate the improperly associated ideas. These two versions of associationism are clearly described by Addison; and he alone in this period impartially employs both Hobbes and Locke. Other writers more or less use only the second or Lockian expression of association. James Arbuckle, for example, describes how habits are formed:

In this last Case one Image of this sort [in a Train of Images] never appears without its whole Retinue; and if a straggling one, in its progress thro' the Brain, chances to strike any of this Chain, all the others will appear, and chime to the last link. These sorts of Chains are what we call Habits; and Temper and Passions strengthen them, and they in grateful return strengthen the Temper and Passions.

[Conduct] proceeds from a fortuitous Concourse of Images, which I call Caprice; or from a Chain of Images link'd together by Chance, which form Custom or Habit.

From their early Infancy they have been inured to the former [customs]; they have associated to them Ideas of Dignity, Beauty, and Convenience, and sometimes of Sanctity and Religion.[1]

Arbuckle's friend, Francis Hutcheson, is the chief exponent of this point of view in taste and criticism.

In the criticism at the turn of the seventeenth century few explicit applications of the association of ideas to literary critical problems were made. Although there is no doubt that the beliefs of Hobbes and Locke thoroughly pervaded the intellectual milieu of the time, yet few references to the psychological theory can be found in the criticism of the well known

1 *Hibernicus's Letters* (London, 1734), II, 188, 189-90 (No. 76, Sept. 10, 1726), II, 304 (No. 89, Dec. 10, 1726). Cf. also II, 191 (No. 77, Sept. 17, 1726): "And what is Education, for the most part, but stocking a Child's Brain with Chains of Images?"

writers. Dryden merely refers to the Hobbesian sequence of continuous ideas while pursuing a train of thought in his informal *Preface to the Fables* (1700).

In the mean time, to follow the thread of my discourse (as thoughts, according to Mr. Hobbes, have always some connexion,) so from Chaucer I was led to think of Boccace, who was not only his contemporary, but also pursued the same studies.[2]

Thus Dryden superficially indicates his awareness of the psychology of association. He is evidently unaware of its potentialities for literature and does not use the doctrine for literary purposes in a manner more seriously than this. Instead, like Blackmore, Dryden turned to logic to objectively explain dramatic unity of action; the term he used, "cause and effect", is interesting only because Hume later used it as a law of subjective association that might explain unity of action. Unconsciously, therefore, Dryden perhaps contributed a small share to associationist criticism. For example, in his *Epistle Dedicatory of the Rival Ladies* (1664), he described the structure of the play and the difficulties of verisimilitude. Asserting that the stage can hardly be more exact than life itself, he deduced that the dramatist must be allowed a margin of error in his difficult task of plotting naturally; so

that when the whole plot is laid open, the spectators may rest satisfied that every cause was powerful enough to produce the effect it had; and that the whole chain of them was with such due order linked together, that the first accident would naturally beget the second, till they all rendered the conclusion necessary.[3]

[2] W. P. Ker, *Essays of John Dryden* (Oxford, 1900), II, 248.

[3] Ker, I, 2; cf. *An Essay of Dramatic Poesy* (1668), I, 60: The French "do not embarrass, or cumber themselves with too much plot; they only represent so much of a story as will constitute one whole and great action sufficient for a play; we, who undertake more, do but multiply adventures; which, not being produced from one another, as effects from causes, but barely following, constitute many actions in the drama, and consequently make it many plays." Blackmore, *Preface to King Arthur* (1695) in Spingarn, *Critical Essays of the Seventeenth Century* (Oxford,

Dennis is perhaps the first to rely upon the doctrine of associated ideas for the explanation of special esthetic problems. But, again, as with Dryden, there is only a suggestion of the theory; and if it is felt that his views on the sublime were only accidentally associationist, it must also be remembered that they exerted some influence upon later writers who were consciously associationist and in whose critical systems the theory of association was of central importance. If only for this fact, we must include Dennis among the associationist critics.

In Dennis's criticism there are a few loci where the psychology of Hobbes and Locke appears. But while in these places the language of Hobbes on fancy and judgment is parroted, there is no suggestion in his discussion of an operation of mind according to associating ideas. For example, in his earliest critical preface (1692), Dennis points out that "no sort of imagery can be the Language of Grief". Grief constricts the mind and fixes it upon a single object; therefore figures of speech would be entirely unnatural because they show the mind in motion. This idea is not new; Dryden, the Earl of Mulgrave, Boileau, Rapin, Blackmore, and Trapp all objected to simile in the language of passion. [4] Dennis grounds his objection on Hobbes's psychology:

For to be in a capacity to make a good similitude, the mind must have several qualifications and two more particularly; which are utterly inconsistent with that Passion. First, The Soul must be susceptible of a great many Idea's, and the Imagination capacious of a great many Images. For the Fancy can start a hint from them, which may carry

1908), III, 237: "That which makes the Unity of the Action is the regular Succession of one Part or Episode to another, not only as Antecedents and Consequents, but as it were Causes and Effects, wherein the Reader may discern that the former Episode makes the following necessary; and the Connection between them is such that they assist and support each other as the Members of the Body do, no Episode being out of its place."

[4] Cf. *The Critical Works of John Dennis*, ed. E. N. Hooker (Baltimore, 1939-43), I, 424; Blackmore, *Essays upon Several Subjects* (London, 1716), I, 83; Trapp, *Lectures on Poetry* [1711] (London, 1742), pp. 138-9.

with it that appearance of likeness, which may afterward by the Judgment be improved to an exact resemblance (not but that I know very well, that the Soul on those occasions acts with that prodigious Celerity, that it is its self insensible of the degrees of its own motion).[5]

Here Dennis is certainly echoing *The Answer to Davenant* (1650), wherein Hobbes describes the roles of fancy, judgment, and memory. However, Hobbes's conception of swift, inventive fancy, operating through the associative laws of the mind, is not to be found in Dennis.

Another close resemblance to Hobbes's (and Dryden's) metaphorical description of the ranging memory is in Dennis's analysis of invention (1729). Hobbes and Dryden use a figure taken from hunting; Dennis takes one from hawking.

For Memory may be justly compar'd to the Dog that beats the Field, or the Wood, and that starts the Game; Imagination to the Falcon that clips it upon its Pinions after it; and Judgment to the Falconer, who directs the Flight, and who governs the whole.[6]

This is reminiscent of Hobbes's concept of ranging memory and fancy controlled by association; but, like Dryden's metaphorical description, it suggests little of the way the associationist mind functions, and so suffers from vagueness. Again, in his arguments against rhyme in the larger poetic forms and the drama (1704), Dennis seems to borrow directly from Locke's chapter on the association of ideas. The popular taste for rhyme is false and its persistence can only be accounted for, Dennis thinks, by "the Prevalence of Prejudice, and the Force of Custom. They who read poetry, have been us'd to rime

[5] "Preface to the *Passion of Byblis*", Hooker, I, 2. In his "Essay at a Vindication of the Love-Verses of Cowley and Waller" [*Miscellaneous Letters and Essays* (London, 1694), pp. 217-9], Gildon takes issue with this psychology that Dennis employs. Gildon quotes from Locke (*Essay*, II, i, 11) and Le Clerk on the constant succession of ideas in our minds in order to support his view that similes are natural even in heats of passion or states of pain.

[6] "Remarks upon the *Dunciad*", Hooker, II, 363.

from their Infancy; and what cannot long Habitude render agreeable?"[7] The decay of this unnatural taste for rhyme is confidently predicted by Dennis; the false custom cannot endure, and by 1750, he continues, it will be broken by the influence of Milton and tragic blank verse. Indeed, this explanation of popular taste is reminiscent of Locke's analysis of the difficulty in both recognizing and avoiding unnatural and false associations that have become habitual.

More than once, then, especially in connection with simile, invention, and rhyme, Dennis comes close to the theory; but he never really satisfies us by definitely mentioning it. But while it is not possible to arrive at safe conclusions about Dennis's debts to the associationism of Locke or Hobbes, yet we can agree to a general psychological influence that led critics of the time to explore for themselves the mysteries of the mind and to apply their results to an analysis of literary effects. [8] Clearly, such is the case with Dennis, for he is an original thinker independently using philosophic concepts that were at the time new and fashionable and that could perhaps best explain the mysteries of criticism or taste. In particular, Dennis's originality is found in an analysis of the sublime; and it is not surprising to find that in dealing with the sublime effects of objects upon the mind of the subject Dennis again approaches the association psychology.

With Dennis the sublime is the poetic passion *par excellence*; in theorizing over this emotional concept, he faintly suggests associationism. Moreover, his attempts at explaining sublimity in poetry with reference to the enthusiastic emotions take on added interest in that we know that Wordsworth himself owed something to Dennis's critical acumen, and perhaps found

7 "Preface to *Britannia Trimphans*", Hooker, I, 378.

8 Cf. H. G. Paul, *John Dennis, His Life and Criticism* (New York, 1911), p. 131 and *passim;* S. H. Monk, *The Sublime* (New York, 1935), pp. 45-54; C. D. Thorpe, *The Aesthetic Theory of Thomas Hobbes* (Ann Arbor, 1940), pp. 221-59; E. N. Hooker, *The Critical Works of John Dennis* (Baltimore, 1939-43), Vol. II, "Introduction".

foreshadowings of his own views on the way the mind associates ideas in times of poetic excitement. Further suggestions of associationism in Dennis's criticism occur in two of his most important essays, *The Advancement and Reformation of Modern Poetry* (1701) and *The Grounds of Criticism in Poetry* (1704).

In the *Advancement* Dennis tries to explain poetry almost entirely by reference to passion. "Passion is the principal Thing in Poetry", he writes; and he comes to believe that "Poetry is Poetry, because it is more Passionate and Sensual than Prose." [9] Laying such emphasis upon the strong emotions, Dennis is led to state the difference between ordinary and enthusiastic passion.

> I call that ordinary Passion, whose Cause, is clearly comprehended by him who feels it, whether it be Admiration, Terror, or Joy; and I call the very same Passions Enthusiasms, when their Cause is not clearly comprehended by him who feels them.[10]

The difference, then, between common and poetic emotion is one of degree and depth of feeling. The latter is deeper and greater than the former because its "Cause is not clearly comprehended", or, in short, because the poetic feeling is aroused by secret and irrational operations of mind. These operations suggest the presence of the association psychology, for, as Dennis continues, some ideas, thoughts, and images, especially those of religious poetry, produce the deeper feeling and may be the chief source of or "the cause of Poetical Enthusiasm .... because we are not us'd to them, *and because they proceed from Thoughts, that latently, and unobserv'd by us, carry Passion along with them.*" [11] However imperfect Dennis's language is, we can catch in it a faint glimmering of a Wordsworthian association of image and emotion; and

[9] Hooker, I, 199, 215. Cf. again (I, 217): "Passion is the Characteristical Mark of Poetry".

[10] Hooker, I, 216.

[11] Hooker, I, 217. My emphasis.

this association helps explain the incomprehensible and wonderful operations of the mind, responsive and creative.

Moreover, with this notion of the associationist sublime, Dennis introduces the subjective element into criticism. The effects that things have upon us, Dennis declares, are dependent upon the type of thoughts we form and their attendant emotions. All esthetic experience depends on our thoughts.

> The same sort of Passions flow from the Thoughts, that would do from the Things of which those Thoughts are Ideas. As for Example, If the Thing we think of is great, why then Admiration attends the Idea of it, and if it is very great, Amazement. If the Thing is pleasing and delightful, why then Joy and Gaiety flow from the Idea of it; if it is sad, Melancholy; if 'tis mischievous and powerful, then the Imagination of it is attended with Terror.[12]

How this subjective associationism, if such it may be called, affects the neoclassical doctrine of the distinction of genres – the precept that literature is divided into distinct categories and forms, each with a specific purpose and effect to achieve, – Dennis himself now shows. A religious association can uplift any form of poetry, however humble: "In short, any Thing that immediately concerns Revelation, has so great an Influence upon Poetry, that it is able to change even the Nature of Writing, and exalt that very sort of poetry, which by its Character is Low and Humble; as for Example, The Eclogue." Dennis is certainly capable of writing like a subjective Alisonian associationist: "Let us consider beside, what prodigious Force all this must have in the Connexion, where Religion adds to the Terror, increases the Astonishment, and augments the Horror." [13]

Perhaps a clearer explanation of what Dennis apparently thinks are the mysterious ways of association is found in the later essay, which Dennis planned carefully as his *magnum opus*, *The Grounds of Criticism* (1704). In this essay, he again

[12] Hooker, I, 217.
[13] Hooker, I, 233, 222.

approaches the problem of distinguishing between esthetic and common emotions; and he also explains more clearly as a subjective element in taste the association of image and emotion.

Dennis begins with the distinction between "Vulgar Passion" and "Enthusiasm". The cause of the former, he avers, is clearly understood and of everyday occurrence. It "is that which is moved by the Objects themselves, or by the Ideas in the ordinary Course of Life; I mean that common Society which we find in the World." On the other hand, the latter or enthusiastic passion is unusual and found only in the mind.

> Enthusiastick Passion, or Enthusiasm, is a Passion which is moved by Ideas in Contemplation, or the Meditation of things that belong not to common Life. Most of our Thoughts in Meditation are naturally attended with some sort and some degree of Passion; and this Passion, if it is strong, I call Enthusiasm.[14]

The nature of this meditation is interesting; but Dennis does not completely explain it. Yet the word in context does suggest why the source of enthusiastic emotion is not clearly perceived by him who feels it: the mind loses itself in deep thought, during which it is carried away in a flurry of associated ideas and emotions. And so Dennis's statement resembles Wordsworth's belief that the origin of poetry is in emotion recollected in tranquility. That Dennis further approximates, albeit vaguely, the "primary law of our nature" which describes "the manner in which we associate ideas in a state of excitement", can be seen in Dennis's illustrations of the subjective effects of poetic enthusiasm.

> As for example, the Sun mention'd in ordinary Conversation, gives the Idea of a round flat shining Body, of about two foot diameter. But the Sun occurring to us in Meditation, gives the Idea of a vast and glorious Body, and the top of all is the visible Creation, and the brightest material Image of the Divinity.

[14] Hooker, I, 338.

Here, obviously, the original perception or the original image is entirely unlike any image in the excited mind. From excited contemplation of the image, the mind can advance to a state of poetic fury and beget by means of association with great ideas, the sublime. In another example, Dennis shows how terror is produced by the mental idea of great danger.

So Thunder mention'd in common Conversation, gives an Idea of a black Cloud, and a great Noise, which makes no great Impression upon us. But the Idea of it occurring in Meditation, sets before us the most forcible, most resistless, and consequently the most dreadful Phaenomenon in Nature: So that this Idea must move a great deal of Terror in us, and 'tis this sort of Terror that I call Enthusiasm.[15]

In these illustrations Dennis foreshadows not only Wordsworth but also Burke. By associating personal dread and danger with an object Dennis paves the way for Burke's sublime terror, an emotion which is formed by similar associations of fear and danger.[16] No one in English criticism, as Monk has observed, attempted what Dennis only half succeeds in doing in these two significant essays. Certainly, Dennis's explanation is not entirely satisfactory. Yet it was his original but vaguely expressed idea that became unmistakably of central importance in the consciously applied associationism of Burke and Wordsworth. All this perhaps allows us to conclude that association was present as the nucleus, despite our difficulties in isolating it, in Dennis's theory of the poetic sublime.

[15] Hooker, I, 339. The quotation from Wordsworth is from "The Preface to the Lyrical Ballads", *Wordsworth's Literary Criticism,* ed. N. C. Smith (London, 1925), p. 14. That Wordsworth was acquainted with Dennis's theory is proved by the reference to Dennis's distinction in a letter to Mrs. Clarkson, December, 1814 [*Letters of William and Dorothy Wordsworth* (Oxford, 1937), II, 617]: "Poetic passion (Dennis has well observed) is of two kinds; imaginative and enthusiastic, and merely human and ordinary." For a short comparison of Dennis and Wordsworth see Hooker, II, cxxv. Hooker adapts appropriate sections from R. D. Havens's *The Mind of a Poet* (Baltimore, 1941), Ch. ii, "Passion".

[16] Dennis anticipates Burke in associating the instinct of self-preservation, as well as danger, with terror in the *Grounds of Criticism.* Hooker, I, 356, 362. Dennis's sublime is grounded entirely upon terror.

In Dennis, then, it cannot be said with certainty that the principle of association was applied to criticism or taste. Yet because his imperfect but independent analyses subsequently were paralleled by those of Wordsworth and Burke, they become significant in the history of associationist criticism in the eighteenth century. It was Dennis's type of subjective association, implicit in his theory of enthusiastic poetry, that helped liberate the esthetic emotions from the authorized channels of neoclassical literary theory, that, in fact, vitiated the doctrine of the distinction of the genres. And it was, no doubt, just this subjectivism that made Dennis appear quite modern to Wordsworth a century later.

Dennis's speculation upon the emotional effects of images upon the mind is taken up by Addison in his papers on the pleasures of the imagination. But where Dennis gropes, is confused and fragmentary, Addison speaks with certainty, is lucid and complete. Addison's series of papers on the imagination gives perhaps the first complete statement of an esthetic theory in England. And in his system the theory of association finds its proper place among "the several Sources of that Pleasure which rises in the Mind upon the Perusal of a noble Work". [17]

Following a hint from Locke's division of matter into primary and secondary qualities, Addison distinguishes between primary and secondary pleasures of the imagination. The former "entirely proceed from such Objects as are before our Eyes", while the latter "flow from the Ideas of visible Objects, when the Objects are not actually before the Eye, but are called up into our Memories, or formed into agreeable Visions of Things that are either Absent or Fictitious".[18] The primary pleasures arise from the sight of what is great or sublime, uncommon or novel, and beautiful in nature, landscape gardening, or architecture. But the secondary esthetic pleasures arise from objects that once sensed by sight "are afterwards

[17] *Spectator 409* (VI, 51), ed. G. Gregory Smith (Everyman Library).
[18] *Spec. 411* (VI, 57).

called up into the Mind either barely by its own Operations [through memory], or on occasion of something without us, as Statues or Descriptions".[19] Having noticed that the esthetic responses, especially those known as the secondary pleasures of the imagination, vary according to individual taste, Addison proceeds to speculate briefly on the reason for this diversity of taste over words or descriptions. Addison's answer to the problem of diversity is in accordance with Locke's doctrine of the association of ideas. The cause for variety in taste, he writes, is an association of different ideas by different men to the same words. "This different Taste must proceed either from the Perfection of Imagination [i.e. imaging, sensation] in one more than in another, *or from the different Ideas that several Readers affix to the same Words.*" Continuing in the English tradition begun by Hobbes and Locke, Addison adds that in order to have true taste and right judgment, one must first be born with a good imagination, and must then study the propriety and decorum of words "so as to be able to distinguish which are most significant and expressive of their proper Ideas, and what additional Strength and Beauty they are capable of receiving from Conjunction with others." [20] Addison is here perhaps the first to do what later neoclassical associationists, Gerard and Kames, for example, were to do about the middle of the century. Attempting to set up a single standard of good taste, they all came to believe the discerning judgment to be fundamental in deciding upon the proper connections between ideas. In all three writers there is a suggestion of the reconciliation of neoclassic formalism with the associationist psychology.

[19] *Spec. 416* (VI, 73). Hutcheson also employs this division. He calls them absolute or original and relative or comparative beauty. See *Inquiry into the Original of our Ideas of Beauty and Virtue* [1725] (London, 1720), Sec. I, Art. 17, pp. 14-5. Similar divisions are in Gerard, Kames, Alison, etc.

[20] *Spec. 416* (VI, 76). In his *Logick* [1725] (London, 1772), Pt. I, Sec. 8, p. 67, Isaac Watts also mentions how errors and mistakes arise because "different Persons . . . affix different Ideas" to the same word. But he does not apply this concept to art as does Addison.

Spectator 416 concludes with this brief discussion. Immediately following, in the beginning of the next number, Addison considers the effects of trains of ideas in the mind from the point of view of the creative writer and the responsive reader. In accounting for the diverse effects of the connection or conjunction of ideas upon taste and describing the duty of judgment in maintaining propriety among the ideas, Addison makes a perfect transition to the first subject of *Spectator 417:* "How a whole Set of Ideas Hang together, etc."[21] To be specific, Addison describes how a subjective train of ideas in the memory, recalled through contiguity in space and time, increases imaginative pleasure.

We may observe, that any single Circumstance of what we have formerly seen often raises up a whole Scene of Imagery, and awakens numberless Ideas that before slept in the Imagination; such a particular Smell or Colour is able to fill the Mind, on a sudden, with the Picture of the Fields or Gardens, *where we first met with it, and to bring up into View all the Variety of Images that once attended it.*

The motion of the imagination through the scenes in memory is, as the next quotation shows, strongly flavored with Hobbes's description of the fancy traveling through the realm of memory's registered or associated images. It is this subjective operation of mind or memory, representing associated pictures for the fancy, that increases the delight over the original image.

Our Imagination takes the Hint, and leads us unexpectedly into Cities or Theatres, Plains, or Meadows. We may further observe, when the Fancy thus reflects on the Scenes that have past in it formerly, those, which were at first pleasant to behold, appear more so upon Reflection, and that the Memory heightens the Delightfulness of the Original.[22]

The lucidity of Addison's brief account of the ways of associa-

[21] *Spec. 421* (VI, 95), from the "Table of the principal Contents".
[22] *Spec. 417* (VI, 77).

tionism was not surpassed by writers up to the time of Alison. It will also be seen that later writers, Kames, Alison, Wordsworth, do not fundamentally differ from Addison's concise description of the effects of recollection upon the imagination.[23] Clearly, Addison falls within the associationist tradition in English criticism and taste – the tradition of which the sources are in Hobbes and Locke. However, Addison steps momentarily out of the native English tradition when he assigns a "Natural Cause" for the succession of ideas according to the physiological explanation of a Cartesian: "A Cartesian would account for both these Instances in the following Manner."[24] But this movement out of the native tradition is more apparent than real. It should be noted that Addison merely reinterprets the accepted phenomenon of mental association according to Cartesian mechanism. This is a far cry from saying that he found the principles of association in Descartes; he says explicitly that "a Cartesian would", not that a Cartesian *does* explain it physiologically.[25] And his application of the methods of "these Physiologists" is neither original nor unusual. He might have read

[23] Cf. C. D. Thorpe, "Addison and Hutcheson on the Imagination", *ELH*, II (1935), 225, fn. 37: "It is instructive to note that in his exposition of the phenomena of association with relation to aesthetic pleasure, Addison is not only foreshadowing the later 18th-century school of associationists culminating in Alison, but is stating in brief, three quarters of a century before Wordsworth, a doctrine of pleasure through recollected emotion."

[24] *Spec. 421* (VI, 95). Addison's hypothetical Cartesian accounts for the chain of associations by the "Texture in the Brain": "The Sett of Ideas which we received from such a Prospect or Garden, having entered the Mind at the same time, have a Sett of Traces [tracks, channels, canals, courses] belonging to them in the Brain, bordering very near upon one another; when, therefore, any one of these Ideas arises in the Imagination, and consequently dispatches a flow of Animal Spirits to its proper Trace, these Spirits, in the Violence of their Motion, run not only into the Trace, to which they were more particularly directed, but into several of those that lye about it: By this means they awaken other Ideas of the same Sett, which immediately determine a new Dispatch of Spirits, but in the same manner open other Neighboring Traces, till at last the whole Sett of them is blown up, and the whole Prospect or Garden flourishes in the Imagination."

[25] Cf. Worsfold and Saintsbury who were misled into thinking that Ad-

in Locke's chapter on the association of ideas about "tracks" and about "trains of motions in the animal spirits ... [that] may help us a little to conceive of intellectual habits, and of the tying together of ideas".[26] Moreover, Addison could not have found his description of the theory of association paralleled in Descartes, because it does not definitely appear in that philosopher's works.[27] Therefore, all that can be said for the sources of Addison's ideas in the first part of *Spectator 417* is that they are composite. The principle of association remains of Eng-

---

dison used the "Cartesian doctrine of association". W. Basil Worsfold, *The Principles of Criticism* (London, 1897), p. 105; George Saintsbury, *A History of Criticism* (London, 1904), II, 444.

[26] Locke, *Essay,* II, xxxiii, 6. For short accounts of Descartes' mechanical conception of memory and imagination see *The History of the Works of the Learned,* VIII (1706), 94; XI (1709), 260-1. Shaftesbury [*Characteristicks, Advice to an Author* (Dublin, 1743), Pt. III, Sec. 1 (Vol. I, pp. 291ff.)] had nothing but contempt for "these Physiologists". But Watts more than once gives assent to the Cartesian doctrine of the spirits. See his *Philosophical Essays* [1733] (London, 1742), Ch. xvii, in *The Works of Isaac Watts* (London, 1813), VIII, 121: "It is most probable that those very fibres, pores or traces of the brain, which assist at the first idea or perception of any object, are the same which assist also at the recollection of it." James Arbuckle, *Hibernicus's Letters* (London, 1734), II, 188-9 (No. 76, Sept. 10, 1726) gives a humorous account of Cartesian memory: "We must consider that the first Image which an outward Object imprints on our Brain is very slight; it resembles a thin Vapour which dwindles into nothing, without leaving the least track after it. But if the same Object successively offers itself several times, the Image it occasions thereby increases and strengthens itself by degrees till at last it acquires such a consistency (if I may so call it) as makes it subsist as long as the Machine itself. A stock of Images having been acquired, they each have their respective little Cell or Lodge, where they go and hide ... and if one of them chances to go by the Cell or Lodge of another which has the least real or imaginary conformity with it, out pops the retired Image, and immediately joins the wandering one." Satire against the physiologists is also in the *Memoirs of Martinus Scriblerus* [*The Works of Alexander Pope,* ed. Elwin and Courthope (London, 1886), X, 334-5].

[27] G. S. Brett, *A History of Psychology* (London, 1921), II, 210-11, notes only one implication of "the general principle of association" in Descartes' *Passions of the Soul* (1649), Pt. II, Art. 107. But it is far removed from Addison's understanding of association. The closest approach to Addison's psycho-physical explanation of association is in Pt. I, Art. 42, "How we find in the memory the things which we desire to remember."

lish origin and can be traced to Hobbes and Locke. That Addison himself was certainly aware of Locke's description of the association of ideas is proved by unmistakable evidence.[28] But the novelty of Addison's description lies in the way in which the doctrine of association is more completely explained by Descartes' physiological hypothesis. As a result of this synthesis, Addison anticipates Hartley's physiological associationism by about thirty years.

In Addison the two significant uses of association throughout the course of eighteenth-century criticism can already be perceived. First, Addison resorts to association as the explanation of improper connections between ideas and of diversity in taste; secondly, he believes that the succession of associated ideas in the memory accounts for the *increased* pleasures of imagination, those imaginative pleasures which are "the very Life and highest Perfection of Poetry".[29] Like Locke and Hobbes, he urges judgment to test the propriety of ideas in conjunction, so that a true taste can be established. In this respect, Addison betrays his neoclassic roots. And, like his predecessors in philosophy, he also makes no mention of the imagination as either combining or compounding ideas through association.[30] Of course it will be conceded that the principle of association is not of central importance in Addison's poetics; but that it is found at all and found closely related to the notion of the perceptive imagination is prophetic of its future

[28] In *Spec. 110* (II, 103) Addison quotes from Locke's chapter on association in order to explain how darkness comes to be associated with ghosts and sprites.

[29] *Spec. 421* (VI, 92).

[30] Addison's active, compounding imagination that "has something in it like Creation" appears in *411* (VI, 56), *416* (VI, 73-4), *421* (VI, 92), and invention or the fairy way of writing in *419* (VI, 84ff.). The word *range* appears too and is barely reminiscent of Hobbes's ranging succession of ideas; see *417* (VI, 78): A "noble Writer should be born with this Faculty [Imagination] in its full strength and Vigour, so as to be able to receive lively Ideas from outward Objects, to retain them long, *and to range them together, upon occasion, in such Figures, and Representations as are most likely to hit the Fancy of the Reader.*"

importance as the means by which the intricacies of taste and the imagination were to be explained. Addison's application of the two fundamental meanings of association to an understanding of diversity in taste and of esthetic response is followed with few fundamental changes up to the time of Archibald Alison at the end of the eighteenth century.

In the early eighteenth century Berkeley also lent strength to the tradition and maintained the continuity of associationist thought, although he did not apply the theory to taste or criticism. Berkeley relies upon the concept of associationism for the explanation of what he considers to be the psychological phenomenon of vision in his first published work, *An Essay towards a New Theory of Vision* (1709). Distance is perceived and visual judgments can be made only as a result of experience, writes Berkeley; the visual impressions become habitually associated with tactile sensations and with the sensations accompanying the movements of the pupils, when we make the necessary ocular adjustments in looking at far or near objects. This theory is enunciated again and again in Berkeley's writing.[31] In itself it is not significant for criticism, but it becomes significant as it incidentally introduces association into the discussion of language and so influences Burke.

In order to have his theory of vision more easily understood, Berkeley draws upon what might have appeared at the time to be a simple and common illustration and draws an analogy with the association of word to sound: ". . . . Just as, upon

[31] A note on association as the cause of visual judgment appears in the earlier *Commonplace Book* [*Complete Works*, ed. A. C. Fraser (Oxford, 1901), I, 75]: "Qu. Whether the sensations of sight arising from a man's head be liker the sensations of touch proceeding from thence or from his legs? Or, Is it onely the constant & long association of ideas entirely different that makes me judge them the same?" Cf. *Theory of Vision,* Sec. 16-17, 25, 26, 28 (I, 131-2, 134-5), and *passim*; *The Principles of Human Knowledge* (1710), Secs. 30-2, 59, 64-5 (I, 273-4, 290, 293-4); *Three Dialogues between Hylas and Philonous* (1713), I, 415-6, 464; *Alciphron* (1732), Dialogue 4, Sec. 8 (II, 165); *Theory of Vision Vindicated* (1733), Secs. 39-40 (II, 397-8). Hartley is indebted to Berkeley for his own theory of vision; cf. *Observations on Man,* Props. 30, 58.

hearing a certain sound, the idea is immediately suggested to the understanding which custom had united with it".[32] In the "Introduction" to the later *Principles of Human Knowledge*, this analogy is extended and developed into an attack upon Locke's theory of abstract ideas. Asserting that these abstract ideas are impossible to form and are void of all meaning, Berkeley would rather try to reduce the problem of abstraction to the mere matter of language. In short, Berkeley views language or words as the source of abstract ideas. We learn through experience and custom, says Berkeley, to "annex" meanings to words until the process of association becomes so habitual and automatic that understanding can be effected through suggestion. In time, therefore, the ideas originally represented by the words can be omitted. "And a little attention will discover that it is not necessary (even in the strictest reasonings) that significant names which stand for ideas should, every time they are used, excite in the understanding the ideas they are made to stand for." When words are used for their own sake alone, "abstract" ideas can be produced. Now, this associationist theory of language allows for "the communication of ideas marked by words"; but far more significant than this is the fact that it also shows how passion may be raised without intermediary ideas. It is precisely at this point that Burke comes closest to Berkeley, and, as Mr. Dixon Wecter alleges, "Burke might have discovered his clue for this theory of non-imagistic

[32] *New Theory of Vision,* Sec. 17 (I, 132); see also Sec. 51 (I, 151); "No sooner do we hear the words of a familiar language pronounced in our ears but the ideas corresponding thereto present themselves to our minds: in the very same instant the sound and the meaning enter the understanding; so closely are they united that it is not in our power to keep out the one except we exclude the other also"; and Sec. 147 (I, 199-200). See also *Alciphron,* Dialogue 4, Sec. 8 (II, 165); "We perceive distance, not immediately, but by mediation of a sign, which hath no likeness to it, or necessary connexion with it, but only suggests it from repeated experience, as words do things"; and Sec. 11 (II, 169): "There must be time and experience, by repeated acts, to acquire a habit of knowing the connexion between the signs and things signified; that is to say, of understanding the language, whether of the eyes or of the ears." See also *Alciphron,* Dialogue 7, Secs. 5, 14 (II, 324-9, 344); *Theory of Vision Vindicated,* Secs. 39-40 (II, 397-8).

language which rouses emotion" in the "Introduction" to the *Principles.*

I entreat the reader [says Berkeley] to reflect with himself, and see if it doth not often happen, either in hearing or reading a discourse, that the passions of fear, love, hatred, admiration, and disdain, and the like, arise immediately in his mind upon the perception of certain words, without any ideas coming between. At first, indeed, the words might have occasioned ideas that were fitting to produce those emotions; but, if I mistake not, it will be found that, *when language is once grown familiar, the hearing of the sounds or sight of the characters is oft immediately attended with those passions which at first were wont to be produced by the intervention of ideas that are now quite omitted.*

And even proper names can have this effect upon certain men; for example, Aristotle: "So close and immediate a connexion may custom establish betwixt the very word Aristotle and the notion of assent and reverence in the minds of some men".[33]

The key to this discussion, it will be readily agreed, is the association of ideas. Similarly, the association of ideas is at the base of Burke's theory of words and emotions. This important fact receives no consideration in Mr. Wecter's article.[34] Although Burke might have adapted only Berkeley's associationism, it is also interesting to note that the comprehension of words through the experience of constant association of sign or sound to meaning or emotion was not unknown to many other writers in this period.[35] It may be, then, that

[33] "Introd.", Secs. 19-20 (I, 251-3). See D. Wecter, "Burke's Theory of Words, Images, and Emotions", *PMLA,* LV (1940), 174.

[34] The author perhaps unconsciously puts Burke's theory in the tradition by closely following Burke's associationist explanation [*PMLA,* LV (1940), 172]: "Burke maintains that compound abstracts do not raise images in the mind – but that through long use, and *association with good or evil or 'other interesting things or events,'* these words are able to stir emotion merely by 'the sound, without any annexed notion' (*Inquiry,* V, ii)." For Burke's theory see below, pp. 143-6.

[35] In addition to Berkeley, Hutcheson and Watts may be mentioned. Hume expresses this theory as clearly as Berkeley; see *Works,* ed. Green and Grose, I, 325, 328-31, 393-4, 510. A. C. Fraser, *Complete Works of Berkeley,* I, 200 fn. 1, also cites Robert Smith, *Optics. – Remarks* (1738), p. 29.

the important thing to remember about Burke's theory of cloudy, imaginative words packed with feeling is not the belief that the theory might have been suggested only by Berkeley, but the fact that it was grounded on an eighteenth-century associationist commonplace. And the very same associationist view of language enabled Wordsworth to use a new poetic diction. Long before Wordsworth, however, Burke applied this aspect of associationism to the practice of poetry and so produced a romantic poetics.[36]

Although Burke might have found in Berkeley's associationist theory of language a suggestion for a romantic conception of art, others might have found that Berkeley could equally well have supported neoclassic notions about literature. For example, in Section 10 of his *Principles of Human Knowledge* (1710) Berkeley equates the laws of association with the regular laws of nature. This paragraph is interesting solely because it illustrates the attitude of those critics, like Hobbes and Hume, who examine art and the ways of imaginative creation in accordance with neoclassic rules reinforced with an associationist conception of human nature.

> The ideas of Sense are more strong, lovely, and distinct than those of the Imagination; they have likewise a steadiness, order, and coherence, and are not excited at random, as those which are the effects of human wills often are, but in a regular train or series – the admirable connexion whereof sufficiently testifies the wisdom and benevolence of its Author. Now the set rules, or established methods, wherein the Mind we depend on excites in us the ideas of Sense, are called the laws of nature; and these we learn by experience, which teaches us that such and such ideas are attended with such and such other ideas, in the ordinary course of things.[37]

[36] For Wordsworth's comment on the word *idiot,* see his "Letter to John Wilson" (1800) in *Wordsworth's Literary Criticism,* ed. N. C. Smith (London, 1925), p. 9: "I must content myself simply with observing that it is probable that the principal cause of your dislike to this particular poem lies in the *word* Idiot. If there had been any such word in our language, *to which we had attached passion,* as lack-wit, half-wit, witless, etc., I should have certainly employed it in preference; but there is no such word."

[37] Ed. Fraser, I, 273.

It is a commonplace in histories of philosophy to describe how Hume, who of all Berkeley's contemporaries perhaps understood him best, developed Berkeley's philosophical idealism into the extremes of skepticism. But Hume's debt to Berkeley goes further than this: he seized upon Berkeley's notion of the association of two senses and extended it to apply to the association of emotions and to the formation of complex ideas, and he also carried Berkeley's description of regular connection of ideas into the realm of literary criticism.

Although his tutor Locke had enunciated the theory of association, Shaftesbury found no room for it in his moral and esthetic system of thought. In clear opposition to Locke's doctrines, he believed that we possess an innate or instinctive taste or sense for certain harmonies and forms – "that which Nature teaches, exclusive of Art, Culture, or Discipline".[38] Consequently, his philosophy did not compel him to consider the extent to which our ideas of beauty may be influenced by associations with other ideas and emotions. As an illustration of Shaftesbury's belief that we have an innate sense of beauty, the dialogue between Theocles and Palemon in *The Moralists* should be adequate.

"'Tis enough," [said Theocles,] "if we consider the simplest of Figures; as either a round Ball, a Cube, or Dye. Why is even an Infant pleas'd with the first View of these Proportions? Why is the Sphere or Globe, the Cylinder and Obelisk preferr'd; and the irregular Figures, in respect of these, rejected and despised?" "I am ready," ... [replied Palemon,] "to own there is in certain Figures a natural Beauty, which the Eye finds as soon as the Object is presented to it." "Is there then, said he, a natural Beauty of Figures? ... No sooner the Eye opens upon Figures, the Ear to Sounds, than straight the Beautiful results, and Grace and Harmony are known and acknowledg'd."[39]

[38] *The Moralists* (1709) in *Characteristicks* (London, 1737), Pt. III, Sec. 2 (II, 411). McKenzie incorrectly includes Shaftesbury among the associationists: see "Lord Kames and the Mechanist Tradition", *Essays and Studies, University of California Publications in English,* XIV (1943), 121. Cf. Brett, "The Third Earl of Shaftesbury as a Literary Critic", *MLR,* XXXVII (1942), 135: Shaftesbury "repudiates the whole associationist conception of the human mind and vigorously asserts the existence of innate ideas".

[39] *Ibid.*, Pt. III, Sec. 2 (II, 414).

However, Shaftesbury's neglect of association and emphasis upon the natural and immediate taste for beauty indirectly began the tradition of opposition to association as the foundation and measure of taste and beauty. In the eighteenth century Burke was perhaps the leading anti-associationist critic. But there were some, among whom even Burke may be numbered, who compromised with the theory and did not completely reject it. Francis Hutcheson is the first to come to a compromise with Shaftesbury and Locke. After having accepted the notion of the intuitive sense of beauty, Hutcheson proceeded to account for the apparent diversity of effects upon this uniform sense by means of the principle of association. The problem of diversity was ignored by Shaftesbury; but Hutcheson, his disciple, was able to cope with the problem by falling back upon and exploiting the psychological theory of Locke.

Hutcheson divides Shaftesbury's single sense or instinct which responds equally to the beauties of harmony and virtue into two distinct senses, an internal sense of beauty and a moral sense. The first has the "Power of perceiving the Beauty of Regularity, Order, Harmony" and produces the pleasures of the imagination; the second is "that Determination to approve Affections, Actions, or Characters or rational Agents, which we call virtuous".[40] We are concerned here only with the internal sense of beauty to the discussion of which Hutcheson

[40] Francis Hutcheson, *An Inquiry into the Original of our Ideas of Beauty and Virtue* [1725] (London, 1729), p. xiii; Sec. I, Arts. 9-10. The first treatise on beauty will be referred to unless otherwise noted. As Thorpe has showed in his article, "Addison and Hutcheson on the Imagination", *ELH,* II (1935), 219-20, 221-2, Hutcheson uses interchangeably in his later works the pleasures of the internal sense of beauty with Addison's pleasures of the imagination; cf. below p. 64, fn. 56. James Arbuckle, [*Hibernicus's Letters* (London, 1734), II, 107-8 (No. 67, July 9, 1726)] Hutcheson's friend, also alleges that the taste for the "Pleasures of the Imagination" is original and natural, i.e., with us from birth. In his later *Essay on the Nature and Conduct of the Passions* (London, 1728), pp. 5-6, Hutcheson breaks down the senses into five categories: external senses, internal sense for pleasures of the imagination, public sense or *sensus communis,* moral sense, and sense of honor.

devotes the first treatise of his *Inquiry*, "Concerning Beauty, Harmony, Design".

The meaning that Hutcheson gives to the internal sense of beauty in this treatise cannot be mistaken.

> But let it be observ'd here once for all, "That an internal Sense no more presupposes an innate Idea, or principle of Knowledge, than the external." Both are natural Powers of Perception, or Determinations of the Mind to receive necessarily certain Ideas from the Presence of Objects. The internal Sense is, a passive Power of receiving Ideas of Beauty from all Objects in which there is Uniformity amidst Variety.[41]

It is, therefore, not very much unlike the external senses, except that it is the special capacity for the exquisite sensation of beautiful forms, harmonies, and proportions. It is also as natural in all men as their five senses, for it is supposed to give immediate pleasure without benefit of rational reflection on the cause of the feeling: its effects strike "us at first with the Idea of Beauty".[42] The last important point made about this sense is that there is as much agreement in men over this natural sense of beauty as over the external senses.[43] In making this assumption Hutcheson is compelled to come to grips with the problem of the diversity of opinion concerning beautiful effects. Why, the question may be legitimately raised, if this sense is the same in everyone, is there so much disagreement about the kinds of objects that may give it pleasure? Hutcheson's answer is unambiguous: the cause for exceptions to nature's rule, he believes, is associations of ideas. "The Association of Ideas . . . is one great Cause of the apparent Diversity of Fancys in the Sense of Beauty, as well as in the external Senses".[44]

41 *Inquiry,* Sec. VI, Art. 10, p. 80.

42 *Ibid.,* Sec. I, Arts. 6, 13, pp. 4, 11.

43 *Ibid.,* p. xvi.

44 *Ibid.,* Sec. VI, Art. 11, p. 80. Cf. *Essay on Passions,* p. 127: "To compare these several Pleasures and Pains [of the senses] as to their Intenseness, seems difficult, because of the Diversity of Tastes, or Turns of Temper given by Custom and Education, which make strange Associations of Ideas, and form habits; from whence it happens, that, tho all the several kinds of original Senses and Desires seem equally natural, yet some are

All the senses, therefore, can be influenced by association. The five external senses produce simple ideas; the cause, then, for the different "fancies" produced by these senses and for the variety of reactions to simple sensations is an "accidental Conjunction of a disagreeable Idea".

The simple Ideas rais'd in different Persons by the same Object, are probably some way different, when they disagree in their Approbation or Dislike; and in the same Person, when his Fancy at one time differs from what it was at another. This will apear from reflecting on those Objects, to which we have now an Aversion, tho they formerly were agreeable: And we shall find that there is some accidental Conjunction of a disagreeable Idea, which always recurs with the Object; as in those Wines to which Men acquire an Aversion, after they have taken them in an Emetick Preparation, we are conscious that the Idea is alter'd from what it was when that Wine was agreeable, by the Conjunction of the Ideas of Loathing and Sickness of Stomach.[45]

Nor is the internal sense of beauty unaffected by association; for the "Diversity of Fancy" concerning the complex ideas of beautiful objects, such as dress, is accounted for "from a like Conjunction of Ideas". [46] Hutcheson does not draw further

---

led into a constant Pursuit of the Pleasures of one kind, as the only Enjoyment of Life, and are indifferent about others."

[45] *Inquiry,* Sec. I, Art. 7, pp. 4-5. Along with Hobbes and Locke, Hutcheson believes these simple ideas can be compounded into complex ones (Sec. I, Art. 3, p. 2): "The Mind has a power of compounding Ideas, which were receiv'd separately." He does not suggest that compounding can occur by associating ideas. The insidious effects of "casual associations" are also described by Watts in his *Logick* [1725] (London, 1772), Pt. II, Ch. iii, Sec. 1, p. 194: "The casual Associations of many of our Ideas becomes the Spring of another Prejudice or rash Judgment, to which we are sometimes exposed. If in our younger years we have taken Medicines that have been nauseous, when any Medicine whatsoever is afterward proposed to us under Sickness, we immediately judge it nauseous: Our Fancy has so closely joined these Ideas together, that we know not how to separate them .... The best relief against this Prejudice of Association is to consider, whether there be any natural and necessary Connection between those Ideas, which Fancy, Custom or Chance, hath thus joined together; and if Nature has not joined them, let our Judgment correct the Folly of our Imagination, and separate these Ideas again."

[46] *Inquiry,* Sec. I, Art. 7, p. 6: "Thus, if either from any thing in Nature, or from the Opinion of our Country or Acqaintance, the fancying of

upon "art" for examples of the effects of association; instead, he gives common examples to illustrate how special associations affect a few things: love, melancholy, and religion affect our reactions to trees and woods; and dim light is associated with religion through constant connection with dark gothic churches. "We know the like Effect in the Ideas of our Churches, from the perpetual use of them only in religious Exercises. The faint Light in Gothick Buildings has had the same Association of a very foreign Idea, which our Poet shews in his Epithet – A Dim religious Light." This quotation from Milton's *Il Penseroso* is Hutcheson's sole excursion into literature for the purpose of explaining the association of ideas.[47] In his *Cyclopaedia* (1727) Ephraim Chambers uses the same illustration and almost the same language:

---

glaring Colours be look'd upon as an evidence of Levity, or of any other evil Quality of Mind; or if any Colour or Fashion be commonly us'd by Rusticks, or by Men of any disagreeable Profession, Employment, or Temper; these additional Ideas may recur constantly with that of the Colour or Fashion, and cause a constant Dislike to them in those who join the additional Ideas, altho the Colour or Form be no way disagreeable of themselves, and actually do please others who join no such Ideas to them." Kames and Alison explain fashion in dress along these associationist lines originated by Hutcheson.

[47] *Inquiry,* Sec. VI, Art. II, p. 81. Writing as usual in a very abstract manner, Hutcheson again mentions metaphors in connection with associations [*A System of Moral Philosophy* (London, 1755), I, 29-30]: "We shall only take notice here, that by certain associations of ideas, and by frequent comparisons made in similes and metaphors, and by other causes, some inanimate objects have obtained additional ideas of dignity, decency, sanctity; some appear as mean and despicable; and others are in a middle state of indifference." The *System of Moral Philosophy* was published posthumously. According to the studies of William R. Scott [*Francis Hutcheson* (Cambridge, 1900), pp. 113, 210], this work was begun and completed between 1733-7. It is substantially the same as Hutcheson's written lectures delivered while he occupied the Chair of Moral Philosophy at the University of Glasgow. A parallel to these passages in the *Inquiry* and the *System* is that in an essay on laughter in *Hibernicus's Letters* (London, 1734), I, 88-9 (No. 11, June 12, 1725). The essays on laughter were assigned to Hutcheson by James Arbuckle, the editor and the author of most of the letters, in the last number [II, 429 (No. 102, March 25, 1727)]. Dennis, too, was aware of the effect of religious ideas upon other ideas; see *ante,* p. 42.

This association of ideas makes many objects beautiful and pleasant. The beauty of trees, their cool shades, and their aptness to conceal from observation, have made groves, and woods, the usual retreat of those who love solitude, especially the religious, the pensive, the melancholy, and the amorous: and do not we find, that we have so joined the ideas of those dispositions of mind, with those external objects, that they always occur to us along with them? And according as the habits, or passions contracted, or gratified therein give us pleasure, or pain, remembrance is pleasurable or painful. The dim light in Gothic buildings has had an association of a very foreign idea, which Milton expresses by his epithet, *a dim religious light*. After the like manner, the casual conjunction of ideas gives us disgust where there is nothing disagreeable in the form itself.

But this illustration is scarcely prophetic of the time when Hutcheson's Scottish followers, Gerard, Kames, and Alison, will examine literature and art almost entirely from the associationist point of view.

Thus, although the complex ideas are the sources of the greater pleasures of the imagination or internal sense – the "higher and more delightful Perceptions of Beauty and Harmony", – yet they, like simple ideas received by other senses, are subjected to the influence of pleasing and displeasing associations "according to Persons Tempers and past Circumstances".[48] It is these associated ideas, remote from ideas of beauty, that cause such wide disagreement among several imaginations. Naturally, a single standard of taste cannot possibly be secure under such conditions wherein taste is diversely affected by the whimsical and subjective associations of several people. It is therefore somewhat strange to find that alongside his neoclassic inclination to set up an objective standard – "Uniformity amidst Variety", – Hutcheson is driven by the psychological tradition which he implicitly accepts to admit that even our tastes and distastes are produced by subjective associations: "Associations of Ideas make Objects pleasant, and delightful, which are not naturally apt to give any such Pleasure; and the same way the casual Conjunction of Ideas may give a Disgust,

[48] *Inquiry,* Sec. I, Art. 12, p. 10; Sec. VI, Art. 12, p. 83.

where there is nothing disagreeable in the Form itself". [49]

Hutcheson has not advanced very far from Locke. Applying Locke's version of association to taste, he tries hard to convince us that the principle of association cannot be a natural basis for the pleasures of imagination; he does recognize, however, its profound influence in changing tastes. He is constantly aware of exceptions to the responses of the internal sense to uniformity; but, like Locke, he seems to minimize the importance of association. The associations are almost always "strange", "confused", and "vain Associations of Ideas", or "foolish Conjunctions of Ideas". [50] A good example of his deprecatory attitude towards associations is found in his discussion of horror. Supposedly horrible objects, Hutcheson states, can give pleasure only when a "foolish" association is removed.

There are Horrors rais'd by some Objects, which are only the Effect of Fear for our selves, or Compassion, towards others, when either Reason, or some foolish Association of Ideas, makes us apprehend Danger, and not the Effect of any thing in the Form it self: for we find that most of those Objects which excite Horror at first, when Experience, or Reason has remov'd the Fear, may become the occasions of Pleasure; as ravenous Beasts, a tempestuous Sea, a craggy Precipice, a dark shady Valley.[51]

[49] *Inquiry,* Sec. VI, Art. 3, p. 73; cf. also Sec. VI, Art. 4, p. 256 of the second treatise where it is pointed out that these subjective associations can make any gesture and motion beautiful and an object of taste. In the *Essay on Passions,* pp. 93-8, Hutcheson explains how our passions or appetites "may be strengthened or weakned and variously alter'd by Opinion, or ['confused and wild'] Associations of Ideas".

[50] E.g., *Essay on Passions,* p. 9: "The Laws or Customs of a Country, the Humour of our Company may have made strange Associations of Ideas, so that some Objects, which of themselves are indifferent to any Sense, by reason of some additional grateful Idea, may become very desirable; or by like Addition of an ungrateful Idea may raise the strongest Aversion." Cf. also Hutcheson's essays on the *Fable of the Bees* in *Hibernicus's Letters,* I, 372, 373, 375 (No. 45, Feb. 4, 1725/6).

[51] *Inquiry,* Sec. VI, Art. 2, p. 72. Chambers borrows this passage without any verbal change for his article on "Deformity". Although in the *Inquiry* he does not entirely accept association as the ground of taste, yet in later works Hutcheson admits that it plays an important part in normal life. Herein he shows an advance over Locke. See *A System of Moral Philos-*

It is interesting to note how this explanation of what the marginal gloss describes as "Approbation and Dislike from Associations of Ideas" differs from Burke's systematic analysis of sublime terror. Hutcheson lays emphasis on accidental, unnatural associations, not long before described by Locke. These associations are the sources for displeasure or horror, and must be removed. Burke, on the contrary, accepts the association of personal danger because when terror produces the pleasures of the sublime, the painful object is first removed to a safe distance away from the spectator. Therefore a personal association of the idea of fear or danger is the only means left, so Burke implies, whereby the distant object can retain its terrible significance. Thus, while Burke's terror is sublime and pleasing through a necessary and subjective association of danger, Hutcheson's sense of beauty cannot be pleased by horrible objects until either reason removes the associations of fear, or experience (i.e. custom or habit) makes these terrifying associations pass by unnoticed. No doubt Burke, who was separated from Hutcheson by a quarter of a century, had to contend with a stronger and more respected tradition that was favorable to association in the middle of the century. Perhaps because of the strength of associationist belief at the

---

ophy, I, 31: "Tho' many miseries and vices spring from this fountain [association of ideas], we may see the absolute necessity of this determination. Without it we could have little use of memory, or recollection, or even of speech. How tedious would it be to need a particular recollection upon each word we hear or desire to speak, to find what words and ideas are joined by the custom of the language? it must be as tedious a work as decyphering after we had found an alphabet. *Whereas now the sound and idea are so associated, that the one ever is attended with the other.*" See also *Essay on Passions,* pp. 10-11: "Should any one be surprised at this Disposition in our Nature to associate any Ideas together for the future, which once presented themselves jointly, considering what great Evils, and how much Corruption of Affections is owing to it, it may help to account for this Part of our Constitution to consider '*that all our Language and much of our Memory depends upon it*:' So that were there no such Association made, we must lose the use of Words, and a great part of our Power of recollecting past Events." Certainly, Burke might have discovered some clues for his theory of non-imagistic language in this associationist understanding of language.

time, Burke was led to compromise so significantly with the theory of association, despite his intense opposition to that theory as a source of the standard of taste.

It is also of interest to note that it is precisely in opposing association as a way in which the standards of taste are formed that Hutcheson anticipates Burke's refutation of the theory. Hutcheson's position is grounded on the belief that the internal sense is original and immediately intuitive, and that it precedes secondary associations: "there is a natural Power of Perception, or Sense of Beauty in Objects, antecedent to all Custom, Education, or Example".[52] This sense operates before associations can be effective. For example, "Custom may connect the Ideas of religious Horror to certain Buildings; but Custom could never have made a Being naturally incapable of Fear, receive such Ideas".[53] Similarly, Hutcheson shows how the natural sense for beauty is prior to any association of ideas established by education.[54] It is now possible to say that the chief sources for Burke's arguments against association can all be found in these paragraphs of Hutcheson's *Inquiry*. Undoubtedly, Burke read this very popular and influential study, which went through five editions from 1725 to 1753 and the title of which so closely resembles that of his own essay.

The application of association of ideas in the *Inquiry* is made, then, according to Locke's understanding of the psychology. Associationism is used by Hutcheson for two closely related

[52] *Inquiry,* Sec. VII, Art. 1, pp. 84-5. Similarly, in the *Essay on Passion* Hutcheson explains man's malicious temper. Our natural inclinations are always good, but secondary associations of ideas confuse and alter them for the worse. In the *Peri Bathous, The Art of Sinking in Poetry* (1727) [*The Works of Alexander Pope,* ed. Elwin and Courthope (London, 1886), X, 348], the wits also adopt Locke's theory for their explanation of sublimity: "*The taste of the Bathos is implanted by Nature itself in the soul of man; till, perverted by custom or example, he is taught, or rather compelled to relish the sublime.* Accordingly we see the unprejudiced minds of children delight only in such productions, and in such images, as our true modern writers set before them."

[53] *Inquiry,* Sec. VII, Art. 3, p. 85. Cf. *System of Moral Philosophy,* I, 32-3, 57; and the second treatise in the *Inquiry,* Sec. I, Art. 7, p. 127.

[54] *Inquiry,* Sec. VII, Art. 3, pp. 87-9.

purposes: it explains apparent differences in taste, and it shows how tastes change because of subjective connections of ideas. Being a neoclassicist, Hutcheson must have been annoyed at the way in which associations of ideas constantly came into conflict with his theory of uniformity. Unwilling to accept the differences in taste that experience constantly pointed out to him, he insisted that "Uniformity amidst Variety" must universally please.[55] Moreover, throughout his treatise he drops variety from his formula and strongly favors the uniformity and the regularity in figures.[56] Thus, as a result of his neoclassic bias, Hutcheson limits the application of the theory to the problem of diversity and change in taste, and concludes that diversifying associating ideas are extraneous to esthetic feeling and cannot be the basis for our sense of beauty. Yet, and this is of great significance to the history of associationism in literary theory, when Hutcheson vacillates and admits that associations may affect the sense of beauty by causing objects to appear differently to different people, he encourages associationists to use a weapon which, by affirming individual sensibility, contributed to the downfall of the universal standard of uniformity and regularity.[57] Finally, although Hutcheson was no doubt aware

[55] Cf. *Inquiry,* Sec. VI, Art. 12, pp. 82-3.

[56] *Inquiry,* Sec. II, Art. 3, p. 17; Sec. VI, Art. 5, pp. 75-7. And mathematical theorems can also be beautiful. See also *Essay on the Passions,* pp. 4-5: "A little Reflection will shew that there are such Natural Powers in the human Mind, in whatever Order we place them. In the 1st Class are the External Senses, universally known. In the 2d, *the Pleasant Perceptions arising from regular, harmonious, uniform Objects;* as also from Grandeur and Novelty. These we may call, after Mr. Addison, the Pleasures of the Imagination; or we may call the Power of receiving them, an Internal Sense." – *Ibid.,* p. 101: "The Regularity, Proportion, and Order in external Forms, will as necessarily strike the Mind, as any Perceptions of the external Senses." – *A System of Moral Philosophy,* I, 15: "Certain forms are more grateful to the eye than others, even abstracting from all pleasure of any lively colours; such complex ones, especially, *where uniformity, or equality of proportion among the parts is observable.*"

[57] Some associationists, however, like Hume and Kames, begin where Hutcheson left off and explain neoclassic regularity according to association. Cf. William R. Scott, *Francis Hutcheson,* pp. 282-3: "Hutcheson's relation to the Associationalist Psychology has both an inner and an outer

of Addison's paragraphs on the increased delights of a succession of associated ideas in the memory, he places emphasis, as we said before, almost entirely on the arbitrariness of foolish and accidental associations and their influence on taste.[58] He definitely insists upon a single standard – "a fine Genius or Taste" is measured by the capacity of its internal sense to receive beautiful ideas, that is, uniformity amidst variety.[59] Unlike Addison, who in part acquiesces to their pleasing effects, Hutcheson recognizes only the disruptive and perniciously anti-classical tendencies of subjective associations of ideas, unstable and diverse, and would have us believe that they are secondary to the universal internal sense for uniform beauty. It was in just such an inferior position that the theory of association of ideas first began to manifest its influence upon taste.

To sum up, then, Hutcheson was partly responsible for the origin of two opposed trends in associationist thought. First, by arguing against association as a way in which standards of taste may be produced, and by founding taste directly on

---

side. The latter is one of hostility; he distrusts its arbitrariness and conventionality and refuses to believe that it can account for any 'sense.' Upon the inner side, again, it has been shown that Hutcheson has no real criterion of a 'sense', and he is driven back upon a plea for its universality. But he is met with contrary cases and exceptions, and to escape this difficulty he uses 'Associations of Ideas.' *If, then, association can explain the exceptions, why may it not account for the rule?*"

58 Only in a few places in the *Inquiry,* such as those mentioned above (p. 61, fn. 49) and one in Sec. VI, Art. 11, p. 81, is there a suggestion of the added pleasures in a succession of ideas: "It is known, That often all the Circumstances of Actions, or Places, or Dresses of Persons, or Voice, or Song, which have occurr'd at any time together, when we were strongly affected by any Passion, will be so connected that any one of these will make all the rest recur. And this is often the occasion of great Pleasure and Pain, Delight and Aversion to many Objects, which of themselves might have been perfectly indifferent to us: but these Approbations, or Distastes, are remote from the Ideas of Beauty, being plainly different Ideas." Also in the *System of Moral Philosophy,* I, 31: "How is it we remember? when we are examined about a past event, the time, or place, some circumstance, or person then present, is suggested in the question, and these bring along with them the whole train of the associated ideas."

59 Cf. *Inquiry,* Sec. I, Art. 10, p. 9.

a natural sense for uniform beauty, he originated the opposition against association as a standard of esthetic judgment. This hostility was later taken up by Burke. Secondly, by adapting Locke, he presented the most thorough analysis of diversifying associations in the early eighteenth century and strengthened those views regarding the influence of associations on ideas of beauty which, as McCosh says, were later held by Turnbull, Beattie, and Gerard, till they culminated in the ingenious but extravagant theories of Alison and Jeffrey.[60]

The last important figure in the history of associationism in the early eighteenth century is Isaac Watts. As a youth, the hymn writer and philosopher was taught at the Dissenting Academy of Stoke Newington by Thomas Rowe (1657-1705), who, as it is said in the *DNB*, was one of the earliest exponents of Locke's mental science. In an ode Watts himself celebrated his "gentle influence" which "bids our thoughts like rivers flow/And choose the channels where they run". It is not surprising, therefore, to find in the enormously popular works of this famous divine that the theory of association is accepted as a psychological fact. But Watts, like Hutcheson in part, had advanced beyond Locke's version of the psychology, for not only does he show how reason can be perverted by the association of accidental ideas, but he also describes how association may improve the mind. We have already mentioned how Watts, along with Addison and Hutcheson, recognized the ill effects of casual associations.[61] Now we shall only show how Watts in the other and more sympathetic way maintained the continuity of the associationist tradition.

Watts, therefore, is interesting for two reasons, although he does not directly apply association to literature. He suggests the use of association in language, and his *Improvement of the Mind* (1741) is the source of Johnson's illustration for the definition of association in the *Dictionary* (1755). Watts's

60 James McCosh, *The Scottish Philosophy* (London, 1875), p. 77.

61 See above, pp. 46, fn. 20; 58, fn. 45.

brief remarks on the problem of language are important only when taken in conjuction with those of Berkeley and Hutcheson, for all together suggest the existence of an associationist convention which Burke accepted as the foundation of poetic diction. In his *Logick* (1725), which was taught in the universities, Watts agrees to Locke's division of the sources of our simple ideas, "Sensible and Spiritual [or Intellectual]", into sensation and reflection. After these ideas have been attained, Watts believes that they may be excited or recollected "afresh by the Use of Names, Words, Signs, or by any Thing else that has been connected with them in our Thoughts; for when two or more Ideas have been associated together, whether it be by Custom, or Accident, or Design, the one presently brings the other to Mind". [62] Moreover, Watts, in common with Addison, lent further respectability to the theory of association by describing at length its constructive achievements. This he did in the book that Johnson eulogized, *The Improvement of the Mind* (1741). [63] It will be noticed, however, that in the following advice for the improvement of memory, Watts adds little to what Hobbes had written long before.

> When you would remember new things or words, endeavour to associate and connect them with some words or things which you have well known before, and which are fixed and established in your memory. *This association of ideas is of great importance and force, and may be of excellent use in many instances of human life.* One idea which is familiar to the mind, connected with others which are new and strange, will bring those ideas into easy remembrance. . . .[64]

[62] *Logick: or the Right Use of Reason* (London, 1772), Pt. I, Ch. vi, Sec. 1. p. 81, where Watts notes how confusion is brought into our ideas by mistaking words for things: "That from Infancy we have had the Ideas of Things so far connected with the Ideas of Words, that we often mistake Words for Things, we mingle and confound one with the other."

[63] *Lives of the Poets,* ed. G. B. Hill (Oxford, 1905), III, 308, 309.

[64] *The Works of Isaac Watts* (London, 1813), VIII, 129-31. Watts also suggests several associative aids to memory – the laws of association – time, place, company or contiguity, and likeness. The italicized sentence was adapted by Johnson for the *Dictionary.* Watts does not describe invention or compounding by means of association. His views on these two

Thus, even in the beginning of the century, Hobbes's views accompanied those of the generally dominating Locke. It was only in the next period, with Hume and others, that the Lockian account of irrational and casual connections was finally matched in strength by the Hobbesian version of orderly and regular connections between ideas. Whereas in this period, the theory of casual and confused associations comes into conflict with and undermines the standards of neoclassic taste, in the next period, the theory of regular and "natural" associations will be used to account for and reinforce reigning neoclassic taste.

Already, then, in the first quarter of the eighteenth century, the psychological principle of the association of ideas was seriously employed by many writers to explain the formation of critical standards and taste. Although Locke only recently coined and described the phrase in the fourth edition of the *Essay concerning Human Understanding* (1700), it was almost immediately picked up and came to be respected as a potent influence upon taste and criticism. In the eighteenth century Dryden is the first critic to mention the theory. But Dryden acknowledges Hobbes as the source of his idea of a series of consecutive thoughts; moreover, the psychology is of no critical importance to an understanding of Dryden's literary tenets. In Dennis, however, the theory receives heavy emphasis more or less successfully. Dennis attempts to account for the deeper imaginative and poetic emotions by reference to the way in which the mind operates. He suggests that poetic enthusiasm, or the sublime, is caused by thoughts in medita-

---

faculties conform to tradition. See e.g., *Logick,* Pt. I, Ch. iii, Secs. 1, 3, pp. 29, 38, and Pt. II, Ch. iii, Sec. 3, p. 201: Ideas "may be treasured up in the Memory, and by the Work of Fancy may be increased, diminished, compounded, diversified, (which we are ready to call our Invention) yet they all derive their first Nature and Being from something that has been let into our Minds by one or other of our Senses. If I think of a golden Mountain, or a Sea of liquid Fire, yet the single Ideas of Sea, Fire, Mountain and Gold, came into my Thoughts at first by Sensation; the Mind has only compounded them." – "It is no wonder therefore if Fancy leads us into many Mistakes, for it is but Sense at second hand."

tion, which, unknown to us, become profoundly moving by being associated with emotions. These incomprehensible and mysterious associations, he believes, might account for the sublime emotions. Dennis's contribution to the history of associationism in English literary theory lies in the notion that ideas in meditation associate with emotion and so become sources for the sublimest emotions of poetry. Wordsworth, holding similar views, was conscious of his affinity with Dennis. Dennis's belief that poetic enthusiasm proceeds from the meditation on lofty images associated with emotion thus foreshadows romantic practice and theory by almost a hundred years. As Monk has pointed out, the striking thing about Dennis is that in his work critical theory was in part turned away from the rules and dogmas of the ancients and was directed, instead, inwards to the analysis of emotions, in short, of the creative and responsive phenomena of the mind. [65] The shift in emphasis in Dennis is from the study of the object of art in accordance with established and preconceived literary standards to an appreciation of the profound emotional effects within the subject. Even as early as *The Grounds of Criticism* can the romantic tendencies of associationism be detected.

Dennis's unusual emphasis on the subjectivism inherent in the associationist approach to art is unique in the first quarter of the century. On the other hand, Addison is concerned with both the diversity of taste rising from wrong associations of ideas and the increase of esthetic pleasure through trains of associated ideas in the mind. In the first place, Addison shows how judgment must control the tendency of the mind to join incorrect ideas to words so that a true and correct taste might be established; in so doing he follows Locke closely. In the second place, however, Addison advances from his sources in the psychology of Hobbes and Locke and, like Dennis, stresses the subjective aspect of the theory of association. Herein, Addison is prophetic of the future importance of associationism in romantic esthetics. In thus relating the scientific psy-

[65] Samuel H. Monk, *The Sublime* (New York, 1935), p. 50.

chology of his day to taste and pleasures of imagination, Addison also contributes to the tendency of supporting critical theory by reference to mental processes.

The diversity of emotions and experiences in real life constantly ruffled the smooth waters of neoclassicism. Addison and his more philosophic follower, Hutcheson, account for this diversity of experience and its effects upon neoclassic taste by the new theory of association. But Hutcheson's emphasis falls almost entirely, as does Locke's, upon the "unnatural" conjunction of ideas, a conjunction of ideas so unnatural as to make taste incorrect. It is interesting to see that Hutcheson does not side with Addison and Locke in demanding a close scrutiny of associations by judgment; he refers instead to the irrational internal sense for uniform harmony and beauty, which he has taken from Shaftesbury. But whereas Shaftesbury believes the natural or innate propension of the mind for beauty to be universal, Hutcheson is disquieted by observing variations of opinion. These differences had to be explained somehow; therefore, all delinquencies from the esthetic norm were accounted for by the casual intrusion of improper and extraneous associations of ideas. Hutcheson, then, is an amalgam of Locke, Addison, and Shaftesbury. In the history of critical theory in the eighteenth century, Hutcheson's development of association is important for the influence it exerted upon Burke, Gerard, and many others.

The associationist tradition, only in its infancy in the first quarter of the eighteenth century, even at this time is markedly evident in the works of many writers and thinkers of national importance. There is no hiatus in the continuity of the tradition from its inception with Hobbes and Locke to its development by Hutcheson. And this continuity is maintained, it will be seen, to the peak of its literary application by Wordsworth. Naturally, the theory was constantly undergoing change throughout the century, as each writer saw new and varied opportunities for its application. This accretion of thought, to which the literary figures immediately following Locke contributed no small share, produced the associationist climate of opinion that was responsible for the ways in which many writers – Addison, Hutcheson, Hume, Hartley, Kames, Gerard, Beattie, Alison, Wordsworth, Coleridge, Hazlitt, Jeffrey, *et al.* – habitually resorted to associationist thinking.

IV

THE SEVENTEEN-FORTIES

In the second quarter of the eighteenth century the psychology of associationism increases as a vital and influential force in critical thought. As we have seen, it is of outstanding signifiance in the neoclassic esthetics of Francis Hutcheson, and it exerts some influence upon Addison's conception of taste and the imagination and upon Dennis's analysis of the sublime in poetry. The pattern of associationist ideas to which critics can refer when applying the psychology to critical problems is almost wholly complete. In the next chronological period, there is one addition to this pattern of associationism in critical theory. This addition is made by Hume and Hurd who both employ the psychology to reinforce their neoclassic points of view: the one to apply it to unity of action and the other to uniform standards of taste. And although Hartley is more concerned with the associationist basis for diversity, he too shows how associationism can be used to support neoclassic uniformity in taste. The theory is also used, in ways previously lighted by Addison and Dennis, in the works of Akenside and Baillie. Akenside's analysis of the inventive imagination is strictly in accordance with the associationist theory; and Baillie clearly introduces the psychology into the sublime. That the theory has evidently become popular and of increasing importance is suggested by its inclusion in the works of such very popular writers as Hume, Akenside, and Hurd, and such minor figures as John Gay, the precursor of Hartley; George Turnbull, the teacher of Reid; and William Shenstone, the friend of Mason and Warburton.

The tendency to think of associations as natural, if not

entirely regular, in operation begins in earnest with the work of the Reverend John Gay. It is Gay's *Preliminary Dissertation concerning the Fundamental Principle of Virtue and Morality* (1731), with its argument for an associationist basis for morality, that, as Hartley admits, led him first "upon considering the Power of Association".[1] In itself, therefore, Gay's work is important only as it opposes Hutcheson's doctrine of casual and "wrong" association and fosters the transition to the type of thoroughgoing universal associationism resorted to by Hume and Hartley. Gay explicitly differs with Hutcheson. Asserting that the theory of the internal and moral sense is occult, Gay resolves "our Approbation of Morality, and all Affections whatsoever ... into Reason pointing out private Happiness", and concludes "that whenever this end is not perceived, they are to be accounted for from the Association of Ideas, and may properly enough be call'd Habits".[2] In his brief essay, Gay limits the operation of association to the formation of moral habits, prejudices, and feelings. His point is that the persistence of an association with the feeling of pleasure produces habits which, in turn, account for various passions and desires. This process, it is seen, originates in an association of idea with feeling:

> We first perceive or imagine some real Good, i.e. fitness to promote our Happiness, in those things which we love and approve of. Hence ... we annex Pleasure to those things. Hence those things and Pleasure are so ty'd together and associated in our Minds that one cannot present itself but the other will also occur. And the Association remains even after that which at first gave them the Connection is quite forgot, or perhaps does not exist, but the contrary.[3]

Probably the most significant and influential figure in the history of associationism in eighteenth-century critical theory is

[1] *Observations on Man* (London, 1749), I, v. Gay's *Dissertation* is prefixed to William King, *An Essay on the Origin of Evil,* translated by Edmund Law (Cambridge, 1731).

[2] P. xxxi. I use the third edition (Cambridge, 1739).

[3] P. lii. Edmund Law himself notes (p. 506n.) that habits and associations raise passions, "and make us constantly proceed upon them for self-evident Principles, and pursue them for ultimate Ends of Action".

David Hume. Hume early evinced an interest in providing criticism with a philosophical basis. In a letter written about March or April, 1734, and addressed to a physician (probably Dr. George Cheyne), the youthful Hume avows his principal intention of studying human nature, for from this source he "wou'd derive every Truth in Criticism".[4] His preoccupation with the philosophic grounds of literary theory is again underscored in the "Advertisement" of his first-born *Treatise of Human Nature* (1739), wherein he plans to include in the treatise an "examination of Morals, Politics, and Criticism". A year later he published the third book of the *Treatise*, a systematic analysis of morals and politics in accordance with his conception of human nature. His philosophic examination of the principles of criticism, however, received no such special attention in the completed *Treatise*, unless we except the fragmentary discussions in Book II, "Of the Passions", and those in the later version of Book I, renamed *An Enquiry concerning Human Understanding* (1748). It is not until the publication in the *Four Dissertations* (1757) of the essays on tragedy and the standard of taste that Hume fulfills to the letter the promise, made almost twenty years before, to examine criticism with an eye to human nature. Nevertheless, even in the fragmentary and relatively minor

[4] *The Letters of David Hume,* ed. J.Y.T. Greig (Oxford, 1932), I, 16. The complete statement is as follows: "I found that the moral Philosophy transmitted to us by Antiquity, labor'd under the same Inconvenience that has been found in their natural Philosophy, of being entirely Hypothetical, and depending more upon Invention than Experience. Every one consulted his Fancy in erecting Schemes of Virtue and of Happiness, without regarding human Nature, upon which every moral Conclusion must depend. This [human nature] therefore I resolved to make my principal Study, and the Source from which I wou'd derive every Truth in Criticism, as well as Morality." For this section on Hume the following works have been very helpful: W. B. Elkin, *Hume: The Relation of the Treatise of Human Nature Book I to the Inquiry concerning Human Understanding* (Ithaca, 1904); C. W. Hendel, Jr., *Studies in the Philosophy of David Hume* (Princeton, 1925); John Laird, *Hume's Philosophy of Human Nature* (London, 1932); N. K. Smith, *The Philosophy of David Hume* (London, 1941); and Harold Taylor, "Hume's Theory of Imagination", *University of Toronto Quarterly,* XII (1942-3), 180-90.

suggestions in the philosophical *Treatise* and *Enquiry,* it is possible to perceive the importance for literary theory with which Hume invests the principles of association – those principles that are fundamental to Hume's conception of human nature. We shall first present Hume's analysis of these principles, and then we shall observe how he applies this associationist conception of human nature to criticism.

Hume "loosen'd" all our particular perceptions; the senses, he believed, "convey to us nothing but a single perception, and never give us the least intimation of any thing beyond." [5] Therefore, since all perceptions are "distinct and separable, . . . and may exist separately", every distinct perception being "a distinct existence", one of Hume's first problems is to show the manner in which the successive ideas in our thought and consciousness are connected, in order that knowledge be possible.[6] For, as Hume says, if these ideas were "entirely loose and unconnected, chance alone wou'd join them", and the result would be chaos. [7]

In the "Appendix" (1740) to the third book of the *Treatise*, he is quick to admit the weakness of the associationist hypothesis insofar as the metaphysical problem of personal identity or self is concerned: "All my hopes vanish, when I come to explain the principles, that unite our successive perceptions in our thought or consciousness. I cannot discover any theory which gives me satisfaction on this head". [8] But although he perceives the weakness of the theory with respect to one problem, Hume does not repudiate it or question its usefulness for the solution of others. On the contrary, he continues to insist in later revisions of his philosophy on the usefulness of the association of ideas as the "uniting principle" by which we feel confusion to be averted. [9] There are three

[5] *The Philosophical Works of David Hume,* ed. T. H. Green and T. H. Grose (London, 1875), I, 479, 559. All references are to this edition.
[6] I, 319, 326, 518, 559.
[7] I, 319.
[8] I, 559.
[9] The *Enquiry* (1748) and "A Dissertation on the Passions" (1757). The

general principles of human nature describing the regular and orderly manner in which ideas, supposedly simple and relationless entities, are associated: resemblance, contiguity, and causality. [10] These so-called "principles of union and coherence" are "the only general principles" of association among ideas in the mind. [11]

Furthermore, Hume claims, these "universal principles" regularize and organize the activity of the imagination. He clearly states that the imagination is gently guided by these universal laws "which render it, in some measure, uniform with itself in all times and places". It is not strange, as we shall see, that Hume should think in accordance with the neoclassic credo of the orderly imagination, uniform in all men, despite his acquiescence to the contrary belief that "nothing is more free than that faculty". [12] Hobbes, it will be remembered, believes that fancy picks out a pattern of ideas from the mass of ideas already associated in the memory. Thus memory, with Hobbes, is the determinant of fancy. But unlike Hobbes, who also sees the need for judgment and reason to check on the wild resemblances of the fancy while memory sets its bounds, Hume assigns to the regular operations of association the task of directly guiding the imagination with absolutely no reference to governing memory and no hindrance from restraining judgment. As a matter of fact, Hume distinguishes between the memory and the imagination, when he says the memory is strictly tied down to contiguity, that is to say, to the order and position of the original impressions. [13]

With Hume, then, the imagination is apparently free to combine ideas in any order at all; but, he qualifies, although we may not be aware of it, the imagination is in fact determined

---

latter, a revision of Book II of the *Treatise,* was published in *Four Dissertations,* together with essays on tragedy, taste, and natural religion.

10 I, 320; II, 82, 101.

11 I, 393.

12 I, 319.

13 I, 318, 386.

by our human nature to operate in certain regular ways. Therefore, the imagination is not considered as something arbitrary in its activity; and it does not require the aid of judgment to remedy its defects, simply because it already operates regularly by means of the uniform laws of association. In Hume's view the imagination for the first time becomes productive, or as eighteenth-century critics say, *inventive*, in terms of the regular laws of association. He states, for example, that the imagination is free to compound ideas:

> Nothing is more free than the imagination; and though it cannot exceed that original stock of ideas, furnished by the internal and external senses, it has unlimited power of mixing, compounding, separating, and dividing these ideas, in all the varieties of fiction and vision.[14]

Yet, he continues, even this synthesizing and compounding of ideas by the imagination is, in great measure, unconsciously subject to and dependent on the principles of association. Thus, despite the great authority of the imagination over ideas, these principles of human nature can and do still exert their guiding and regularizing power:

> But notwithstanding the empire of the imagination, there is a secret tie or union among particular ideas, which causes the mind to conjoin them more frequently together, and makes the one, upon its appearance, introduce the other. Hence arises what we call the *apropos* of discourse: hence the connection of writing: and hence that thread, or chain of thought, which a man naturally supports even in the loosest reverie.[15]

[14] *Enquiry,* IV, 40. This statement is perhaps the source of parallel well-known observations by Burke and Reynolds. Cf. also *An Abstract of A Treatise of Human Nature 1740,* ed. J. M. Keynes and P. Sraffa (Cambridge, 1938), p. 31: "There are no ideas that are different from each other, which it cannot separate, join, and compose into all the varieties of fiction." This *Abstract* is an epitome written by Hume of what he himself considered the most striking parts of the *Treatise.*

[15] *Abstract,* pp. 31-2; cf. also *Enquiry,* IV, 24: "By means of that relation alone [cause and effect] we can go beyond the evidence of our memory and senses." See C. W. Hendel, Jr., *Studies,* pp. 73,99; Harold Taylor, "Hume's Theory of Imagination", *Univ. of Toronto Quarterly,* XII (1942-3), 181: "Though the imagination, considered as a kind of fancy, may seem

The three different principles governing the connection of ideas in the imagination are first listed and described in the *Treatise* (Bk. I, Pt. i, Sec. 4): "The qualities, from which this association arises, and by which the mind is after this manner convey'd from one idea to another are three, *viz.* Resemblance, Contiguity in time or place, and Cause and Effect". He now proceeds to the description of these laws. The first law is resemblance: " 'Tis plain, that in the course of our thinking, and in the constant revolution of our ideas, our imagination runs easily from one idea to any other that *resembles* it, and that this quality alone is to the fancy a sufficient bond and association". The second is contiguity: " 'Tis likewise evident, that as the senses, in changing their objects are necessitated to change them regularly, and take them as they lie *contiguous* to each other, the imagination must by long custom acquire the same method of thinking, and run along the parts of space and time in conceiving its objects".[16] Of the three laws, cause and effect is the strongest and the most extensive. " 'Tis sufficient to observe, that there is no relation, which produces a stronger connexion in the fancy, and makes one idea more readily recall another, than the relation of cause and effect betwixt their objects .... Of the three relations above mention'd this of causation is the most extensive". One object is the cause of another when it produces either the actions and motions or the existence of the other, or when it has a power of producing it. Hume finds evidence of this law in government and society.[17]

---

free to juggle ideas in a variety of ways, Hume discovered that actually it operates in a regular manner, according to certain conditions of human nature and natural instinct."

[16] I, 319-320.

[17] I, 320-1; see also I, 392-3. Of course, when in one of his most celebrated critiques Hume later reduces causality to merely constant conjunction, repeated contiguity, or custom, he has apparently contradicted himself. This confusion in Hume's terminology has been noted by his opponent Thomas Reid more than once. See *Essays on the Intellectual Powers of Man* (1785) in *The Works of Thomas Reid*, ed. Sir William Hamilton (Edinburgh, 1872), I, 386b: "Causation, according to his philos-

Near the conclusion of this section, Hume draws two analogies: imagination is compared with memory, and association is compared with gravitation: these three "principles of union or cohesion among our simple ideas and in the imagination supply the place of that inseparable connexion by which they are united in our memory". Thus, as we noticed before, the imagination is no longer under the jurisdiction of memory. Hume then draws the analogy between the way "one idea naturally introduces another" and the operation of Newtonian gravity. This "gentle force which commonly prevails" is "a kind of *Attraction*, which in the mental world will be found to have as extraordinary effects as in the natural, and to shew itself in as many and as various forms".[18] This comparison proves the importance of association to Hume – it is as if Hume were to compare his "discoveries", had he been living today, with Einstein's revolutionary physical and mathematical discoveries.

Finally, Hume adds, while "its effects are everywhere conspicuous", the original causes of associations rest in human nature and "are mostly unknown". Yet when he dwells on a "most fertile source of error", the failure to distinguish between closely related ideas, he falls back upon the Cartesian

ophy, implies nothing more than a constant conjunction observed between the cause and the effect, and, therefore contiguity must include causation, and his three principles of attraction are reduced to two." Cf. also I, 294b: "We may here observe, by the way, that the last of these three laws seems to be included in the second, since causation, according to him, implies no more than contiguity in time and place." See also *The Letters of David Hume,* ed. Greig (Oxford, 1932), I, 155-6: "You ask me, If the idea of Cause & Effect is nothing but Vicinity, (you should have said constant Vicinity, or regular Conjunction), I would gladly know whence is that farther Idea of Causation against which you argue? This Question is pertinent; but I hope I have answer'd it. We feel, after the constant Conjunction, an easy Transition from one Idea to the other, or a connexion in the Imagination. And as it is usual for us to transfer our own Feelings to the Objects on which they are dependent, we attach the internal Sentiment to the external Objects. If no single Instances of Cause & Effect appear to have any Connexion, but only repeated similar ones, you will find yourself oblig'd to have Recourse to this Theory" (March 10, 1751)

[18] I, 319, 321; II, 87.

explanation advanced by Locke and Addison. This is a marked exception, however, for Hume generally renounces the physiological explanation of association.[19]

Although the original causes of association then, are for the most part unknown, Hume believes it entirely possible to give a mechanist account of the mental constitution by means of the principles of association. At the conclusion of the section, "Of the Connexion or Association of Ideas", he anticipates Hartley, for example, by stating that association is (what it never was with Locke) the mechanism by which complex ideas are formed from simple ones:

> . . . and 'tis impossible the same simple ideas should fall regularly into complex ones (as they commonly do) without some bond of union among them, some associating quality, by which one idea naturally introduces another.
>
> . . . nature in a manner pointing out to every one those simple ideas, which are most proper to be united in a complex one.
>
> Amongst the effects of this union or association of ideas, there are none more remarkable, than those complex ideas, which are the common subjects of our thoughts and reasoning, and generally arise from some principle of union among our simple ideas.[20]

Moreover, Hume explains the formation of the "indirect" passions, pride and humility, hatred and love, by a complex double process of association.

It is in connection with the enquiry into the production of passions that Hume describes the three *types* of association,

[19] In the *Treatise,* Bk. I, Pt. ii, Sec. 5 (I, 364-5), Hume conjectures that the ultimate basis of the principles of association may be physiological, although formerly he has said that the cause of association must be resolved into "original qualities of human nature", which he does not pretend to explain (I, 321). Sceptical about the truth of the Cartesian hypothesis, Hume nevertheless offers it as a solution to the problem of error. In the *Enquiry,* Hume entirely avoids the explanation of the causes of association. Instead he gives a popular treatment of its effects as illustrated in literature. He thus hoped to open a field of speculation that would be "entertaining" and "instructive".

[20] I, 319, 321. Cf. Hartley, *Observations on Man,* Prop. 12: "Simple Ideas will run into complex ones, by means of Association."

or "properties of human nature", that "have a mighty influence on every operation both of the understanding and the passions". The first property is, as he said before, the union of *ideas* through the associative laws of resemblance, contiguity, and causality. The second is the association or chain of "*impressions*", by which Hume here intends to signify the passions, operating only in accordance with the principle of resemblance. The succession of passions from one to another is described as follows:

The second property I shall observe in the human mind is a like association of impressions. All resembling impressions are connected together, and no sooner one arises than the rest immediately follow. Grief and disappointment give rise to anger, anger to envy, envy to malice, malice to grief again, till the whole circle be completed. ... 'Tis evident, then, there is an attraction or association among impressions, as well as among ideas; tho' with this remarkable difference, that ideas are associated by resemblance, contiguity, and causation; and impressions only by resemblance.[21]

In addition to the association of ideas and of passions, Hume also observes that the independent processes of association of ideas and of passions may "assist and forward each other, and that the transition is more easily made where they both concur in the same object".

Thus a man, who, by any injury from another, is very much discompos'd and ruffled in his temper, is apt to find a hundred subjects of discontent, impatience, fear, and other uneasy passions; especially if he can discover these subjects in or near the person, who was the cause of his first passion. Those principles, which forward the transition of ideas, here concur with those, which operate on the passions; and both uniting in one action, bestow on the mind a double impulse. The new passion, therefore, must arise with so much greater violence, and the transition to it must be rendered so much more easy and natural.[22]

21 II, 82.

22 II, 82-3, 87-8. It is interesting to notice that Hume cites a paragraph from Addison's *Spectator 412* as an example of "this phaenomenon" of "the association both of impressions and ideas, as well as the mutual assistance they lend each other". The quotation from the *Spectator* follows (II, 83): "Upon this occasion", writes Hume, "I may cite the authority of

This process of double association, barely suggested by Dennis in the first decade of the century, is central to Hume's exposition of the complex esthetic pleasure aroused by tragedy. The combination of pleasing ideas and painful emotions is described as the basis of the tragic feeling which it is the business of the poet to excite: "The whole heart of the poet is employed, in rouzing and supporting the compassion and indignation, the anxiety and resentment of his audience". The poet can succeed in pleasing only by the "sentiments of beauty" he employs in expressing these passions: "The force of imagination, the energy of expression, the power of numbers, the charms of imitation" which "are naturally, of themselves delightful to the mind".[23] Thus the painful emotions aroused by the scene ordinarily will cause pain and displeasure but are converted into a source of deep pleasure by an association with the delight in art. The ingenious philosopher explains this conversion into esthetic pleasure in a way not unlike Baillie's conception of the method by which a variety of sublime emotions may be produced:

> The same force of oratory, employed on an uninteresting object, would not please half so much, or rather would appear altogether ridiculous; and the mind, being left in absolute calmness and indifference, would relish none of those beauties of imagination and expressions, which, if joined to passion, give it such exquisite entertainment. The impulse or vehemence, arising from sorrow, compassion, indignation, receives a

---

an elegant writer, who expresses himself in the following manner. 'As the fancy delights in every thing that is great, strange, or beautiful, and is still more pleas'd the more it finds of these perfections in the same object, so it is capable of receiving a new satisfaction by the assistance of another sense. Thus any continu'd sound, as the music of birds, or a fall of waters, awakens every moment the mind of the beholder, and makes him more attentive to the several beauties of the place, that lie before him. Thus if there arises a fragrancy of smells or perfumes, they heighten the pleasure of the imagination, and make even the colours and verdure of the landscape appear more agreeable; for the ideas of both senses recommend each other, and are pleasanter together than when they enter the mind separately: As the different colours of a picture, when they are well disposed, set off one another, and receive beauty from the advantage of the situation.' " Cf. Akenside, *post,* pp. 103-4, fn. 68.

[23] III, 258, 263-4 ("Of Tragedy").

new direction from the sentiments of beauty. The latter, being the predominant emotion, seize the whole mind, and convert the former into themselves, at least tincture them so strongly as totally to alter their nature.[24]

In addition to the applications of associationism to passions and understanding, Hume uses it to explain sympathy, belief, inference and probability, and, as we have already noticed, errors in thinking.[25] If the theory of association does provide a plausible solution to so many philosophical problems, then Hume has more than proved his contention that the association of ideas has in the mental world as manifold and as noteworthy effects as gravity in the physical world. Truly, as the rationalist Reid indignantly comments, man is but a puppet without a mind and all of human nature is reduced to the mechanical association of ideas and emotions: "By this system, three laws of association, joined to a few original feelings, explain the whole mechanism of sense, imagination, memory, belief, and of all the actions and passions of the mind. Is this the man that Nature made?"[26] And critical theories, too, especially with respect to the norms, sublimity, fitness, and unity of action, are explained by means of the mechanical association of ideas or of emotions.

In connection with his associationist approach to the sublime, Hume considers this special phenomenon: "Why a very great distance encreases our esteem and admiration for an object". In other words, why does distance lend sublimity to an object?[27] Hume answers by saying that whenever "any very distant object is presented to the imagination, we naturally reflect on the interpos'd distance, and by that means, conceiving something great and magnificent, receive the usual satisfaction".[28] This satisfaction arising from "greatness", he explains,

[24] III, 261.
[25] II, 112-4, 142; I, 392ff., 396-7, 411, 428-9.
[26] *The Works of Thomas Reid,* ed. Sir William Hamilton (Edinburgh, 1872), I, 103.
[27] Cf. Monk, *The Sublime,* p. 64.
[28] II, 209-10.

"enlarges the soul, and gives it a sensible delight and pleasure". The process of double association of idea-plus-passion is the source of the sublime of distant objects. Hume describes the process and, incidentally, illustrates the subjective aspect of associationism.

> But as the fancy passes easily from one idea to another related to it, and transports to the second [idea] all the passions excited by the first, the admiration, which is directed to the distance, naturally diffuses itself over the distant object. Accordingly we find, that 'tis not necessary the object shou'd be actually distant from us, in order to cause our admiration; but that 'tis sufficient if, by the natural association of ideas, it conveys our view to any considerable distance.[29]

A person such as "a great traveller" or an object such as "a Greek medal", associated to the idea of distance, "by a natural transition, conveys our view to the distance", and thereupon excites admiration which, in turn, returns to the original source of the idea. Thus by a cumulative process of association, objects, near as well as far, may awaken sublime emotions in the soul. This is an early and interesting effort, writes Monk, to analyze psychologically the experience then called sublime. Hume's remarks on the sublime may be incomplete, "but they are none the less new departures, for they are concerned in the main not with the object *qua* object, but with the experiences of the mind that perceives the object".[30] It is Hume who begins clearly the application of psychology to the discussion of the sublime. Baillie carries on in the next decade and Burke takes it to exhaustive lengths in his associationist conception of the terrible sublime.

Hume makes another original contribution to the development of associationism in critical theory. Although he discusses at great length the utilitarian basis of beauty, generally omitting the principle of association, yet once he does clearly join the idea of utility with that of beauty when he states his belief that "the imagination is influenced by associations of

[29] II, 210.
[30] *The Sublime*, p. 65.

ideas" and that "personal beauty arises very much from ideas of utility".[31] This view, a departure in the direction of the Alisonian association of fitness – the fitness that augments the beauty of an object through associations – develops the remarks in Berkeley's *Alciphron* (1732) and begins serious discussion of the influence of fitness on taste in the middle of the century.[32] Spence regarded fitness as an association that influences ideas of beauty: "Sometimes an Idea of Usefulness may give a Turn to our Ideas of Beauty; as the very same Things are reckoned Beauties in a Coach-horse, which would be so many Blemishes in a Race-horse".[33] But Burke, as we shall see, fiercely denied utility a place in esthetics.

Indeed, it is difficult to assess accurately the enormous debts owed Hume by his horde of literary followers, Scottish and English. Hume is perhaps neither immodest nor incorrect in believing himself to be an innovator in the mental world as Newton was in the physical world. For us, his egoism, unfairly attacked in an early review of the *Treatise*, is justified insofar as he "give[s] new hints which men of genius may carry further", that is to say, as he discovers new fields wherein the association of ideas may be useful for writers interested in critical theory.[34]

Thro' this whole book, [Hume writes of his *Treatise*,] there are great pretensions to new discoveries in philosophy; but if any thing can intitle the author to so glorious a name as that of an *inventor,* 'tis the use he makes of the principles of the association of ideas, which enters into most of his philosophy... 'Twill be easy to conceive of what vast consequence these principles must be in the science of human nature, if we consider, that so far as regards the mind, these are the only links that bind the parts of the universe together, or connect us with any person or object exterior to ourselves. For as it is by means of

[31] IV, 199. See, e.g., IV, 202-17 for Hume's more generally held beliefs. Other accounts of sympathy and utility and the idea of beauty appear in II, 95ff., 150-2, 336.

[32] Ed. A. C. Fraser, II, 133.

[33] Joseph Spence, *Crito: or a Dialogue on Beauty* [1752] in Dodsley's *Fugitive Pieces* (London, 1761), I, 47.

[34] The review appeared in *The History of the Works of the Learned* (London, Nov. & Dec., 1739), II, 353-404.

thought only that any thing operates upon our passions, and as these are the only ties of our thoughts, they are really *to us* the cement of the universe, and all the operations of the mind must, in a great measure, depend on them.[35]

For literary theory, it is more pertinent to remember that Hume conceives association as something almost purposeful, especially as the guide of the artistic imagination. Proof of this point may be found in his third original contribution to the development of the associationist psychology in critical theory – his reliance upon association in an examination of literary genres and unity of action. [36]

Hume's best and most extensively original application of the associationist fancy to literary problems occurs in the *Enquiry concerning Human Understanding* (1748). There is in this work a lengthy passage in which he conservatively argues against mixture of genres. This he does by stating the case for strict neoclassic unity of action in accordance with the theory of associations of ideas and emotions. It is interesting to note, however, that a short passage in the *Treatise* (Bk, II, Pt. ii, Sec. 8) foreshadows the position later to be taken in the *Enquiry*:

When the fancy, in the comparison of objects, passes not easily from the one object to the other, the action of the mind is, in a great measure, broke, and the fancy, in considering the second object, begins, as it were, upon a new footing. The impression, which attends every object, seems not greater in that case by succeeding a less of the same

[35] *Abstract,* pp. 4, 31-2. In the eighteenth century Gerard appears to have corroborated Hume's pretensions as the discoverer of the several principles of association [*Essay on Genius* (London, 1774), Pt. II, Sec. i, p. 124]: "Though association of all the kinds that have been mentioned, is natural to all men, yet every man is so far from knowing the qualities and relations of ideas which produce association, that the enumeration of them is but a recent discovery among philosophers themselves."

[36] Hume even goes so far as to speak of the swift associating activity in the imagination as "genius", or "a kind of magical faculty in the soul" that collects ideas by means of resemblance. Here he anticipates Gerard, whose *Essay on Genius* (1774) is the most extensive associationist analysis of this character in the eighteenth century. See *Treatise,* I, 331; C. W. Hendel, Jr., *Studies,* p. 102.

kind; but these two impressions are distinct, and produce their distinct effects, without any communication together. The want of relation in the ideas breaks the relation of the impressions, and by a such a separation prevents their mutual operation and influence.[37]

Ideas and passions are deprived of the advantage of affecting each other, "unless they be united together by some relation, which may cause an easy transition of the ideas, and consequently of the emotions or impressions, attending the ideas; and may preserve the one impression in the passage of the imagination to the object of the other".[38] There is, then, a distinct advantage in maintaining the association between the ideas and emotions. For, if the ideas are not connected, the advantage of emotional accretion will vanish, and the over-all effect will be attenuated. Hume makes the obvious application of this principle to literary criticism. Nothing in the arts, he deduces, should be contrary to the rules – especially the rule of unity – for they are founded on "the qualities of human nature".

Shou'd an author compose a treatise, of which one part was serious and profound, another light and humorous, every one would condemn so strange a mixture, and wou'd accuse him of the neglect of all rules of art and criticism. These rules of art are founded on the qualities of human nature; and the quality of human nature, which requires a consistency in every performance, is that which renders the mind incapable of passing in a moment from one passion and disposition to a quite different one.

Here, nature and associationism and neoclassicism all merge. Hume illustrates these theoretical remarks with two literary references:

Yet this makes us not blame Mr. Prior for joining his *Alma* and his *Solomon* in the same volume; tho' that admirable poet has succeeded perfectly well in the gaiety of the one, as well as in the melancholy of the other. Even supposing the reader shou'd peruse these two compositions without any interval, he wou'd feel little or no difficulty in the

37 II, 163.
38 II, 165.

change of the passions: Why, but because he considers these performances as entirely different, and by this break in the ideas, breaks the progress of the affections, and hinders the one from influencing or contradicting the other?

An heroic and burlesque design, united in one picture, wou'd be monstrous; tho' we place two pictures of so opposite a character in the same chamber, and even close by each other, without any scruple or difficulty.[39]

Hume unmistakably supports the neoclassic position: "But though poetry can never submit to exact truth, it must be confined by rules of art, discovered to the author by genius or observation". [40]

All these remarks are further elaborated in the early editions of the *Enquiry,* where Hume seriously exploits associationism in order to explain the production of regular works of art by the imagination.[41] But before he applies the psychology to the arts, Hume analyzes it. In the *Treatise,* he writes that the "*qualities* from which this association arises" are resemblance, contiguity, and causality. In the *Enquiry*, these qualities are called "*principles* of connexion". Hume also states that these principles may produce sequences of ideas as well as mere connections or coexistences (complex ideas). Moreover, another law is suggested: contrast or contrariety, which, Hume believes, is a mixture of causation and resemblance. Yet except for the fact that the treatment of association in the *Enquiry* consists largely of popular illustrations, the position of the *Treatise* and the *Enquiry* on the subject of the association of ideas coincides almost exactly.

"It is evident", Hume begins in the *Enquiry*, "that there

[39] II, 163-5. Most of this is repeated in the "Dissertation on the Passions", IV, 160-1.

[40] III, 270 ("Of the Standard of Taste").

[41] Originally, the passages on literature in the *Enquiry* constituted no less than five-sixths of Section 3, "Of the Connexion of Ideas", as first composed and as given in all editions up to and including that of 1770. When these passages were omitted from the posthumous edition of 1777, the section was reduced to three short paragraphs. L. A. Selby-Bigge follows the text of the last or 1777 edition for his (Oxford, 1894) reprint. He gives no explanation or notification of the omission. The text may be found in the footnotes of the *Enquiry,* ed. Green and Grose, IV, 19-23.

is a principle of connexion between the different thoughts or ideas of the mind, and that in their appearance to the memory or imagination, they introduce each other with a certain degree of method and regularity".[42] Like Hobbes, he reflects on the connected succession of ideas in serious thinking, dreams, and reveries, and then illustrates the three principles of association:

A picture naturally leads our thoughts to the original (resemblance): The mention of one apartment in a building naturally introduces an enquiry or discourse concerning the others (contiguity): And if we think of a wound, we can scarcely forbear reflecting on the pain which follows it (cause and effect).[43]

Hume's great enthusiasm for association is evident from that which follows this definition. He translates at length and far more thoroughly and explicitly than Hobbes the three principles in terms of unity in drama, poetry, and history. Not caring to search into the inexplicable original causes of association, Hume is eager to consider "some of the effects of this connexion upon the passions and imagination; where we may open a field of speculation more entertaining, and perhaps more instructive".[44]

Hume begins his critical application by stating that in each work of art where an end is in view, there must be some plan. And though

the writer be hurried from this plan by the vehemence of thought, as in an ode, or drop it carelessly, as in an epistle or essay, there must appear some aim or intention in his first setting out, if not in the composition of the whole work. A production without a design would resemble more the raving of a madman, than the sober efforts of genius and learning.

To avoid chaos, each of the parts in a work of art must be connected and so "form a kind of *Unity*, which may bring them under one plan or view".

42 IV, 17.
43 IV, 18.
44 IV, 19n.

As this rule admits of no exception, it follows, that in narrative compositions, the events or actions, which the writer relates, must be connected together, by some bond or tye: They must be related to each other in the imagination and form a kind of *Unity,* which may bring them under one plan or view.

The three laws of association among ideas are responsible for this unity of subject and of structure. But, Hume continues, "this connecting principle among the several events, which form the subject of a poem or history, may be very different". For example, Ovid's *Metamorphoses* is formed "upon the connecting principle of resemblance" – the fabulous transformations produced by the power of the gods. Histories are limited in accordance with contiguity in time and place. In this way they maintain "a species of unity, amidst all their variety". But causality, the strongest relation or connection, is "the most usual species of connexion among the different events which enter into any narrative composition". [45]

Hume concentrates most of his attention upon the principle of cause and effect, for apparently it explains best the orderly sequence of ideas in a work of art. "Here therefore", Hume suggests, "we may attain some notion of that *Unity of Action,* about which all critics, after Aristotle, have talked so much: Perhaps to little purpose, while they directed not their taste or sentiment by the accuracy of philosophy". Obviously, the phrase "by the accuracy of philosophy" means the doctrine of association. All genres, biographical and historical, epic and dramatic, Hume continues, must employ this unity of connection. The unity in art, however, "is more close", because the associations of ideas in the "enlivened imagination" are reinforced by those of the "enflamed passions".

Hume now goes into detail in order to show why "a stricter and closer unity in the fable" is required in art. Such close unity is a requirement because the action is concentrated and the causes are therefore not traced "to any great distance".

[45] IV, 19n.

And it is also necessary if the associated passions are to fortify the associated events:

'Tis evident, that in a just composition, all the affections, excited by the different events, described and represented, add mutual force to each other; and that while the heroes are all engaged in one common scene, and each action is strongly connected with the whole, the concern is continually awake, and *the passions make an easy transition from one object to another. The strong connection of the events, as it facilitates the passage of the thought or imagination from one to another, facilitates also the transfusion of the passions, and preserves the affections still in the same channel and direction.* Our sympathy and concern for Eve prepares the way for a like sympathy with Adam: The affection is preserved almost entire in the transition; and the mind seizes immediately the new object as strongly related to that which formerly engaged its attention. But were the poet to make a total digression from his subject, and introduce a new actor, nowise connected with the personages, the imagination, feeling a breach in the transition, would enter coldly into the new scene, would kindle by slow degrees; and in returning to the main subject of the poem, would pass, as it were, upon foreign ground, and have its concern to excite anew, in order to take part with the principal actors.[46]

It is interesting to note that here Hume uses the three kinds of association formerly explained in Book II of the *Treatise*, "Of the Passions". The text of the *Enquiry* lacks this analysis. This slight lapse in the unity of Hume's work, later partially amended with the publication of the "Dissertation on the Passions" (the revision of Book II of the *Treatise*), we may correct by the insertion of a short review describing how the mind is conveyed from an idea to an idea, or from a passion to another of a kindred type, and from a passion to an idea and back again. The last type, the association of idea and emotion, it will be noted, is particularly valuable for literary art. For the rule dependent on it, the unity of close connection or of emotional effect, "takes place in dramatic poetry". Regular compositions, Hume writes, do not allow the intrusion of actors imperfectly connected with the principal personages, or the addition of digressive scenes "dis-

[46] IV, 21n. My italics.

joined and separated from the rest. This breaks the course of the passions, and prevents the communication of the several emotions, by which one scene adds force to another, and transfuses the pity and terror, which it excites, upon each succeeding scene". Hume calls attention to this operation among the "many operations of the human mind that depend on the connexion or association of ideas".

Particularly, the sympathy between the passions and imagination will, perhaps, appear remarkable; while we observe that the affections, excited by one object, pass easily to another connected with it; but transfuse themselves with difficulty, or not at all, along different objects, which have no manner of connexion together. By introducing into any composition, personages and actions, foreign to each other, an injudicious author loses that communication of emotions by which alone he can interest the heart, and raise the passions to their proper height and period.[47]

Therefore, a "breach in the connexion of ideas" extinguishes the "warmth of affection". Hume examines the fables of the *Iliad* and *Paradise Lost* in accordance with all the principles discussed and finds in them sufficient unity. In this manner, then, Hume comes to advocate, along with the neoclassicists, the strict and narrow view of unity of epic and dramatic action, which implies, he believes, that "the action be one and simple, in order to preserve the concern or sympathy entire and undiverted".

In short, then, Hume broadly reinterprets and defends the traditional neoclassic literary rule, unity of action. But he is not neoclassical in the sense that he refers to the authority of Aristotle and established classical models or to the determination of reason and judgment. His defense of neoclassic dogma rests solely on the new philosophy of human nature, that of the mechanism of association. Yet, as he disapproves of irregularity and believes that literature should be confined by rules of art, Hume fortifies and at the same time reanimates Aristotelian and neoclassical modes of criticism. Later,

[47] IV, 23n.

in 1761, his good friend, Lord Kames, will likewise attempt to "raise" criticism to the level of science by founding the chief neoclassic doctrines in addition to that of strict unity, verisimilitude and the distinction of genres, upon the associationist conception of human nature. In 1790, another Scotsman, Archibald Alison, will thoroughly apply Hume's discoveries to literature and art. And Alison's fundamental point, one which he never tires of reiterating, is the complex unity of associated ideas and passions which Hume ushered into criticism. In Hume's most systematic application of the theory of human nature to critical theory, associationism supports neoclassicism. We have, therefore, the anomaly of Hume's teachings which reinforce and encourage the tendency to search for subjective effects but which, at the same time, insist upon a formal and objective unifying quality in literature. As in Hobbes, there is in Hume a reconciliation of neoclassic formalism with psychology.

Although Hume is as neoclassical as Hutcheson in his insistence upon unity in art, it is strange that he does not use the theory of association to explain divergencies from neoclassic uniformity of taste in his essay "Of the Standard of Taste" (1757). Unlike Hutcheson who closely follows Locke, Hume takes Locke's phrase "association of ideas" and gives it a new twist. With Locke the association of ideas is largely an "unnatural" and confusing activity of mind. Hutcheson uses this conception of association to explain the lapses of the internal and moral sense for harmony, uniform beauty, proportion, and virtue. But with Hume, who in part closely follows Berkeley's adaptation of the necessary association of two senses for visual perception, it becomes a regular rule, useful and fundamental in many of the activities of the mind. Hume's attitude towards the theory of association thus becomes like that maintained by Hobbes in the seventeenth century. Hobbes believes that the process of successive association of ideas is a "natural" operation in human nature; and this is exactly how Hume conceives it. But Hume differs from Hobbes in that he believes it unnecessary to rely upon either judgment or memory – those faculties that produce orderly transitions or connections of ideas in the fancy by compelling it to remain close to the experience of "normal" human nature. With Hume, the fancy is inventive; it may alone compound ideas according to the synthetic principle – the regular and universal laws of association.

What has happened? What has made Hume use associations to explain the rule, no longer the exception? Perhaps the growing respectability of the concept and its general usefulness in explaining all of human nature, including the imaginative faculties, has much to do with this change in attitude. Much can also be explained by the eager, curious, and original mind of the philosopher, Hume. And, also, we must remember that Hume's discoveries are only part of a larger movement in the history of an idea. Hutcheson, Berkeley, Watts, John Gay, Edmund Law, Turnbull, Akenside, Hartley – all were seriously concerned about the role of association in art and life at the time Hume was writing and thinking. Associationism was in the air; and men of genius were able to revise old conceptions by means of the new psychology.

Although he fails to bring standards of taste within the scope of this psychology, Hume does clearly confine the exercise of imagination to the operation of associating ideas. He differs from his predecessors by even allowing the imagination to join simple ideas into complex ones and into successive trains without being bound by the memory or corrected by the judgment. This new concept of the artistic, associationist imagination is among the chief original contributions made by Hume to the associationist tradition in English critical theory. Hume's other contributions to the associationist approach to critical theory are almost equally significant. His conception of causal association and of the double association of ideas in the imagination and of passions in the soul has enabled him to lay the associationist foundation for neoclassic regularity of structure, that is, of epic and dramatic unity of action. Similarly, this cumulative process of association has enabled him to explain how distance lends sublimity to objects and how tragedy produces esthetic pleasure. Lastly, he indicates, although imperfectly, how the idea of utility may influence ideas of beauty.

Like Hume, Bishop Richard Hurd also has occasion to employ the associationist psychology to reinforce a neoclassic thesis. In a long discourse "On Poetical Imitation" (1751), Hurd defends modern versions of ancient themes from the libel of plagiarism on the grounds that nature everywhere and always is approximately uniform and also that common sense in its operations acts in certain general and regular ways.[48] These principles apply to the pleasure which imagination finds in metaphor and comparison, "the main source of that perpetual usage of indirect and allusive imagery in the writings of the poets".[49] Hurd's problem is to explain why there is such a similarity in the use of these figures in all writers. "This work of comparison", he begins, "is not gone about by the mind causelessly and capriciously". There are, in fact, two controlling factors; and these are (as Hume has shown) the law of resemblance and the law of cause and effect. Hurd summarizes and illustrates each of these laws. The first is resemblance:

> There are certain and obvious and striking resemblances in nature, which the poet is carried necessarily to observe, and which offer themselves to him on the slightest exercise and exertion of his comparing powers. It may be difficult to explain the causes of this established relationship in all cases; or to shew distinctly, what these secret ties and connexions are, which link the objects of sense together, and draw the imagination thus insensibly from one subject to another. The most obvious and natural is that of actual similitude, whether in shape, attitude, colour, or aspect.

Hurd offers some examples of these natural associating resemblances: "As when heroes are compared to gods, – a

[48] This essay appears in Hurd's edition, *Q. Horatii Flacci Epistolae ad Pisones, et Augustum: with an English Commentary and Notes: To which are added Critical Dissertations* (London, 1766), II, 1-146. The essay first appeared in 1751.

[49] III, 93.

hero in act to strike at his foe, to a faulcon stooping at a dove, – blood running down the skin to the staining of ivory, – corn waving with the wind, to water in motion". The second law that brings analogous ideas together in the imagination is cause and effect: "Sometimes the associating cause lies in the effect. As when the return of a good prince to his country is compared to the sun . . . ." [50]

Both types of allusions are common, Hurd claims, and occur in "the greater works of genius", even though the exact causes of these associations may not be entirely known:

But whatever be the causes, which associate the ideas of the poet, and how fantastic soever, or even casual may sometimes appear to be the ground of such association, yet, in respect of the greater works of genius, there will still be found the most exact uniformity of allusion, the same ideas and aspects of things constantly admonishing the poet of the same resemblances and relations.[51]

Thus, he concludes, because of the nature of things there is "a very remarkable correspondence of imagery" in modern and ancient epic poetry:

There are fixed and real analogies between different material objects; between these objects, and the inward workings of the mind; and, again, between these, and the external signs of them. Such, on every occasion, do not so properly offer themselves to the searching eye of the poet, as force themselves upon him; so that, if he submit to be guided by the most natural views of things, he cannot avoid a very remarkable correspondence of imagery with his predecessors.[52]

Hurd's inherent disposition again turns associationism to the support of his neoclassic thesis when he considers the similarity between the Roman and the English style. Ordinarily, critics would emphasize diversity when anatomizing the "*genius* of two people" remote from each other in time and place; Hurd, however, has his thesis in mind. Therefore, he believes, "the corresponding state of the English and Roman people

[50] III, 94-5.
[51] III, 96.
[52] III, 100.

has produced very near the same combinations of ideas". He carries this deduction into the realm of literary style: "May we not carry the conclusion still further on the same principle, that it produced very near the same combinations of words?" Thus, again, he observes, there ought be no suspicion of plagiarism; but, on the other hand, this similarity simply proves the operation of certain "general principles". [53]

At the same time that Hume published his *Treatise of Human Nature* (1739), a Scottish professor, George Turnbull, advertised his forthcoming work on *The Principles of Moral Philosophy*; a year later, when Hume published the third part of the *Treatise,* the *Principles* was published. In Turnbull's work there is a chapter devoted to an analysis of what he thought were two of the major laws of human nature, the association of ideas and the formation of habits. Turnbull is a prolific and indiscriminate borrower; he takes ideas, as he admits, from Berkeley, Shaftesbury, Butler, and, especially from Hutcheson and Locke. His treatment of the law of association derives largely from the last two.

Turnbull defines the association of ideas as "a league, or cohesion, formed by frequent conjunction in the mind". [54] Associations and habits, he insists, must be considered together as they "are very similar or like". The activity of the one presupposes that of the other; for when associations occur, Turnbull avers, habits are also acquired.

> They both include in their nature a certain kind of cohesion with the mind, formed by reiterated conjunction or co-existence between objects really separate and distinct from one another; i.e. that do not necessarily co-exist, or are not naturally parts of one whole. And as they are like to one another, so they must go together; or neither of them can take place in a mind without the other. If habits are contracted by repeated acts, ideas will be joined or mixed by repeated concurrence: and reciprocally, if ideas contract a sort of coherence by being often joined, habits must be formed by frequent repetition of acts.[55]

[53] III, 106-09. In a minor way, this psychology also enters into Hurd's brief against the use of puns in serious poetry; see II, 77-8.

[54] *The Principles of Moral Philosophy* (London, 1740), p. 93.

[55] Pp. 81-2.

Because associated ideas are originally distinct, he deduces that they are then distinguishable from complex ideas. In a complex idea the parts really or naturally inhere and are not necessarily held together by association. To be exact, associations refer not to these coexistent ideas already combined in an object, writes Turnbull; but they are "suggested to, or excited in our imagination by it". They are, he implies, completely subjective, for they "are added by the mind itself". Like Locke and Hutcheson, therefore, he believes that they "have no natural or necessary coherence". [56]

Nevertheless, despite the casual and accidental nature by which associations operate and habits are formed, they are both very important activities of human nature and may have beneficial effects. While it is true that there can be wrong associations which give rise to fantastic imagination and bad habits, they are, Turnbull admits, necessary sources of "habitual knowledge", memory, good taste, invention, – and of the advancement toward moral perfection. [57] Associations influence our emotions; the majority of agreeable or disagreeable perceptions are therefore partially determined by associations. They so influence us "from the very beginning of our existence" that it is extremely difficult ever after to separate them. Philosophy, he continues, is greatly concerned with this problem of separating ideas joined or "confounded" by association.[58] Turnbull mentions one problem that associationism raises in criticism, the association of utility with beauty: "The jangling about beauty among philosophers, whether it is distinct or not from utility, is a sufficient proof of it . . . . There is no reasoning about poetry, painting, or any of the polite arts, or indeed about morality, without being led into it." (i.e. the problem of dissociation). [59] But Turnbull gives no concrete illustrations and makes no detailed literary application of these abstract statements.

[56] Pp. 84-5.
[57] Pp. 83-4, 216.
[58] Pp. 86-7.
[59] P. 87.

Another significant associationist point made by Turnbull concerns diversity. Variety of associations produces variety of temper, he states:

various associations must produce various tempers and dispositions of mind: since every idea, as often as it is repeated, must move the affection it naturally tends to excite; and ideas, with their corresponding affections, often returning, must naturally form inclinations, propensions, or tempers; for temper means nothing else.

And this variety also contributes to the "formation of various genius's among mankind", which "may in general be divided into the aptitude to associate [or wit], and the aptitude to dissociate" [or judgment].[60] Turnbull is here adapting Locke's remarks on wit and judgment to the current understanding of the associationist psychology. "Wit and its instruments, metaphor and simile, are associations", he agrees with Hurd; they depend on the association of resembling ideas:[61]

And how, indeed, do poetry or oratory entertain or agitate, or wherein does their chief excellence consist, whether with respect to soothing and extending the imagination, or bestirring and moving the passions, but in associating the ideas, which being assembled together make agreeable, pleasant, charming, well suited company; in associating ideas which enlighten and set off one another, and by being fitly and closely joined, create great warmth in the mind and put it into agreeable motion.[62]

These are Turnbull's contributions to the history of associationism in critical theory. Only indicating an awareness of the influence of association upon beauty, taste, diversity of genius, wit, simile and metaphor, Turnbull keeps his discussion on a high abstract plane and out of sight of literature. Shenstone and Akenside, however, take association-

60 Pp. 93, 96.
61 Turnbull describes only the law of resemblance (p. 93): "Though frequent concurrence be sufficient, as has been observed, to produce the effect called *association,* yet nothing is more certain, than that association is more easily engendered between ideas that have some affinity or likeness, than between those which have no kindred, no resemblance."
62 P. 96.

ism out of the realm of abstract philosophy and make poetry of it.

Altogether different from Hume's profoundly serious applications of the association psychology are the popular and semi-humorous adaptations of associationism in the poetry of William Shenstone. In a letter Shenstone informs his friend, Richard Graves, that to his Spenserian parody "The School-Mistress" he added "a ludicrous index, purely to shew (fools) that I am in jest".[63] But it is fortunate for us that this index is added to the 1742 edition, for without its explicit commentary, we cannot be sure of the appearance of the psychology in the obscure poetry. The note in the index merely remarks on the casual association of ideas described in the third stanza: "A Circumstance in the Situation of the Mansion of early Discipline, discovering the suprizing Influence of the Connection of Ideas". The event to which this note refers is the terrible association in the mind of a child between the birch-tree and the rod.

> And all in sight does rise a Birchen Tree,
> Which Learning near her little Dome did stow,
> Whilom a Twig of small Regard to see,
> Tho' now so wide its waving Branches flow;
> And work the simple Vassals mickle Woe:
> For not a Wind might curl the Leaves, that blew,
> But their Limbs shudder'd, and their Pulse beat low;
> And as they look'd, they found their Horror grew,
> And Shap'd it into Rods, and tingled at the View.

More obviously associationist remarks not requiring the lucidity of prose commentary appear in another poem by Shenstone, the didactic essay in blank verse named *Oeconomy, a Rhapsody, Addressed to Young Poets* (1742-3).[64] The poet uses the association of ideas only as a helpful figure by which he may give depth and point to the moral he wishes to draw. Like

[63] *Letters of William Shenstone*, ed. Duncan Mallam (Minneapolis, 1939), p. 38.
[64] For date of composition, see *Letters*, pp. 47-8.

Hume, he compares mental attraction with physical attraction:

> Know too by nature's undiminish'd law,
> Throughout her realms obey'd, the various parts
> Of deep creation, atoms, systems, all!
> Attract and are attracted.

He then describes the attraction of ideas in the soul:

> Nor prevails the law
> Alone in matter; soul alike with soul
> Aspires to join; nor yet in souls alone,
> In each idea it [the soul] imbibes, is found
> The kind propensity. And when they meet,
> And grow familiar, various tho' their tribe,
> Their tempers various, vow perpetual faith:
> That, shou'd the world's disjointed frame once more
> To chaos yield the sway, amid the wreck
> Their union shou'd survive; with Roman warmth
> By sacred hospitable laws endear'd
> Should each idea recollect his friend.

The moral in all this popular psychology is that the young poet must shun one idea (profusion, extravagance, pride in clothes) so that he will never be plagued with its "conjoin'd" evil (poverty, shame in rags).[65]

In both of these poems, associationism is incidental to a larger purpose. Shenstone, responding to the associationism discussed in intellectual circles, superficially but plainly employs the psychology. He is interesting because he is perhaps the first to give it such popular literary expression. His poetic applications serve as a fitting introduction to his later and more serious prose remarks,[66] and to the important and far more popular poetic adaptation by Mark Akenside.

Unlike Shenstone, however, Akenside does not employ associationism merely to lend weight to semi-philosophic or moral

[65] *Oeconomy*, "Part the Second", *The Works, in Verse and Prose, of William Shenstone* (London, 1773), I, 283-4.
[66] See below, pp. 152-5.

observations. In his poem, *The Pleasures of Imagination* (1744), the association of ideas is as fundamental to his concept of the imagination as it is to Hobbes's philosophy of the fancy.

Convenient aids to the understanding of Akenside's concept of the imagination are furnished in the prose remarks that accompany the obscure, inflated rhetoric of his poetry. In "The Design" prefixed to this philosophic poem founded upon the writings of Addison, Shaftesbury, and Hutcheson, Akenside clearly points out to his readers that some of the imaginative pleasures arise "from the relations of different objects one to another". As these pleasures, he continues, are apparently in great measure dependent "on the early association of our ideas, and as this habit of associating is the source of many pleasures and pains in life, and on that account bears a great share in the influence of poetry and the other arts, it is therefore mentioned here and its effects described". The importance of association, thus made explicit at the outset, becomes especially obvious in the section of Book III, which the "Argument" explains as "The operations of the mind in the production of the works of imagination described".[67]

The prose remarks suggest the respect in which Akenside holds the psychology of association. His application of associationism to an understanding of his central subject, the nature of esthetic response and of creation, is only further evidence of the significance of the association of ideas for critical theory in the eighteenth century. Akenside believes that the operations of the mind involve the processes of association. That is to say, he maintains that the association of ideas in the memory is an invaluable aid to imagination when the latter selects images for "the curious aim of mimic Art" (III, 354). In this way art's imitations will remain comparable to its source in nature. Equally significant as this Hobbesian concept of the associative memory supplying the imagination with images is Akenside's belief that custom,

[67] *The Poetical Works of Mark Akenside,* ed. Rev. A. Dyce (Boston, 1875), pp. 117, 166.

formed by chance associations of ideas (III, 321ff.), is of fundamental importance in the explanation of man's esthetic responses to natural scenery. These two uses of the theory of association are, it will be remembered, not much unlike Addison's combination of the associationism of Hobbes and Locke.

Why, Akenside begins, do the varied scenes in nature affect the poet with beauty or sublimity? Is the source of their effect in God? "Or rather from the links Which artful custom twines around her [the mind's] frame?" (III, 310-11). The latter conjecture is apparently accepted as the correct one; and Akenside expands upon it as the explanation of the emotional and esthetic effects that several unrelated natural scenes have upon man. The customary association of ideas is described in accordance with Locke's analysis of the way chance associations form habits:

> For when the different images of things,
> By chance combin'd, have struck the attentive soul
> With deeper impulse, or connected long,
> Have drawn her frequent eye. . .

This subjective association of ideas joins ideas of which the sources in nature are really separate and distinct.

> . . .howe'er distinct
> The external scenes, yet oft the ideas gain
> From that conjunction an eternal tie,
> And sympathy unbroken.[68]

[68] III, 312-8. In a comment on other lines but peculiarly appropriate here, Akenside has explained how the subjective habitual associations may produce pleasure from disagreeable objects (p. 189, fn. to I, 234ff.): "Though the object itself should always continue disagreeable, yet circumstances of pleasure or good fortune may occur along with it. Thus an association may arise in the mind, and the object never be remembered without those pleasing circumstances attending it; by which means the disagreeable impression which it at first occasioned will in time be quite obliterated." Other subjective expressions, but not certainly associationist, are in I, 481ff., 526ff. Cf. also III, 462-4: "By what fine ties hath God connected things When present in the mind, which in themselves have no connection." The lines following these (III, 464ff.) give a poetic version of the

These associations then produce a chain of connected ideas. Akenside believes that temper or the prevailing passion determines the movement of this train of ideas in the mind:

> Let the mind
> Recall one partner of the various league,
> Immediate, lo! the firm confederates rise,
> And each his former station straight resumes:
> One movement governs the consenting throng,
> And all at once with rosy pleasure shine,
> Or all are sadden'd with the glooms of care. (III, 318-324)

Like Hume, who compares association to gravity, Akenside compares the associational attraction to an operation in physics, to the effects of magnetic attraction upon two points of a compass.

> . . . whate'er the line
> Which one possess'd, nor pause nor quiet knew
> The sure associate, ere with trembling speed
> He found his path, and fix'd unerring there.[69]

He now borrows from Addison directly [See p. 47, fn. 22] and shows how the associational powers of recollection augment the pleasures of the fancy and so affect the taste for nature.

> Such is the secret union, when we feel
> A song, a flower, a name, at once restore
> Those long-connected scenes where first they mov'd
> The attention: backward through her mazy walks
> Guiding the wanton fancy to her scope,
> To temples, courts, or fields; with all the band
> Of painted forms, of passions, and designs
> Attendant: whence, if pleasing in itself,

---

passage from Addison's *Spectator 412* which Hume used to illustrate the double association of ideas and impressions or feelings. It is not inconceivable, therefore, for Akenside to think likewise of the combination of sensuous effects as operating within the sphere of associationism. See above, p. 81, fn. 22.

[69] III, 334ff. For comment on this figure see A. O. Aldridge, "The Eclecticism of Mark Akenside's *The Pleasures of Imagination*", *JHI,* V (1944), 304.

The prospect from that sweet accession gains
Redoubled influence o'er the listening mind. (III, 338ff.)

Having completed the description of the associational pleasures of the receptive imagination, or taste, Akenside proceeds to the associational pleasures of the inventive imagination.

"These mysterious ties", he continues, hold together the trains of ideas in the memory, so that they may be worked over by the imitative fancy, "mimic art". Indeed, this popular description of association, except for the fact that no laws or principles are mentioned, is hardly different from Hobbes's conception of the associations in the memory aiding the imagination.

By these mysterious ties, the busy power
Of memory her ideal train preserves
Entire; or when they [images, ideas] would elude her
[memory's] watch,
[Memory] Reclaims their fleeting footsteps from the waste
Of dark oblivion; thus collecting all
The various forms of being to present,
Before the curious aim of mimic art,
Their largest choice: like Spring's unfolded blooms
Exhaling sweetness, that the skilful bee
May taste at will, from their selected spoils
To work her dulcet food. (III, 348ff.)

In a note to III, 348ff. Akenside observes, "The act of remembering seems almost wholly to depend on the association of ideas". "The child of fancy" can thus employ his "plastic powers" upon these materials associatively retained in the memory. And fancy, as in Addison's papers on the imagination, compounds, combines, and invents, and even "ranges in fantastic bands". However, in this compounding it is not, as Hume on the other hand affirms, governed directly by the regular laws of successive association.

Now compares
Their different forms; now blends them, now divides,
Enlarges and extenuates by turns;

Opposes, ranges in fantastic bands,
And infinitely varies. (III, 391ff.)

After the completion of the imitative work of art, Akenside describes how the poet judiciously compares his imitation, "line by line", with nature.

In Akenside's *Pleasures of Imagination* the theory of association is for the first time given genuinely popular literary expression in dignified poetry. Like Addison, Akenside has taken this eighteenth-century psychology out of the realm of abstract philosophy and has carried it into mildly intellectual art and literary theory. He has used it to explain the esthetic feelings as well as the processes of artistic invention. In both these applications of the associationist psychology, Akenside keeps well within the bounds of the tradition determined by Hobbes and Locke and affirmed by Addison and Hutcheson. He makes no original contribution; and his contradictory eclecticism is to be blamed for his failure to note how associations may affect the "internal powers" of taste (III, 515ff.).[70]

In his revised version of the poem (1757-70), Akenside also plans to show how the association of ideas affects taste. In the "General Argument", he observes, rather obscurely, that among the causes of imaginative pleasures is "the association of ideas", despite the fact that it is "more limited in [. . .its] operation" than those causes found in nature and art: "To illustrate these [causes], and from the whole to determine the character of a perfect taste, is the argument of the fourth book".[71] Unfortunately, Akenside never completed this book; consequently, we can only guess that perhaps under the impact of the new associationist ideas of Hume *(Treatise* and *Enquiry,* 1739, 1748) and Hartley (*Obs. on Man,* 1749) he might have had more to say about the artistic effects of the association of ideas. But even in the fragment of Book IV (1770), a slight

[70] But Akenside does believe that the Hutchesonian moral sense is "determined by the peculiar temper of the imagination and the earliest associations of ideas". See p. 191, fn. to I, 548ff.

[71] P. 201.

shift from the associationist position in the first published version can be perceived.

In this fragment, it is not strange to find that Akenside again uses association to explain the way the mind functions when in the heat of artistic imitation. But a difference from the first approach can be detected, and perhaps the source of this difference is in Hume and Hartley. He describes, for example, how habits are unconsciously and spontaneously formed and how these habits affect the taste for beauty.

> For thus far
> On general habits, and on arts which grow
> Spontaneous in the minds of all mankind,
> Hath dwelt our argument; and how self-taught,
> Though seldom conscious of their own employ,
> In Nature's or in Fortune's changeful scene
> Men learn to judge of Beauty, and acquire
> Those forms set up, as idols in the soul
> For love and zealous praise. (IV, 58ff.)

Conventionally enough, this is in the Lockean tradition; but what follows is not. It is precisely at this point that Akenside, under the influence of the new ideas about association, leaves the old channels of thought. The "vulgar" and unknowing populace, he states, are blindly controlled by unconscious casual associations of ideas stored in the mind. This is, indeed, reminiscent of Hartlean necessity.

> Yet indistinctly
> In vulgar bosoms, and unnotic'd, lie
> These pleasing stores, unless the casual force
> Of things external prompt the heedless mind
> To recognize her wealth. (IV, 66ff.)

On the other hand, the will of the poet is more powerful than the casual force of associations and can consciously employ "the secret laws Which bind them to each other" in order to frame a work of art. Here the imagination, as Hume thought, directly uses the laws of association without benefit of memory.

> But some there are
> Conscious of Nature and the rule which man
> O'er Nature holds: some who, within themselves
> Retiring from the trivial scenes of chance
> And momentary passion, can at will
> Call up these fair exemplars of the mind;
> Review their features; scan the secret laws
> Which bind them to each other; and display
> By forms or sounds or colours, to the sense
> Of all the world their latent charms display:
> Even as in Nature's frame... (IV, 70ff.)

It is impossible to appreciate Akenside's poetic analysis of the pleasures of imagination without understanding one of the chief influences upon his concept of the imagination, the association of ideas. With the aid of the prose commentary Akenside himself has provided, the associationism embedded in his difficult poetic diction can easily be detected. In the 1744 version of the *Pleasures of Imagination* four closely related associationist concepts are significantly applied to esthetic effects and products. Akenside uses the results of Locke's and Hutcheson's analyses of the customary, chance and casual associations of ideas in order to show how imagination through habitual connections of natural objects comes to be affected by the beautiful and sublime. Following Addison closely, Akenside also relates how the powers of recollection augment the pleasures of the passive imagination. And he clearly falls within the Hobbesian tradition when he describes how the memory helps the plastic powers of imagination "imitate" and remain close to nature. Finally, Akenside has reflected the subjective nature of the associationist psychology as applied to literary theory. In the 1770 version Akenside employs an additional associationist concept. From Hume he borrows the conception of laws of association and describes how the artist uses "secret laws" (no longer "mysterious ties") when producing an imitation that approximates nature's standards.

Again, therefore, as in the works of Hobbes and Hume, there is in the *Pleasures of Imagination* a marked tendency to think of the associations of ideas as something "natural", as the means by which the artist can abide by standards in nature when producing a work of art. The poetic applications of Shenstone and Akenside are evidence of the increasingly important presence of the associationist psychology in the intellectual atmosphere surrounding writers and critics. Evidently, as the abstruse psychology now became popular enough for adaptation by poets, critics also began to introduce it in their work. One such critical application occurs in a little pamphlet on the sublime by Dr. John Baillie.

In *An Essay on the Sublime* (1747), Baillie employs the association psychology to explain a few problems peculiar to his subject. Just as Ephraim Chambers in his *Cyclopaedia* (art. "Deformity") writes that subjective associations can make objects generally disagreeable give pleasure, so in this essay Baillie similarly recognizes the subjective influence of associations as he observes that while the sublime feeling of grand exultation is produced by magnitude and vastness, "small Scenes (except from Association . . .) have never this Effect".[72] This thoroughly subjective associationism which can make almost anything sublime is especially illustrated in the effects of architecture. Buildings, relatively small in comparison with the immensity of nature's works, can effect the sublime through several associations with sublime ideas which transfer their sublime effects to them: "Objects which in Themselves are not great and immense, if long connected with such, will often produce an Exaltedness of Mind". Buildings may produce the sublime sensations when associated with the ideas of great riches, power, and grandeur; and if they have columns, "the Imagination of Strength and Durableness" may produce the same sensation.[73]

"The powerful Force of Connection", Baillie also states, applies to metaphor; for if one idea is pleasing, it will make its associate equally pleasing by a transfer of feeling after pro-

[72] P. 7.
[73] P. 36.

longed association. Again, this shows how continued associations of ideas can modify taste: "Objects in general delight from two Sources; either because naturally fitted to please, from a certain Harmony and Disposition of their Parts, or because long associated with Objects really agreeable; and thus, tho' in themselves there be nothing at first delightful, they at last become so".[74]

Baillie admits that various passions can mix with the sublime and can sometimes change the whole character of the sublime or can, when the sublime remains predominant, produce a variety of sublime sensations. As an illustration of the first effect, he takes the association of dread. If this association becomes excessively strong, the delightful sensation of the sublime is ruined:

> There ever enters in the Description of Storms . . . some small degree of Dread, and this Dread may be so heighten'd (when a Person is actually in one) as intirely to destroy the Sublime. By this means an Object in itself grand may by Association lose most if not all it's (sic) Effect.[75]

In the second case, however, when the sublime is connected with other passions, "from such connections different Kinds of Sublime will arise".[76] There can be, for example, joyous and terrible types of the sublime, depending upon the associations connected with the same object. In the following illustration, the same idea produces these opposite kinds of sublimity because of associated emotions: a wrathful God "armed with thunder" strikes us with the terrible sublime; but when He is regarded as benign and as the source of happiness, we feel "the joyous Sublime". And these associations, Baillie declares, augment the delight: "From these Associations there arises different kinds of Sublime, where yet the Sublime is the Predominant; and from these Associations likewise, results a greater Beauty to it".[77]

[74] Pp. 34-5.
[75] P. 31.
[76] P. 40.
[77] P. 32.

Baillie also comments briefly on the association of virtue and sublimity, "quite different things".

When Virtue is at any time sublime, it is not that she is the same as the Sublime, but that she associates with it, and from this Association each acquires new Charms: Virtue becomes more commanding, the Sublime more engaging.

Thus most of the Sublime Passions, when virtuous, are so by Association and Accident.[78]

Whereas Dennis has only hinted at the associationist basis of the sublime feeling and Hume has only dealt in passing with the sublime of distance, Baillie has more clearly and more effectively integrated the association of ideas with theories of the sublime. He has especially noted its subjective influences; and he does not neglect to mention how it can produce a diversity of taste in the sublime. By thus carrying associationism into the realm of critical theory, Baillie contributes the associationist background of the sublime which will influence Burke and Gerard in the next decade.

In 1747 an anonymous author published "for the use of the young gentlemen at the universities" a searching and comprehensive analysis of the effects of associations upon man's moral, intellectual, and emotional life. His publication, *An Enquiry into the Origin of the Human Appetites and Affections, shewing how each arises from Association*, is a fitting and formidable precursor to the thoroughgoing associationist tract issued by Hartley two years later, as it explains practically all of human behavior by means of the association of ideas with the feeling of pleasure. Like Hartley, the author provides the activity of association with a physical basis in neural "vibrations" and motions:

[78] Pp. 25-7. For another, but very incomplete and entirely inaccurate, reference to the association of moral ideas with ideas of beauty see J. G. Cooper, *The Power of Harmony* (1745), "The Design" and Book II, pp. 519, 524 (col. 2) in *The Works of the English Poets,* ed. Alexander Chalmers (London, 1810), Vol. XV.

By association I mean that power or faculty by which the joint appearance of two or more ideas frequently in the mind, is for the most part changed into a lasting and sometimes into an inseparable union. It is probable association may be the result of, and owing to, that relation, which the soul and body have to each other in their joint incorporated capacity. And since by ideas are understood certain motions of the nerves as felt and perceived by the soul; then, probably, the reason of ideas when once united keeping ever after in company together, is owing to a succession of motions in the body, or, rather, to those motions of the nerves always producing one another.[79]

And, also like Hartley, he appears to accept only the principle of contiguity:

We have observed . . . how the brain acquires a propensity to the particular states a, b, c, d, e, f, etc. according to the degree in which it has been impressed by the objects A, B, C, D, E, F, etc. alternately. Let those impressions be successively repeated a certain determinate number of times, and the tendency to those states will become stronger and stronger, or the dispositions in the medullar particles to receive those impressions will succeed each other in their turn. Supposing therefore the state A to exist, or the brain to be impressed by the object A singly, and the tendency to the states b, c, d, e, f, etc. follows of course, or the motion excited by A, will produce all the rest in the order they used to arise and follow each other, every one of which will accordingly exhibit its correspondent idea to the soul.[80]

Our passions, desires, and principles of virtue rise and are formed, claims this unknown writer, not by divinely implanted Hutchesonian "instinct", but by these associations of ideas which we make ourselves or learn of others from imitation, or which grow out of circumstances we are placed in. Vices, he insists, are derived from wrong or immoral associations or from indulging right ones to excess.[81] He believes and tries to prove that most of our passions are not innate; they are, however, acquired or learned through a complex of associ-

[79] Sec. II, Art. 18, p. 68. The pamphlet may be read in Dr. Samuel Parr's collection, *Metaphysical Tracts by English Philosophers of the Eighteenth Century* (London, 1837), pp. 43-170.

[80] Sec. II, Art. 19, pp. 69-70.

[81] Sec. V, Art. 11, p. 136.

ations beginning in infancy, and these associations produce habits and customs. There is thus no better way to account for the variety of customs and morals in the world than by means of diverse associations of ideas.

> Hence the source of national virtues and vices; and the different, and (sometimes) contrary sentiments and perceptions of them in different ages and countries, according as men's associations have been different. We join the ideas of certain acts to certain qualities in persons; and annex genteelness, worth, and grandeur to objects which in themselves have none; agreeably to what we have seen others do before us, and in conformity with established practice.[82]

Although the author largely concentrates upon the analysis of the growth and formation of the various passions, he does have occasion to throw some associationist light upon other subjects. He writes, for example, of the association of two senses (Sec. II, Arts. 18, 20); he believes that compound ideas can be formed by association (Sec. II, Art. 41), and that the origin of language is in arbitrary associations (Sec. VI, Arts. 6-8); and, as we have already noticed, he points out that diversity in moral sentiments is best explained by acquired associations. Furthermore, he firmly believes in the deliberate and rational application of associations by men who aspire to the perfection in God (Sec. IV). He is, finally, a utilitarian (Sec. IV, Art. 27) and believes that beauty (which he confuses with sublimity) rests on the pleasing association with utility. His discussion of "beauty" is fragmentary and leaves much to be desired. Nevertheless, we must try to reconstruct it because it is certainly one of the links in the long chain of eighteenth-century esthetic associationism.

He explains first "why we are so agreeably charmed with the sight of magnificent palaces and majestic edifices". The association responsible for this esthetic response, later developed by Burke and Alison, is the idea of power. We receive pleasure, he reasons loosely, in the thought of having the means of happiness or misery of others at our disposal. Hence

[82] Sec. II, Art. 43, pp. 86-7.

we thirst after power and "its immediate consequence, the desire of doing such things as are great and uncommon, or of being possessed of it". The pleasure in the power to do much good produces this feeling of grandeur:

And from hence we deduce our first ideas of grandeur, majesty, etc. and being taught as we grow up to admire what is stately and magnificent, and to be pleased with these figures and adjustments of things as are connected with our greatest good, the association keeps insensibly forming till in time it receives such further degrees of strength as to settle in a confirmed habit.[83]

But, he continues, this association of pleasure can be spoiled and, consequently, the esthetic satisfaction diminished, when a part of the edifice is out of proportion. By this statement he does not mean the failure to conform to established rules of architecture; he implies the failure to be properly useful, i.e., "we do not look upon it as a proper means to an end". He concludes this superficial discussion with a statement on diversity of taste: as the associations of pleasure vary in people, so vary their responses to forms.

Most people, I believe, have ideas of certain forms, etc. in their minds, by which their future choice of things and persons is to be determined, so far as they have the means of determining in their own power. And accordingly as those forms . . . differ in men's minds, will some be pleased with this particular shape, size, complexion, etc. others with that; and to this is owing almost that infinite variety of tastes so observable in the world, that the very same things which some stile beautiful shall be construed a deformity by others.

Thus, he says at last, beauty is entirely dependent on taste perceptions determined by association: "Which contrariety of opinion is a demonstrative proof that beauty is nothing positive and independent, but wholly arbitrary and relative to our perceiving faculty; which faculty is of our own creating".[84]

The remarks passed by this anonymous writer on the associationist basis of sublimity and taste remain somewhat ob-

[83] Sec. IV, Art. 28, pp. 115-6.
[84] Sec. IV, Art. 32, p. 117.

scured by his failure to offer concrete illustrations. Nevertheless, as a whole, they are significant, although minor, contributions to the developing history of associationism in critical theory in this part of the eighteenth century. As he plays on the dominant themes, he helps determine the several uses to which the association of ideas can be put by those interested in critical theory. Unlike Hume and the general run of Scottish philosophers, this writer, presumably English, reflects the tendency to understand critical problems with reference to flexible associationist standards. He offers the experience of emotional satisfaction, not established rule, as the criterion for esthetic judgment, and tries to prove that no single and universal standard of taste, or of morals, can legitimately be held. Finally, he tries rather unsuccessfully to explain how sublime effects are formed by an association with the pleasure in power. Insofar as taste is concerned, his point of view is largely maintained by Hartley. And Hartley's associationist system, it will be seen, has much in common with that found in this interesting little treatise.

Though Hume's contribution to the development of the theory of association is not inconsiderable, yet Priestley is able to say, "Compared with Dr. Hartley, I consider Mr. Hume as not even a child".[85] This dictum is to a certain degree just; for Dr. David Hartley is far more penetrating in his associationism than Hume cared to be. However, Hartley's analytical treatise, *Observations on Man, his Frame, his Duty, and his Expectations* (1749) is, as Priestley declares, "clog-

[85] *Letters to a Philosophical Unbeliever* (Birmingham, 1787), I, 126. Priestley also notes the shortcomings in Locke's views [*Hartley's Theory of the Human Mind* (London, 1790), pp. xxv-xxvi]: "The mechanical association of ideas that have been frequently presented to the mind at the same time was, I believe, first noticed by Mr. Locke; but he had recourse to it only to explain those sympathies and antipathies which he calls *unnatural,* in opposition to those which, he says, are born with us; and he refers them to 'trains of motion in the animal spirits'." [Etc.] Priestley quotes a passage from Locke's *Essay* and then remarks, "This quotation is sufficient to show how exceedingly imperfect were Mr. Locke's notions concerning the nature, cause, and effects of this principle."

ged with a whole system of moral and religious knowledge".[86] Indeed, Hartley makes it exceedingly difficult for readers interested in critical theory to struggle through his treatise precisely because of the vast amount of alien territory explored. This encyclopedic work covers practically all of experience, religious and secular, and comprehends it more or less successfully in a single psychological doctrine. After the religion and the physiology are omitted, as in Priestley's more palatable abridged editions, the following thesis can be perceived as obviously central to all his thought concerning the mind: the human mind operates solely through associations of ideas and through these associations builds from originally simple states into more complex ones.

In the "Preface" to his work, Hartley openly admits that the Reverend John Gay's hypothesis made eighteen years before – all intellectual pleasures and pains can be deduced from association, – set him "upon considering the Power of Association".[87] After having patiently given the closest attention to this subject in the course of several years, he published a Latin tract, *Conjecturae Quaedam de Sensu, Motu, et Idearum Generatione*, in 1746.[88] This essay, reworked and enlarged with extended proofs, is reproduced in translation in the first part of the *Observations* in 1749. It is, therefore, to the latter work that we shall give our attention.

The two chief parts of Harley's theory of the mind are embodied in the doctrine of vibration and the doctrine of association. The one refers to the physical or neural nature of all sensation, the other to the combination of the simple elements of sensation, ideas, into complex ideas and states.

86 *Hartley's Theory of the Human Mind* [1775] (London, 1790), p. iii.
87 *Observations on Man* (London, 1749), p. v. For Gay's associationism, see above, pp. 72-3.
88 It was reprinted in Dr. Parr's collection of *Metaphysical Tracts* (London, 1837). The date was ascertained by Benjamin Rand, "The Early Development of Hartley's Doctrine of Association", *Psychological Review*, XXX (1923), 306-20. See R. E. A. Palmer's English translation, Augustan Reprint Society (1959), Nos. 77-78, ed. M. Kallich.

The doctrine of vibration invites comparison with the physical explanations of association previously advanced by Hobbes and the Cartesians. It will be-remembered that Addison had attempted the Cartesian explanation and that Hume had made a few cautious conjectures in this direction in his *Treatise of Human Nature* (1739); but in his later *Enquiry concerning the Human Understanding* (1748), Hume had abandoned the physiological explanation. Hartley is willing to take Cartesian fancy for fact, and even suggests that there is some resemblance between his and the earlier Cartesian views: "It may afford the Reader some Entertainment, to compare my Hypothesis with what Des Cartes and Leibnitz have advanced, concerning Animal Motion, and the Connexion between the Soul and Body. My general Plan bears a near Relation to theirs."[89] Superficially, Hartley's theory of neural vibrations seems to be a "scientific" development of the earlier point of view. But it clearly shares with that view the weakness of being at best but a dubious hypothesis incapable, at the time, of true scientific verification. Like Hume, Hartley frankly admits his uncertainty over the soundness of the physiological part of his theory; he has no doubt, however, about the truth of associationism: "The doctrine of Association may be laid down as a certain Foundation, and a Clue to direct our future Inquiries, whatever becomes of that of Vibrations".[90] And even Joseph Priestley, his disciple and promoter, omits the physiological portions in his two editions of the *Observations* (1775, 1790), considering them of only minimum importance for the understanding of the operations of the mind. Yet, because Hartley differs with Hume and emphasizes the physiological foundation, his theory of association cannot be properly appreciated without first understanding something of its assumed physical basis. Like the anonymous author of the 1747 pamphlet, Hartley thinks of the human organism as a single unit, of the body and mind acting in cooperation.

The doctrine of vibration is developed, Hartley is frank to

[89] Prop. 21 (I, 110-111).
[90] Prop. 11 (I, 72).

say, from hints found in Newton's works: "The First of these Doctrines [vibration] is taken from the Hints concerning the Performance of Sensation and Motion, which Sir Isaac Newton has given at the End of his *Principia*, and in the *Questions* annexted to his *Optics*".[91] This vibration hypothesis is simple: the nerve extremities, or senses, are put into "vibratory motion" by the impression of corpuscular bodies that are also vibrating in the air; these bodies supposedly emanate from the external object. When the object is perceived, the vibratory motion or sensation is freely transmitted by the nerves to the brain and continued there as the vibrations of smaller medullary particles or ideas. There is, then, a continuous stream of vibrations decreasing in intensity from the time the object is sensed until its idea is produced and retained in the mind. Ideas, therefore, are entirely dependent upon the vibrations accompanying previous sensations and are only generated when "sensations ... leave certain vestiges, types, or images of themselves".[92] These faint ideas are, in short, the very same as those formerly described by Hobbes; to be exact, they are only feebler and less intense vibrations, "miniatures" or "vibratiuncles": "The Sensatory Vibrations" beget in the brain "a Disposition to diminutive Vibrations, which may also be called Vibratiuncles and Miniatures, corresponding to themselves". These dispositions, H. C. Warren tries to make clear, are the physical traces of ideas, and the ideas themselves occur and recur as the vestiges or traces left by sensations are again stimulated and set in vibration.[93] In this way, such vibrations and repetitions are also the basis of habits. And, according to Hartley, man lives almost entirely by habit formed by the constant compounding and recompounding of sensations until the natural state in which we are born disappears.

In every creature, writes Hartley, there is from the first a natural disposition, and, consequently, there are "Natural Vi-

[91] Ch. i, p. 5.
[92] Prop. 8 (I, 56).
[93] Prop. 9 (I, 58); H. C. Warren, *A History of the Associationist Psychology from Hartley to Lewes* (Baltimore, 1921), p. 9.

brations" existing in the "Foetus in Utero". "As soon as the Child is born", he continues, "external Objects act upon it violently, and excite Vibrations in the medullary Substance, which differ from the natural ones". These secondary vibrations he calls "preternatural". Continual repetition of these preternatural vibrations explains how habits or dispositions to the preternatural overcome and then permanently displace the natural or original state. This is the essence of empiricism and as perfect a demonstration against the internal sense doctrine of Shaftesbury and Hutcheson in 18th-century psychological theory as one can wish:

> Suppose the same Object to be impressed again and again, for a sufficient Number of Times, and it seems to follow, that the medullary Substance will be longer in passing from *A* [preternatural state] to *N* [natural state], after the second Impression, than after the first, after the third Impression than second, etc. till, at last, it will not return to its natural original State of Vibrations *N* at all, but remain in the preternatural State *A*, after the Vibrations have fallen to a diminutive Pitch, their kind and Place, or chief Seat, and their Line of Direction, continuing the same. This State may therefore be fitly denoted by *a* [ideas, traces], and being now in the Place of the natural State *N*, it will be kept up by the Heat of the Medullary Substance, and the Pulsation of its Arteries.[94]

Thus, as Brett sums up, "This explains the increased facility which is produced by repetition and habit; for *A* supplants *N* permanently, and we have in place of the first nature a second nature".[95]

This is, in short, Hartley's doctrine of vibration. After discussing this physiological foundation and showing the interdependence of body and mind, Hartley is ready for the analysis of the associational processes. His problem is to show how the elements of sensation (miniature vibrations) are related and connected in the mind by the law of association. The doctrine of association is taken, he grants, "from what Mr. Locke, and other ingenious Persons since his Time, have delivered con-

[94] Prop. 9 (I, 60-1).
[95] G. S. Brett, *A History of Psychology* (London, 1921), II, 282.

cerning the Influence of Association over our Opinions and Affections, and its Use in explaining those Things in an accurate and precise Way, which are commonly referred to the Power of Habit and Custom, in a general and indeterminate one".[96] Proposition 10 begins the analysis: "Any Sensations A, B, C, etc. by being associated with one another a sufficient Number of Times, get such a Power over the corresponding Ideas a, b, c, etc. that any one of the Sensations A, when impressed alone, shall be able to excite in the Mind b, c, etc. the Ideas of the rest".[97] It is seen, first, that the succession of ideas is directly dependent on the chance or casual succession of vibrations or sensations. Secondly, the succession of ideas may also be dependent on previously associated ideas:

> When the Ideas a, b, c, d, etc. have been sufficiently associated, . . . if we suppose any single Idea of these, a for instance, to be raised by the Tendency of the medullary Substance that Way . . . this Idea a, thus raised, will frequently bring in all the rest, b, c, d, etc. and so associate all of them still farther.[98]

Hartley recognizes only one principle of association, contiguity [in time] of ideas and sensations; he never employs or mentions any other principle by which associations among ideas are governed, those principles that Hume and the Scottish critics used – resemblance, contrast, and causality. His description of the rise of separate ideas or images is sketched in accordance with the principle of the successive association of contiguous ideas.

Harley also describes the operation of mind in accordance with the principle of "synchronous" or simultaneous association. This principle is to some extent responsible for the formation of complex states and ideas. For example, simultaneous associations occur when sensations are successively transmitted to the *same* region of the brain; thus, as they there tend to modify one another, these sensations ultimately produce a total complex

[96] Ch. i, pp. 5-6.
[97] I, 65.
[98] I, 74.

altogether new and different from any of the original simple ideas: "if any Two [sensations], or more, belong to the same Region, since they cannot exist together in their distinct Forms, *A* will raise something indeterminate between them".[99] Or, again, compound ideas or "miniatures" are produced from a compound impression of simultaneously associated sensation.[100]

And, upon the Whole, [Hartley concludes,] it may appear to the Reader, that the simple Ideas of Sensation must run into Clusters and Combinations, by Association, and that each of these will, at last, coalesce into one complex Idea, by the Approach and Commixture of the several compounding Parts.

It appears also from Observation, that many of our intellectual Ideas, *such as those that belong to the Heads of Beauty*, Honour, moral Qualities, etc. are, in Fact, thus composed of Parts, which, by degrees, coalesce into one complex Idea.[101]

The complex idea of beauty mentioned here is only one among the many complex ideas that upon analysis is proved to be but a composition of elements held together in clusters by habitual associations. When Hartley now concretely endeavors to explain the phenomena of the entire mental world in terms of the fusion and succession of elementary experiences, sensations, and their ideas, it becomes possible to perceive the significance of all this abstract theorizing. More thoroughly than Hume, Hartley examines all mental activity by means of these comprehensive principles. He analyzes the senses in turn: touch, taste, smell, sight, and hearing. Emotions and passions he regards as being derived from ideas; they are merely "Aggregates of simple Ideas united by Association".[102] Memory, reveries, dreams are also said to be controlled by associations. Volition and judgment are governed by association too; and belief, and assent and dissent, are studied as the products of association with the idea of truth. Religion, morality, and

[99] Prop. 12, Case 1 (I, 73).
[100] Prop. 12, Case 4 (I, 74).
[101] Prop. 12, Case 5 (I, 74-5). Emphasis mine.
[102] Prop. 89 (I, 368).

the doctrine of necessity and perfectibility (which Godwin made so much of) are also thoroughly examined and their associationist foundations unveiled. And what is chiefly of interest to us, he discusses the associationist foundation of the "intellectual Ideas and Pleasures", among which are those of the imagination. The discussion of the imagination and the "Pleasures of the Imagination" makes clear Hartley's associationist position with regard to critical theory.

Except in the case of novel or first sensations (and so opening the way for Burke's critique of associationism), the imagination, Hartley believes, is governed by association of ideas:

> The Recurrence of Ideas, especially visible and audible ones, in a vivid manner, but without any regard to the Order observed in past Facts, is ascribed to the Power of Imagination or Fancy. Now here we may observe, that every succeeding Thought is the Result either of some new Impression, or of an Association with the preceding.[103]

Invention, which Hartley distinguishes from this conception of the merely fanciful imagination, is dependent on memory's "Stock of Ideas": "A strong and quick Memory is necessary, that so [sic] the Ideas of the Poet or Philosopher may depend upon, and be readily suggested by, each other. . . And the Nature of this Faculty seems as reconcileable with, and deducible from, the Power of Association, and the Mechanism of the Mind here explained, as that of any other".[104] Evidently, Hartley does not differ very much from Hobbes who, it will be remembered, similarly described in his *Answer to Davenant* (1650) the operation of the fancy.

Hartley's other application of the theory of association to critical theory is found in the section devoted to an analysis of the pleasures of the imagination. These pleasures, which are among the "intellectual Pleasures and Pains", have their origin in "the general law of Association".[105] The discussion

[103] Prop. 91 (I, 383).
[104] Prop. 94 (I, 434-5).
[105] Ch. iv (I, 416). There is an ascending scale of pleasure according to Hartley's system. First come the sensible pleasures; they are the founda-

of the manner in which the imagination is esthetically satisfied by the influence of several types of associated elements of experience fills more than twenty pages. It is an esthetic treatise in little, written in conformity with the theory of association previously submitted. In it is the first real attempt made by Hartley to solve concrete problems of criticism. The method he observes is generally as follows: he lists many of the separate elements that are known to contribute to esthetic pleasure and then shows how they are united and cemented together in the indivisible complex state – "the general indeterminate Aggregate" – by association.[106]

Among the first species of imaginative pleasures to which Hartley applies this system are the "Pleasures arising from the Beauty of the Natural World". In a paragraph that distinctly echoes Addison's remarks in the beginning of *Spectator 417,* Hartley writes of the tranquil beauties of a rural scene. The esthetic pleasure experienced at the sight of such a natural scene is originally derived from the pleasure found in several associated ideas:

> The pleasant Tastes, and Smells, and the fine Colours of Fruits and Flowers, the Melody of Birds, and the grateful Warmth or Coolness of the Air, in the proper Seasons, transfer Miniatures [i.e. ideas] of these Pleasures upon rural Scenes, which start up instantaneously so mixed with each other, and with such as will be immediately enumerated, as to be separately indiscernible.[107]

---

tion of the intellectual ones, "which are formed from them in Succession, according to the law of association" (II, 213). And then the more complex intellectual pleasures combine and recombine through association in order to progress from lower states to higher ones, from imagination, ambition, moral sense, sympathy, self-interest, to theopathy. See Vol. II, Ch. iii, Sec. 3, Props. 55-61, pp. 242-58. A thorough exposition of the association between ideas of beauty and of morality is also made by David Fordyce [*The Elements of Moral Philosophy,* Bk. III, Sec. i, pp. 342-51, in *the Preceptor,* ed. Robert Dodsley (London, 1748), Vol. II]. It is this association of ideas in the mind that provides the basis for Hartley's system, that system which describes the progress of taste from intellectual pleasures to higher moral ones.

[106] Prop. 94 (I, 421). All of Hartley's critical theory is included in this proposition.

[107] I, 419.

Thus, we may conclude, a combination of associated ideas is the source of the complex delight in the beauty of nature.

The sublimity of nature, on the other hand, is somewhat more complex. It is produced by an association with fear; but this fear passes into pleasure when security from danger is suggested. This theory exactly corresponds with that propounded by Burke less than ten years after.

If there be a Precipice, a Cataract, a Mountain of Snow, etc. in one Part of the Scene, the nascent Ideas of Fear and Horror magnify and enliven all the other Ideas, and by degrees pass into Pleasures, by suggesting the Security from Pain.[108]

The sublime in painting can also be partially explained by a similar association:

The Representation of Battles, Storms, wild Beasts, and other Objects of Horror, in Pictures, please us peculiarly, partly from the near Alliance which the Ideas suggested bear to Pain, partly from the secret Consciousness of our own Security, and partly because they awaken and agitate the Mind sufficiently to be strongly affected with the other Pleasures, which may then be offered to it.[109]

Hartley also declares that the traditional neoclassic dualism, uniformity and variety, is a principal source of the pleasures of beauty in external nature. But it is not immediately and intuitively pleasing, as Shaftesbury and Hutcheson affirm; and it does not, Hartley implies, make an original and natural appeal to the imagination. Associationism thus invades the last stronghold of the Hutchesonian school of the internal senses. For three associations are the sources of the pleasures of uniformity and variety: nature, art, and fitness.

Uniformity and Variety in Conjunction are also principal Sources of the Pleasures of Beauty, being made so partly by their association with the Beauties of Nature; partly by that with the Works of Art; and with the many Conveniences which we receive from the Uniformity and Variety of the Works of Nature and Art. They must transfer part of the

108 *Ibid.*
109 I, 428.

Lustre borrowed from the Works of Art, and from the Head of Convenience, upon the Works of Nature.[110]

These three examples suffice as illustrations of the way in which Hartley believes a taste for nature is developed. Many other associated elements that may be included in this complex pleasure are merely listed. Some of these are certainly prophetic of Wordsworth's views and experiences: they are poetry, sports and health, tranquillity, innocence as contrasted with the corruption of populous cities, mirth, retirement, God as Author of nature. All these kinds of associations contribute to the pleasures of imagination. As a result of these diverse sources, Hartley deduces, diverse tastes are necessarily produced:

> And upon the Whole, the Reader may see, that there are sufficient Sources for all those Pleasures of Imagination, which the Beauties of Nature excite in different Persons; and that the Differences which are found in different Persons in this respect, are sufficiently analogous to the Differences of their Situations in Life, and of the consequent Associations formed in them.[111]

By explaining in this manner the presence of diversity in taste, Hartley conforms to the general practice of writers, beginning with Hutcheson, who resolve divergencies from standards into associations of ideas.

In more or less the same fashion, Hartley briefly applies his method to the next group of esthetic pleasures, to the "Beauties of the Works of Art", such as buildings and furniture. The various elements that can be associated for the production of this complex pleasure are also listed. Among them may be found "the strong Associations with Religion, Death, War, Justice, Power, Riches, Titles, High-Birth, Entertainments, Mirth, etc." Architectural proportions are first determined "in a gross way" by the needs of utility. "Afterwards these Proportions become associated so often with a Variety of Beauties in costly Buildings, that they could not but be thought naturally beautiful

[110] I, 419.
[111] I, 421.

at last".[112] Hartley also summarily considers music and painting and the several types of associations and elements in combination that can make these arts sources of esthetic pleasure. And he also discusses poetry.

The three chief beauties of the complex pleasure in poetry are, writes Hartley, the harmony, regularity, and variety of numbers and rhyme, the "Fitness and Strength of the Words and Phrases", and the invention and judgment exerted by the poet in regard to the subject. Association, he adds without going into detail, unites these elements: "And the Beauties arising from each of these are much transferred upon the other Two by Association".[113] Again, he is led to state the case for diversity in taste, because of the manifold influences of association; this time, however, it is with respect to taste in figures of speech. The diverse taste in these figures, he observes, is subject to various associational influences, which, naturally, undermine fixed standards for the determination of this beauty.

> As the various Figures used in Speaking and Writing have great Influences over each other, alter, and are much altered, as to their relative Energy, by our Passion, Customs, Opinions, Constitutions, Educations, etc. there can be no fixed Standard for determining what is Beauty here, or what is the Degree of it. Every Person may find, that his Taste in these Things receives considerable Changes in his Progress through Life; and may, by careful Observation, trace up these Changes to the Associations that have caused them.[114]

Accordingly, the possibility for an infinity of tastes, as Jeffrey was later willing to allow, is enormous. But Hartley is unwilling to draw this radical conclusion. Undoubtedly inhibited by the times in which he lived, and under the influence of neoclassic opinion, education, and temper, he is of the firm opinion that "there will be some general Agreements about these Things common to all Mankind". A practical criterion can be

112 I, 424-5.
113 I, 428.
114 I, 430.

found in common consent, that is, in the common associations of mankind. Indeed, this is an interesting way of expressing the neoclassic *consensus gentium*, the neoclassic assumption that because human nature is nearly the same everywhere and at any time, certain standards may be fixed. This is exactly the argument that Hurd uses.

And yet, since Mankind have a general Resemblance to each other, both in their internal Make, and external circumstances, there will be some general Agreements about these Things common to all Mankind. The Agreements will also become perpetually greater, as the Persons under Consideration are supposed to agree more in their Genius, Studies, external Circumstances, etc. Hence may be seen, in part, the Foundation of the general Agreements observable in Critics, concerning the Beauties of Poetry, as well as that of their particular Disputes and Differences.[115]

Although, then, the esthetic judgment depends largely upon ideas in association, Hartley does not, as A. C. Smith declares he does, completely deny *all* fixed standards of taste.[116] The notion of common associations implies the existence of several standards among various classes or nations of men and also among various age levels. Alison develops this point of view in his *Essays on Taste* (1790). Although Hartley is not so explicit as Alison, it cannot be denied that he provides the means by which complete subjectivity of taste can be limited. Arguments, pro and con, concerning associationism as the source of variations in taste and the source of its stabilization are supplied by many writes after Hartley, – Burke, Kames, Priestley, Alison; but to Hartley belongs the honor of being the first to give clear expression to two contradictory associationist positions and to effect between them some sort of a compromise satisfactory to neoclassical taste.

Hartley's final view concerning the instability and relativity of taste is more in accord with Mr. Smith's observation.

115 I, 430.
116 A. C. Smith, *Theories of the Nature and Standard of Taste in England, 1700-1790* (Chicago, 1937), p. 150.

And this is the extreme view of subjective associationist diversitarianism that Priestley and Jeffrey will later expound.

> We may now observe upon the Whole, that according to the foregoing History of the Pleasures of Imagination, there must be great Differences in the Tastes and Judgments of different Persons; and that no Age, Nation, Class of Men, etc. ought to be made the Test of what is most excellent in Artificial Beauty; nor consequently of what is absurd.[117]

In these ways, Hartley maintains the continuity of the associationist tradition in English critical theory. Although he is greatly concerned with other problems, such as showing that the association of ideas corresponds to the connection of neural traces, that its one law is chance contiguity, and that religion and morality have an associationist basis, he does turn his attention fully to beauty and art at least once. On the whole, his critical theorizing is not flattering to him as an original thinker, nor is it often significantly at variance with that of his predecessors and contemporaries. He expounds an exclusively associationist psychology of taste. And it is also true that his analysis of the sublime anticipates Burke's association of terror with this esthetic emotion. But his views on imagination or fancy and imaginative invention are definitely unoriginal and can be traced ultimately to Hobbes. Generally in his final statement he supports those who deny fixed and uphold relative standards of taste; and while his arguments for relativity and diversity of taste are forcibly presented and logically sound, they derive from numerous contemporary associationist arguments for relative measures. But it is interesting to note that he does provide for the limitation of complete diversity in taste by holding to the neoclassic concept of the *consensus*

[117] I, 442. I cannot reconcile what Hartley previously has written concerning the dependence of uniformity and variety upon associations with what he says immediately following this quotation. "The Only Things", he continues, "that can be set up as natural Criterions here seem to be Uniformity with Variety, Usefulness in general . . .". These "natural Criterions" are Hutcheson's and Shaftesbury's internal senses for beauty of form and morals. Certainly this contradicts the associationist exposition of these elements which Hartley himself presents only a few pages before.

gentium. In critical theory, then, Hartley is more or less limited by the statements of poets, critics, and philosophers preceding him. As H. C. Warren has commented: "He gathered together the hints which were scattered through the writings of his predecessors, and wove them into a sightly fabric".[118] This observation applies equally to his section on taste and imagination, – for although it exhibits little fresh thinking, it provides an excellent systematization of the associationist position. As the *Observations on Man*, therefore, is (up to its time) the most penetrating and consistent, methodized and exhaustive of associationist treatises, it cannot help reinforcing associationist opinion during the eighteenth century and also, consequently, exerting some influence upon critical theory.

Yet it is difficult to discover any tangible influence by Hartley upon critics and writers who employ associationist concepts in the latter half of the century. It is not until Priestley becomes his disciple about twenty-five years after the publication of the *Observations* that Hartley apparently first begins positively to influence English thought. And it is Priestley's two editions of Hartley's book that had the greatest circulation and influence in the latter part of the century. Priestley himself wonders that none of the Scottish writers, who, as we have seen, are traditionally attracted to this psychology, take note of Hartley. He excepts only Beattie.[119] But Beattie, as well as Reid

118 *History of the Association Psychology,* pp. 113-4.

119 Priestley, *An Examination of Dr. Reid's Philosophy* [1774] (London, 1775), p. 101: "That our author [Reid] is extremely ignorant of what has been written by others on the subject of the human mind, is evident, not only from his total silence concerning Dr. Hartley (whose name, however, appears to have reached Scotland; for his work is quoted with some degree of respect by Dr. Beattie) but from his gross mistake concerning the hints that Newton and others have dropped on the subject." For other references to the Scottish writers, see pp. 170-1, 176, 319. In another volume [*Letters to a Philosophical Unbeliever* (Birmingham, 1787), I, 126, 224] Priestley attacks Hume: Hume, he says, "seems not to have given himself the trouble so much as to read Dr. Hartley's *Observations on Man,* a work which he could not but have heard of, and which it certainly behoved him to study. The doctrine of association of ideas, as explained and extended by Dr. Hartley, supplies materials for the most satisfactory solution of almost all the difficulties he has started, as I could easily show

(and Abraham Tucker), mentions Hartley only to point out his weaknesses. On the whole, Hartley's work seems to have attracted little favorable attention until the late eighteenth and early nineteenth century in the writings of Godwin, the Belshams, Darwin, Wordsworth, and Coleridge, and of those interested mainly in psychology, James Mill and others.[120] W. L. Sperry imagines that Wordsworth read Hartley in Priestley's second edition printed by J. Johnson, in whose shop Wordsworth "foregathered with his malcontent friends".[121] In a letter written to Richard Sharp in 1808, Wordsworth speaks of Hartley as one among the "men of real power, who go before their age" and exclaims of the *Observations*, "How many years did it sleep in almost entire oblivion!"[122] And before he finally foreswears associationism, Coleridge also pays tribute to him "of mortal kind Wisest" in his *Religious Musings* (1794-6):

> . . . and he of mortal kind
> Wisest, he first who marked the ideal tribes
> Down the fine fibres from the sentient brain
> Roll subtly surging.

---

if I thought it of any consequence; so that to a person acquainted with this theory of the human mind, Hume's *Essays* appear the merest trifling. Compared with Dr. Hartley, I consider Mr. Hume as not even a child." Tucker is interesting for three reasons: he criticizes Hartley in his *Light of Nature Pursued* [1768] (London, 1805), Vol. I, chs. iii and iv and Vol. II, ch. xv, for regarding the mind as merely a passive receiver of impressions; and, also, Coleridge at one time proposed to write a prefatory essay on Hartley to be included in a new edition of Tucker's work; and, lastly, Hazlitt did write an introductory essay for the new edition of Tucker's work. When Reid noticed Hartley in his *Essays on the Intellectual Powers of Man* (1785) [*Works,* ed. Hamilton (Edinburgh, 1872), I, 249-52], it was only to cast ridicule on Hartley's fabulous vibratiuncles.

120 Warren offers some conjectures upon Hartley's influence but does not support them with concrete evidence (p. 117); "The contemporaries and successors of Hartley must have derived their well-rounded notion of association mainly from him, since most of them assume it without independent analysis, and their broad treatment is not to be found in the earlier authorities."

121 *Wordsworth's Anti-Climax* (Cambridge, Mass., 1935), pp. 126-7.

122 *The Letters of William and Dorothy Wordsworth,* ed. De Selincourt (Oxford, 1937), I, 242.

Additional evidence of Hartley's popularity and influence can be found in the letters and works of many other writers at the turn of the century, – Samuel Rogers, Lamb, Hazlitt, and De Quincey.[123]

Certainly, Hartley's conclusions about the nature of the pleasures of imagination and about standards of taste must have had little influence upon Wordsworth, Coleridge, and the others. With respect to critical theory, Hartley's conclusions are the typical products of his age. If he had written only on the esthetic problems about which his contemporaries were concerned – imagination, invention, sublimity, beauty, diversity of taste, – he might never have appeared so fascinating a figure to Wordsworth. What Wordsworth sought and found in Hartley was what many of the liberal and radical writers of his age found in associationism, not so much support for a theory of taste as a thorough explanation of the development of man's mental powers, an explanation that had moral, pedagogical, and political ramifications. The *Observations on Man* provided Wordsworth with a method and a system by which he could dramatically portray the growth of the complex imagination, sensitive both to beauty and morality, from its associated elements of simple sensation and idea, and, also, by which he could account for the genesis of poetry. Undoubtedly, therefore, it is the dynamics of the associationist creed as interpreted by Hartley that gripped Wordsworth and enabled him to reveal how the mind of the poet develops from the state of infancy to that of adult manhood, from sensation to imagination, and, finally, to the perfect moral state in God.

In Hartley's complex system the associationist psychology has come a long way from its simple beginnings in the philosophy of Hobbes and Locke. It was not long ago that these

[123] Cf. Arthur Beatty, *William Wordsworth, His Doctrine and Art in their Historical Relations* (Madison, 1927), Ch. vi, esp. pp. 109ff. In this chapter Beatty draws an elaborate parallel between the views of Hartley and Wordsworth and infers that Hartley is the chief and probably the only influence upon Wordsworth's associationism. In the light of current knowledge concerning the associationist climate of opinion at the turn of the century, such an inference is entirely unwarranted.

philosophers used the theory of association to explain only the operations of memory and recollection or the "unnatural" habits of the mind. The development of these notions in the works of several significant thinkers in the first and second quarters of the century gradually placed the association of ideas among the outstanding characteristics of all normal mental behavior, in short, of human nature. Some popular writers were quick to apply to critical theory and to poetry the current understanding of human nature. As we have seen, such applications occur in the works of Akenside, Shenstone, Hurd, and Baillie. Other and far more profound thinkers, represented by Hume and Hartley, apply the associationist conception of nature to almost every mental operation that man is capable of, including those of imaginative invention and esthetic judgment. Hume and Hartley regard association as the chief synthetic principle of the mind. After their statement and examination, and their characteristic application of the theory to criticism, the way is open for the elaborate associationist critical theories to be propounded in the next few decades.

V

THE PSYCHOLOGICAL CRITICISM

After the psychological criticism essayed by Hume and Hartley, many important critics became devout adherents to the psychological method. Attempts at establishing the associationist principles of human nature as standards of criticism are therefore not uncommon in this – the third – quarter of the eighteenth century. Burke, Shenstone, Reynolds, Gerard, and Kames are the more significant figures who are seriously engaged in applying this psychology to critical theory. It is apparent as one reads the critical works of Kames and Gerard, for example, that the system of Aristotle is displaced by an altogether different system, that of Hume. Aristotle, it is true, presented critics with rules founded upon the practice of the ancient authors; but neither classical authority nor classical rules satisfy these psychological critics. They do not aim, however, to subvert Aristotelian order and structure and the rules for judging and creating regular works of art, but to ground critical theory anew upon Hume's "discoveries" in the philosophy of human nature. In short, these critics wish to explain the processes of artistic creation with special regard to the way in which the imagination associates ideas. The imagination, according to Gerard and Kames, is not wild or irregular in its operation; on the contrary, it is, they believe, regular and is controlled by the universal and immutable laws of association.

As we have pointed out before, the associationist psychology may not only sustain neoclassic uniformitarianism, but also may cripple it. In Reynolds, Shenstone, Adam Smith, John Brown, and even Gerard, the theory of association is used to explain, in traditional Hutchesonian fashion, diversity and relativity of taste. All these writers show how tastes are formed by habitual associations of ideas and have attributed the great variety of tastes throughout the world to the different ideas constantly associated by different nations and peoples. Some of these writers, however, are unwilling to believe completely in relative standards of taste. Gerard, for example, identifies universal, habitual associations with human nature and uses this psychological and, at the same time, neoclassic conception of nature as a standard for criticism. These general or widespread associations of ideas are merely the psychological version of the *consensus gentium* which we have noticed in Hurd and Hartley. Reynolds and Smith assert that different associations form only the varying tastes for a species of beauty; but, they continue, beauty itself is the general or common idea of nature, the central form of the species. Shenstone and John Brown unqualifiedly present the diversitarian thesis and ground it upon the variety of associated ideas.

The extent to which associationism affected critical theory in the middle of the century is interestingly illustrated by Burke's short essay "On Taste" (1759) and his longer and more famous *Philosophical Enquiry into . . . the Sublime and Beautiful* (1757). In both essays, Burke opposes the associationist current and argues against the theory of association as the basis of taste; in the *Enquiry* he deliberately opposes it as the origin of the taste for the beautiful. Burke is not, however, consistent in his assaults against the theory of association, for he cannot deny that it is the source of the taste for the sublime. Indeed, he is often explicit in claiming a subjective association of fear or danger as the origin of the sublime. Moreover, in the obscure fifth part of the *Enquiry*, associationism is also used as the basis for the refutation of the theory of imitation and the Horatian *ut pictura poesis* precept. Burke is excellent evidence of the fact that, in the middle of the century, the influence of associationism on criticism is irresistible and that any writer seriously concerned with critical problems is obliged in one way or another to comment on its significance.

Thus, after Hume applies the principles of association to

critical theory, the psychological method is firmly established, and associationist critical convictions become common property and are given a chance for further development. In general, this theory of the mind is applied to an understanding of romantic diversity or to a new understanding of neoclassic uniformity. Many of the chief critics of distinction after the middle of the century follow either of these trends and present a psychological, particularly an associationist, interpretation of critical problems. Foremost among these critics is Edmund Burke.

As we have noticed in passing, Burke's critical theory has often been anticipated in the first half of the eighteenth century. Many writers who have used associationism to explain the nature of language – Berkeley, Watts, Hume, and Hartley – have formed a tradition which is the background of Burke's romantic theory of poetic diction. Similarly, Dennis (in part), Baillie, and Hartley anticipate Burke's use of the association of danger and fear for the explanation of the sublime terror. Moreover, the arguments of Hutcheson against association are borrowed whosesale by Burke for his refutation of the associationist theory as the basis of taste. Despite such unoriginality, Burke is still interesting, because he appears to sum up in his esthetic theory fifty years of associationist thought and because he clearly employs the associationist psychology with relation to a romantic point of view, especially to violent romantic emotion, terror and sublimity. Thus, with the aid of the contemporary psychology, Burke strengthens the tendency during the middle of the century to give respect to the profoundly emotional and irrational elements of art, that tendency which runs counter to the neoclassic and rational associationism of Hume, Hartley, Hurd, Kames, and Gerard.

Burke tries to arrest the tendency towards diversity and variety in the standards of taste by opposing to the varying standards permitted by the associationist psychology a species of stable emotional naturalism. His critical works present perhaps the only noteworthy anti-associationist argument in the eighteenth century from the time of the chief exponent of the internal sense doctrine, Francis Hutcheson, to that of Thomas

Reid. In order to understand Burke, it must constantly be borne in mind that in his critical system he is largely concerned with the *origin* of esthetic ideas and emotions, for he contends that the origin can be found only in "nature", by which he means the immediate and spontaneous emotional experience – Hutcheson's internal sense. In his terminology, the spontaneous reaction of the emotions represents the way that is approved by "nature". Consequently, this natural reaction supersedes reasoning or judgment and the mental operation known as the association of ideas, because they are of secondary significance, temporally speaking, in the forming of an immutable, uniform, and original standard of taste. Because they also differ in men, Burke feels that understanding and associations become sources of complexity and diversity. Like Shaftesbury and Hutcheson, Burke insists that beauty originates in the immediate pleasing effects uniformly produced by certain properties of objects and uninfluenced by the mediation of either reason or association, "properties that operate by nature, and are less liable to be altered by caprice, or confounded by a diversity of tastes than any other".[1] And like Hutcheson and Hogarth, he tries to fix taste by founding it upon the "sensibilities", or the natural or original pleasures and pains of the senses. The *Enquiry* is thus deliberately restricted to sensations and concomitant emotions: "When we go but one step beyond the immediate sensible qualities of things, we go out of our depth". And for this reason Burke believes it possible, "by looking into physical causes, . . . to give taste a sort of philosophical solidity".[2]

Attempting therefore to be simple and sensuous, in his introductory remarks Burke reduces the origin of esthetic emotions to the two effects of pleasure and pain. From the former spring the beautiful emotions which refer to the impulse towards love

[1] III, xviii, 222-3. Part, section, and page are given; the pagination is that of the London, 1798 reprint. The essay "On Taste" also appears in this edition.

[2] IV, i, 243; "Preface", p. ix.

and society; from the latter, when it is limited by "a sort of Privation",[3] spring the stronger sublime emotions which relate to the impulse towards self-preservation. By privation, Burke means "the removal or moderation of pain"; it is this moderation that results in "delight", a term Burke finds necessary to introduce in order to explain the peculiar intensity of the terrible sublime. Unlike beauty and ordinary pleasure, this feeling of terror or sublimity is a relative pleasure; that is to say, it exists only with a relation to pain, or, as Burke says, it "accompanies the removal of pain or danger". Therefore, the delight of terror cannot be felt when the sources of the emotion "press too nearly", because then they will have full effect and be absolutely painful or terrible. This relation to a state of mind makes Burke's sublime wholly subjective; for it is in effect nothing but this: anything which may "excite the ideas of pain and danger, that is to say, whatever is in any sort terrible, or is conversant about terrible objects, or operates in a manner analogous to terror, is a source of the *sublime;* that is, it is productive of the strongest emotion which the mind is capable of feeling".[4] On the other hand, contrasted with the subjectivism of the sublime is the objective nature of the beautiful. This notion of beauty seems to be Shaftesburian; it rests partly on the qualities of things and partly on the immediate emotional reaction of affection or tenderness. Because both these emotional experiences are either partly or wholly the guides to taste, Burke feels that every man can see his way clear to the approximation of a standard: "The true standard of the arts is in every man's power".[5]

It is the subjective conception of the sublime delight that perhaps inadvertently injects the associationist idea into Part II of Burke's treatise. Certainly, in view of the hostility to

[3] I, iv, 52.

[4] I, vii, 58.

[5] I, xix, 91. Cf. *A Vindication of Natural Society,* ed. Dodsley, II, 70: "The Pleasures, which are agreeable to Nature, are within the reach of all, and therefore can form no Distinction in favour of the Rich." And "On Taste", p. 24: "So far as Taste is natural, it is nearly common to all."

associationism expressed in Part IV, Section ii, and in the essay on taste, Burke could not help knowing that his critical system was marred by a theoretical flaw. Moreover, it is indeed surprising to find that numerous, albeit minor, concessions to associationist methods appear throughout the *Enquiry*. The presence of associationism in Burke's work only points to its pervasive influence in critical thought. Burke himself is evidence of the fact that even writers who are opposed to the psychology are often influenced by it despite themselves. Although in Part II Burke is unwilling to acknowledge association forthrightly, he nevertheless resorts to the style and language of the writers in the psychological tradition. For example, he states that the suggestion of danger rouses fear or terror and can thus make objects of all kinds produce the sublime. He carries Baillie's subjective associationist contention – that sublime objects may not be restricted to the grand or vast – to almost ridiculous lengths.[6] Hence, small serpents, as they threaten men with danger, can be considered objects of terror and are capable of raising sublime ideas. "And to things of great dimensions, *if we annex an adventitious idea of terror*, they become without comparison greater". A great level plain is therefore less sublime than the ocean, because the latter is associated with the terror of peril or danger.[7] Ugliness, too, he adds later, may become agreeably sublime through an association with terror: "Ugliness I imagine likewise to be consistent enough with an idea of the sublime. But I would by no means insinuate that ugliness of itself is a sublime idea, *unless united with such qualities as excite a strong terror*".[8]

It is strange to find these admissions or inconsistencies in the text, while we know that Burke constantly strives to explain esthetic emotions in terms of uniform and spontaneous effects. According to Burke's central thesis, objects should induce emotional states through the senses, without the intervention

6 II, ii, 96-7. Cf. John Baillie, *An Essay on the Sublime* (1747), pp. 7, 36.
7 II, ii, 97. Emphasis mine.
8 III, xxi, 226.

of latent associations in the mind. The associationist and the naturalist or sensuous methods may readily be confused – as they are by Gordon McKenzie [9] – in that both are subjective: the emotions felt, not the form of the object that produced them, are the standards for the two methods, and they allow for more liberal thinking in criticism and give validity to freer practices in art. But, as we have suggested, the assumptions of the one, in the system of Shaftesbury and Hutcheson particularly, are inconsistent with those of the other. And, as we shall soon see, Burke himself, feeling that associationism sooner permits diversity in taste than do "natural" or sensuous effects which, he believes, are the same in all men, finds it necessary to argue formally against the theory and to minimize the role of associations.[10]

As he believes that the sublime is terrible in one form or another, Burke is able to comprehend sublime effects in the notion of a subjective association with terror or danger. Although he does not succeed with greatness of dimension, magnificence, and light, he does successfully interpret power, darkness, vastness, infinity, and certain awful sounds and stenches and tastes, in accordance with the basic association with terror. Of course, Burke is not explicit about the presence of associationism in all of these qualities; we must discover for ourselves the association of danger that is the source of the sublime. He is once, however, unmistakably positive about associationist effects when he discusses, almost in Hutcheson's fashion, tastes and smells. He notes that the effects of these senses are often corrupted by vitiating associations; these associations, he continues, may be counteracted by dignified and grand ones which can thereby strengthen the potential of these senses as sources of the sublime:

[9] "Lord Kames and the Mechanist Tradition", *Essays and Studies, University of California* (Berkeley and Los Angeles, 1943), pp. 93-121.

[10] Monk has commented on the suggestion of association in II, ii, *(Sublime,* p. 93): "Burke is careful in his use of association, and . . . refuses to follow Hartley in adopting it as the sole explanation of our mental processes. He helps, however, to establish it definitely in speculation against the time when Alison exploits it fully."

If the sentiment stood nakedly by itself, it would be subject, at first view, to burlesque and ridicule; but this I imagine would principally arise from considering the bitterness and stench in company with mean and contemptible ideas, with which it must be owned they are often united; such an union degrades the sublime in all other instances as well as in those. But it is one of the tests by which the sublimity of an image is to be tried, not whether it becomes mean when associated with mean ideas; but whether, when united with images of an allowed grandeur, the whole composition is supported with dignity.[11]

In Part III of the treatise, Burke's subject is beauty. Here Burke describes the manner in which the milder emotion of beauty is immediately and directly affected through the senses by various qualities – smallness, smoothness, gradual variation, and delicacy of form and color. In the analysis of beauty, Burke is far more consistently anti-associationist than in that of sublimity. He defines beauty as something wholly sensuous; secondary associations are deliberately excluded:

By beauty I mean that quality or those qualities in bodies, by which they cause love, or some passion similar to it. I confine this definition to the merely sensible qualities of things, for the sake of preserving the utmost simplicity in a subject which must always distract us, *whenever we take in those various causes of sympathy which attach us to any persons or things from secondary considerations,* and not from the direct force which they have merely on being viewed.[12]

Fitness, acceptable to Hume, Spence, Hartley, and, later, Alison, as an associational source of beauty, is consequently ruled out by Burke, as it must utilize reason to investigate means to ends. Nor can proportion be a basic determinant of beauty, since it too is indirect and secondary and lends confusion to what otherwise can be simple and sensuous. Neither can be a primary cause acting on the senses and imagination, only

[11] II, xxi, 157.

[12] III, i, 162. Cf. III, xii, 210: "Beauty is, for the greater part, some quality in bodies acting mechanically upon the human mind by the intervention of the senses."

because it must be rationally understood through relation to convenience or use (III, ii, vii). It is self-evident, Burke further argues, that custom, which is responsible for the beauty of certain proportions, operates slowly through habit formation; it therefore is secondary and not a natural and original source of beauty (III, v). And utility, moreover, is rejected by Burke as a constituent of beauty for the reason that it is not a cause but "only a concomitant". Adaptability for purpose, or means to ends, so runs his argument, is totally independent of the natural effect of beauty; and when this principle is applied to the parts of certain animals, such as "the wedge-like snout of a swine", its utter absurdity is easily demonstrable.[13]

Unlike his acceptance of sublimity as relative and associationist "delight", Burke cannot accept relative or associationist beauty. For him, beauty can only be intrinsic or limited to the objective qualities of smallness, smoothness, and gradual variation, and cannot involve the mind because its effect precedes any operation of the intellect and any association of ideas.

In Part IV, Section ii, entitled "Association", Burke answers the associationist objections to a single standard of taste. Clearly aware of the problem raised by associationist diversity, he takes a stand and urges his uniformitarian thesis. Associations are made at an early age when we are unaware of them, he observes; and so, after some time, they tend to become confused with the natural effect: "For besides such things as affect us in various manners, according to their natural powers, there are associations made at that early season, which we find it very hard afterwards to distinguish from natural effects".[14]

[13] III, vi, 192. Alison takes Burke to task for not allowing fitness to be a source of beauty. See *Essay on Taste* (Edinburgh, 1790), pp. 341 ff.

[14] IV, ii, 245. This idea is restated in IV, xv, 276-7. In proving that we can experience certain pleasures and pains independently of association, Burke offers evidence in a boy with newly restored vision. This boy experiences black for the first time with a sense of pain; he did not previously connect other disagreeable ideas to black, since there was no time for habits or associations to be formed. The simple and "natural" sense of color was the sole cause of pain.

Although Burke is compelled to admit the authority and validity of associationism, he still differs from Hartley by denying its claim as the source of taste. The sole source is, he avers with Hutcheson, the original and natural emotional effect which is experienced before any associations can be made. In this critical system, associations are assigned a place as subordinate modifiers of the passions.

But as it must be allowed that many things affect us after a certain manner, not by any natural powers they have for that purpose, but by association; so it would be absurd, on the other hand, to say that all things affect us by association only; since some things must have been originally and naturally agreeable or disagreeable, from which the others derive their associated powers; and it would be, I fancy, to little purpose to look for the cause of our passions in association, until we fail of it in the natural properties of things.[15]

Yet, as we have intimated, despite this inferior and secondary position, associations are not entirely renounced in the *Enquiry*; but, on the contrary, they are at the core of the terrible sublime. Unequivocal proof of the presence of the association of danger or terror in Burke's conception of the sublime appears often in the very same fourth part where Burke argues against the associationist hypothesis concerning the origins and the diversity of taste.

With regard to such things as affect by the associated idea of danger, there can be no doubt but that they produce terror, and act by some modification of that passion.

A mode of terror or pain is always the cause of the sublime. For terror, or associated danger, the foregoing explanation [of privation and delight] is, I believe, sufficient.

Whatever is fitted to produce such a tension [of fibres and nerves] must be productive of a passion similar to terror, and consequently

---

[15] IV, ii, 245-6.

must be a source of the sublime, though it should have no idea of danger connected with it.[16]

This subjective association of danger (that can do no real hurt) thereby becomes the source of the sublime and parallels in importance the natural emotional reactions to certain qualities – those reactions that are the sources of beauty. Without the distance that such habitual mental association permits, terror will be merely painful and will give no pleasure. This point will become clearer if we reconstruct Burke's thesis in relation to the sublimity of night and darkness.

Darkness and night, Burke states, are painful "by their natural operation [on the senses], independent of any associations whatsoever".[17] But if darkness be esthetically agreeable or sublime, the cause must be an associated idea of danger. Burke now takes issue with Locke, who suggests that the associations of ghosts and goblins make night horrible. Objecting to the *kind* of association, not to the *theory* of association, Burke suggests that a more fundamental association, one that is common to all men, is responsible for the feeling of terror.

But, with all deference to such an authority, it seems to me, that an association of a more general nature, an association which takes in all mankind, may make darkness terrible; for in utter darkness, it is impossible to know in what degree of safety we stand; we may every moment strike against some dangerous obstruction. . . .[18]

When taken in conjunction with the sections on "Terror" and "Obscurity" (II, ii, iii), in which the significance of danger and fear to the sublime is discussed, this statement clearly demonstrates the importance of the special subjective associations of danger and fear to Burke's conception of the terrible sublime.

In the fifth and last part of the *Enquiry*, Burke takes issue with the Horatian maxim, *ut pictura poesis*; and by so doing

16 IV, v, 252, 253; IV, viii, 258.
17 IV, xv, 275.
18 IV, xiv, 273-4.

he is again compelled to employ the associationist psychology. In connection with his thesis that darkness is terrible through the broad association with danger, Burke develops in this part of his work the idea that obscurity in poetic language is far more affecting than clarity. He maintains that compound-abstract words, such as virtue, honor, persuasion, and docility, do not necessarily raise images of clear ideas in the mind. These words, however, through custom and association with good and evil or "other interesting things or events", can stir emotion by "the sound, without any annexed notion".

> Such words are in reality but mere sounds; but they are sounds, which being used on particular occasions, wherein we receive some good, or suffer some evil; or see others affected with good or evil; or which we hear applied to other interesting things or events; and being applied in such a variety of cases, that we know readily by habit to what things they belong, they produce in the mind, wherever they are afterwards mentioned, effects similar to those of their occasions. The sounds being often used without reference to any particular occasion, and carrying still their first impressions, they at last utterly lose their connection with the particular occasions that give rise to them; yet the sound, without any annexed notion, continues to operate as before.[19]

That is to say, the ideas associated to the words fade away in the process of time and leave the emotion, so that, when the sound is heard, only the emotion will be raised. It is obvious that Burke is indebted to the many associationist discussions of the nature of language for this theory.

Applied to poetic diction this theory of emotion means that words may, after their associated ideas dissolve, immediately excite emotions of beauty and sublimity without raising definite pictures or images (V, v). Therefore, writes Burke, "poetry and rhetoric do not succeed in exact description so well as painting does; their business is, to affect rather by sympathy than imitation, to display rather the effect of things on the mind of the speaker, or of others, than to present a clear idea

[19] V, ii, 316. See Dixon Wecter, "Burke's Theory of Words, Images, and Emotion", *PMLA*, LV (1940), 172; and above, pp. 51-4 (on Berkeley).

of the things themselves".[20] In explaining the manner in which poetry can best move the passions, Burke relies directly upon the principles of the association of ideas. And here he proves his awareness of Hume's principles of association, those principles that govern the shaping imagination.

> The truth is, if poetry gives us a noble assemblage of words, corresponding to many noble ideas, which are connected by circumstances of time or place, or related to each other as cause and effect, or associated in any natural way, they [words] may be moulded together in any form, and perfectly answer their end. The picturesque connection is not demanded; because no real picture is formed; nor is the effect of the description at all the less upon this account.[21]

The argument that we do not picture or supply a clear image for every word we read is thus extended by Burke to a non-imagistic understanding of practically all poetic diction. Burke's point is that poetry simply does not depend for its effects on exact imitation or the power of raising images. He believes that the effect of poetry is explicable by the principles of association, and cites, in particular, contiguity and causality.

Burke's theory of words and emotions is admittedly the most abstract and difficult of all the theories in the treatise. It certainly is not explicit enough, as Shenstone wrote to his friend Graves in 1759; but Shenstone also added, "And yet there seems to be something right about it".[22] We like to think that what Shenstone referred to as right are the accepted "truths" of the associationist psychology, those truths that supported a more emotional and more personal approach to the criticism of art. Certainly, this psychology does shed some light on the way in which Burke refutes the neoclassic theory of exact imitation of nature. If we do not perceive that associationism provides the basic concepts for his romantic theory of poetic diction, this theory must remain obscure

[20] V, v, 332.

[21] V, v, 330.

[22] *Letters of William Shenstone,* ed. D. Mallam (Minneapolis, 1939), p. 377.

as well as difficult of comprehension. Associationism cannot be ignored; it is as essential to this critical theory of poetic language as it is to that of the terrible sublime.

In the introductory essay "On Taste" (1759), prefixed to the second edition of the *Enquiry*, Burke repeats all his arguments against diversifying associations. As in the *Enquiry*, he also realisitically agrees that differences of taste are caused by later associations, although, at the same time, of course, he argues strongly in favor of the stable uniformity of the "natural" emotional reactions preceding the formation of associations. Burke founds taste, like the beautiful, on sensuous experiences which, he believes, are common to all men and operate similarly in all of them.[23] Custom and habit, he asserts, repeating the statement in the *Enquiry*, are temporally acquired, while, on the other hand, natural taste is eternally constant. The acquired and the natural "relish", he further insists, should not be confused. Although deviations from natural pleasures have been caused by custom, "the power of distinguishing between the natural and the acquired relish remains to the very last".[24] An acquired taste can be subject to dispute, since it is largely determined by habit, temper, and prejudice. Natural, original taste, however, as it appeals directly to the senses, is immutable and authoritative.

Sight, Burke continues, differs from the other senses in that it is less easily tainted by adventitious associations. But, he claims with Hartley, the palate is formed by "degrees, and by force of these associations", – the associations of nutrition and health.

> The pleasures of the sight are not near so complicated, confused, and altered by unnatural habits and associations, as the pleasures of the taste are; because the pleasures of the sight more commonly acquiesce in themselves; and are not so often altered by considerations which are independent of the sight itself.[25]

23 P. 8. The pagination is again that of the London, 1798 reprint.
24 P. 9.
25 P. 12.

Burke is clearly aware of the problem raised by associationism, and therefore cannot easily admit it into his system: "This does not in the least perplex our reasoning; because we distinguish to the last the acquired from the natural relish".[26]

It is obvious that the relativist theory of taste, as it is supported by associationism, is the target of Burke's criticism. Like Hutcheson, he tries to fix fluctuating taste by emphasizing the natural predilections, by which he means the original feelings anterior to any use of reason or to any association of ideas. As incontrovertible proof that the theory of association cannot account for all taste, Burke adduces the experience of novelty. Only the senses, and their concomitant emotions, can be the criterion of novelty, because associations or habits have not had time to be formed. This argument, of course, had already been stated in the *Enquiry*.

There is in all men a sufficient remembrance of the original natural causes of pleasure, to enable them to bring all things offered to their senses to that standard, and to regulate their feelings and opinions by it. . . . For in judging of any new thing, even of a Taste similar to that which he has been formed by habit to like, he finds his palate affected in the natural manner, and on the common principles.[27]

Burke's views obviously parallel those of the internal sense dogma. With him, the senses and their uniform reactions are the "great originals" of our esthetic ideas, and are prior to association and custom, the sources of diversity. Because he believes

[26] P. 13.
[27] P. 14. Dugald Stewart similarly tempers associationism is his *Elements of the Philosophy of the Human Mind* [1792] (London, 1802), p. 372: "The influence of association on our judgments concerning beauty or deformity, is still more remarkable than on our speculative conclusions; a circumstance which has led some philosophers to suppose, that association is sufficient to account for the origin of these notions, and that there is no such thing as a standard of Taste, founded on the principles of the human constitution. But this is undoubtedly pushing the theory a great deal too far. The association of ideas can never account for the origin of a new notion; or of a pleasure essentially different from all the others which we know." Cf. also the blind boy in Burke's *Enquiry,* IV, xv, 276.

that the spontaneous experiences of the senses are invariable, he is able to deduce that a true and single standard can perhaps be best founded on them: "The pleasure of the senses ... is the same in all, high and low, learned and unlearned".[28] This naturalism results in a completely democratic understanding of taste. Contrasted with this esthetic theory is the associationism of Hartley, Hurd, Kames, and Gerard, which, although not inconsistent with the concept of the *consensus gentium*, yet remains strongly neoclassic and therefore aristocratic. Hartley, however, has demonstrated how associations can furnish standards for several grades of taste democratically stratified among several classes of people. And this synthesis of uniformity and diversity is the compromise that was finally to be accepted by Alison at the close of the century.

In his essay on taste, Burke examines the association of ideas from the narrow view; that is to say, like the reason or understanding (with which it is put on the same secondary and inferior plane), it is considered merely as succeeding original sensuous experience and is therefore disapproved of for being the cause of diversity of taste. Here, then, in the matter of standards of taste, Burke conservatively follows Hutcheson and Locke and appears to be unaware of the numerous other uses of the associationist psychology which Hume and his followers Kames and Gerard employed in their esthetics. In the more important *Enquiry*, however, associationism contributes no little share to the liberation of critical theory from classic shackles. First, Burke uses it entirely for its subjective approach in order to bolster a characteristically romantic standard – emotional effects. To be exact, he employs it to explain the manner in which certain objects produce esthetic delight from a species of painful terror. This delight in terror, he believes, is the source of sublimity, and is, he further claims, the product of a special association with danger. Secondly, at the conclusion of his treatise, Burke uses the new Humean principles of association to implement his refutation of the

[28] P. 15.

theory of imitation and the *ut pictura poesis* precept. In accordance with these associationist principles, he finds it possible to argue against exact imitations and descriptions and to state a new principle for the appreciation and shaping of a work of art. This principle is the same that Edward Young advocates in his *Conjectures on Original Composition* (1759) – the romantic notion of approximating the spirit of things rather than of copying accurately and perhaps coldly.

But despite the positive significance of associationism in the *Enquiry*, it is also true that Burke is not entirely an associationist. With Hutcheson, Burke believes that the origin of our taste for beauty is in the uniform and immediate reactions of the senses. In his analysis of the sense of beauty – especially with relation to novelty and fitness – Burke is most successfully anti-associationist. Generally, his opposition to the association of ideas as the basis of taste emanates from his desire to move away from secondary causes, complexity and diversity, and to get on the firmer ground of "nature", which he defines in typical neoclassic fashion as the uniform, simple and sensuous, reactions of everyone.

Burke's outstanding contribution to critical theory is his systematic examination of terror. He thus provides a respectable, although abstract, esthetics for the growing contemporary cult of terror manifested in the works of the descriptive poets – Thomson, Mallet, Dyer, Akenside, Savage, etc. – as well as for the fashionable taste for the melancholy type of garden and irregular or picturesque natural scenery. All this has been said countless times before and is now an old story. But the part that the eighteenth-century philosophy of human nature, associationism, has played in these new prominent tastes has generally been slighted. More evidence of the importance of the association of ideas with regard to profoundly emotional effects appears soon after the publication of the *Enquiry*, when the association of melancholy ideas is appropriated by Shenstone (and in part by Kames), who adapted this associationism to the rationale of ruins in the theory and the practice of the new English Garden.

But before these new illustrations of the associationist psychology are discussed, mention must be made of another "protest" against the exaggeration of the associational process in taste. Following the thought of Hutcheson and Burke, James Usher develops in *Clio: or a Discourse on Taste* (1767) a thesis that accidental associations explain the variation from a fixed, determinate standard founded on the uniform and universal reactions of an innate sense of beauty. In order to demonstrate the soundness of this thesis, Usher makes a distinction between certain objects, the "native beauty" of which uniformly strikes all men, and other objects "naturally indifferent or disgusting; and yet that come into value and reputation on account of an association they happen to be in with original beauty". This distinction, he is confident, explains the fixity of judgment in some matters of taste and the fluctuation in others. The main point that he makes is that man must not be deceived by the accidents of beauty produced by errant associations, but must carefully separate from false associations or "casual adjuncts" the "native or unborrowed beauty" which always and invariably pleases.[29]

Like Hutcheson and Burke, he believes that a taste for universal beauty is originally and uniformly implanted in man by nature and that it operates instantaneously.[30] The observation of diversity in the standards of taste is, he makes clear, no argument against the uniform and natural sense of beauty, but may only be proof of the activity of ephemeral associations. Thus, the method that Usher urges in his refutation of the diversitarians or relativists, whom he identifies as Hobbes, Locke, and Mandeville, is the very same as that used by Hutcheson and Burke. In this method, associations do not explain the rule, but the exception: "All the confusion this ingenious and subtile author [Mandeville] has shewn within the boundaries of beauty, may be taken away, by distinguishing between

[29] Pp. vii-viii. I use the second edition, "With large Additions" (London, 1769).

[30] Pp. 1-10, 36.

real beauty, that is for ever engaging, and the adjuncts, or habitual associates of beauty, that pleases (sic) us only accidentally". A dress, for example, may give esthetic pleasure by its accidental and casual association with youth, an idea that is really and permanently beautiful. When such ideas as those of dress and furniture, which have no permanence, are perceived by themselves, they are indifferent; or "when [they are] joined to disagreeable ideas, they become disgustful". Blemishes, too, may often be admired "on account of an association with some superior beauty". And Homer's faults have been idolized on this principle.[31]

To give his uniformitarian point of view more emphasis Usher also distinguishes between *real* and *mixed* taste. Real taste is the property of all men, "the savage and courtier, the rustic and philosopher, the Indian and European", and is affected by "real beauty, the object of the taste I treat of". Mixed taste, on the other hand, is the product of "the casual likings and aversions in matters naturally indifferent, such as the modes of dress and furniture, which by an accidental association are become objects of preference and disgust".[32] The former is, we may infer, the true taste latent in every one: "True taste and sentiment lie deep in the mind, often incorporated with prejudices; and it requires vast judgment to bring the beauteous ore to light, and to refine it."[33]

But despite his antipathy to associationism, Usher, like Burke, is forced to rely on the associationist psychology for the explanation of the sublime. Closely following Burke, Usher believes that the sublime is defined in terms of a feeling of alarm and horror, this horror being produced by an association of immense power with mountains, oceans, cataracts, thunder, and night: "all these produce the sublime by the association of the idea of invisible immense power". And, Usher concludes, "as the

[31] Pp. 22-26. Usher also discusses (p. 78) the ways in which complexion, "a kind of beauty that is pleasing by association", becomes beautiful by association with ideas constantly pleasing.

[32] Pp. 34-5.

[33] P. 92.

soul of man naturally pays homage to unseen power", this special association naturally raises a religious passion, which "is the source of the sublime sensation".[34] Bishop Usher stops short at Burke's secular association of fear.

In the first part of the fifth decade, Shenstone responded to the discussions of associationism by plainly describing its operations in poetry. About fifteen or twenty years later, he again describes, but in prose, the effect of association upon taste. As in his earlier works, Shenstone here offers no really sustained presentation of the associationist approach. Nevertheless, by keeping the idea alive in the mind of the literary public, and by conveying the author's sentiments on the subject more explicitly and penetratingly, these unfinished single and unconnected thoughts do serve better than his verse to carry on the associationist tradition in critical theory. Shenstone's prose applications of the psychology may be found in "Unconnected Thoughts on Gardening" and fragments towards an essay "On Taste".

In the former essay, he tells how a ruin pleases the imagination not only by its variety and irregularity but also by a connection with ideas that rouse pleasing melancholy reflections. This pleasure in associations is distinct from grandeur, beauty, or variety.

> There seem, however, to be some objects, which afford a pleasure not reducible to either of the foregoing heads. A ruin, for instance, may be neither new to us, nor majestick, nor beautiful, yet afford that pleasing melancholy which proceeds from a reflexion of decayed magnificence. For this reason, an able gardiner should avail himself of objects, perhaps, not very striking; if they serve to connect ideas, that convey reflexions of the pleasing kind.[35]

Similarly, Kames is led to reflect on the unique emotional effects of suggested ideas:

[34] Pp. 109-110.

[35] William Shenstone, *Works, in Verse and Prose* (London, [1764], 1773), II, 111-2.

Whether should a ruin be in the Gothic or Grecian form? In the former, I think; because it exhibits the triumph of time over strength; a melancholy, but not unpleasant thought: a Grecian ruin suggests rather the triumph of barbarity over taste; a gloomy and discouraging thought.[36]

Shenstone expands this associationist theory with some practical hints for gardeners. He points out that ruins derive their power of pleasing by their surface irregularity and by "the latitude they afford the imagination ... to recollect any events or circumstances appertaining to their pristine grandeur". It is necessary, Shenstone advises, to provide suitable background scenes for these melancholy pleasures that are excited by the associated idea of passing grandeur:

Events relating to them [ruins] may be simulated by numberless little artifices; but it is ever to be remembered, that high hills and sudden descents are most suitable to castles; and fertile vales, near wood and water, most imitative of the usual situation for abbeys and religious houses; large oaks, in particular, are essential to these latter;

> Whose branching arms, and reverend height,
> Admit a dim religious light.[37]

In effect, such practical hints recall Hume's application of associationism to the unity of emotional effect required in literary works of art.

Also in the associationist tradition is Shenstone's conception of the formation of taste. Although in his fragmentary essay on taste there is no sustained presentation of the associationist position, Shenstone does consider the association of ideas as among the chief determinants of taste. Associations are equally productive of beauty, he implies, as are the formal and objective elements, color, smoothness, proportion, variety, and uniformity.

Every thing seems to derive its pretensions to beauty, on account of its color, smoothness, variety, uniformity, partial resemblance

[36] *Elements of Criticism* (Edinburgh, [1762], 1769), II, 446.
[37] Shenstone, II, 117.

to something else, proportion, or suitableness to the end proposed, *some connexion of ideas,* or mixture of all of these.[38]

He briefly details the effects of colors, resemblance, and proportion; and then he expatiates upon "connexion of ideas" by noticing how habits affect standards of taste. At the core of habit, it will be remembered, lies the frequent association of ideas in the mind from the time of birth. Although it is not explicitly stated, such may be the basis of Shenstone's conception of habit:

Habit, herein, seems to have an influence to which we can affix no bounds. Suppose the generality of mankind formed with a mouth from ear to ear, and that it were requisite in point of respiration, would not the present make of mouths, have subjected a man to the name of Bocha chica?

It is probable, that a clown would require more color in his Chloe's face, than a courtier.

We see daily the strange effects of habit, in respect of fashion. To what colors, or proportions, does it not reconcile us! [39]

Like Reynolds (in *Idler 82,* 1759), Shenstone makes habit responsible for a good many taste preferences. For example, habit is the source of the taste for uniformity and regularity in certain objects.

I am much inclined to suppose our ideas of beauty depend greatly upon habit – what I mean is, upon the familiarity with objects which we happen to have seen since we came into the world – Our taste for uniformity, from what we have observed in the individual parts of nature, a man, a tree, a beast, a bird, or insect, etc. – our taste for regularity from what is within our power to observe in the several perfections of the whole system.[40]

But, as he mentions before in the essay on gardening, habit also reconciles taste to irregularity in nature: "We form our

[38] II, 269.
[39] II, 270.
[40] II, 281.

notions from what we have seen; and though, could we comprehend the universe, we might perhaps find it uniformly regular; yet the portions that we see of it, habituate our fancy to the contrary".[41]

Diversity of taste is easily produced by various associations of ideas: "Our taste of beauty is, perhaps, compounded of all the ideas that have entered the imagination from our birth. This seems to occasion the different opinions that prevail concerning it. For instance, a foreign eye esteems those features and dresses handsome, which we think deformed".[42] Finally, going to almost ridiculous extremes, Shenstone believes anything can become an object of beauty by means of an association of ideas. It is obviously impossible to maintain objective criteria by means of these subjective associations. This position is the antithesis of that held by Burke.

People of little or no taste, commend a person for its corpulency. I cannot see, why an excrescence of belly, cheek, or chin, should be deemed more beautiful than a wen on any other part of the body. *Through a connexion of ideas, it may form the beauty of a pig, or an ox.*[43]

The associationist tradition in critical theory is fast becoming conventional. But in addition to all the old ideas about the ways in which habitual associations may produce a diversity of taste, a new application can be seen in Shenstone. He uses an association of ideas to explain the pleasing esthetic effect of artificial ruins and shows also how the melancholy emotional effect can be best maintained by providing for a unity of associated melancholy ideas drawn from external nature. The novel application of the psychological theory to gardening and ruins proves how pliable the theory can be, and foreshadows an associationist explanation of the picturesque.

The association of ideas can therefore be used in diametrically opposed critical systems. It can be exploited for its uniformi-

[41] II, 115.
[42] II, 282.
[43] II, 272.

tarian and neoclassic attributes (as in Hobbes and Hume, and later, in Kames and Gerard); and it can also provide the rationale for the pleasures of romantic feeling and for a wide diversity in the standards of taste. In Shenstone the romantic approach is emphasized. In John "Estimate" Brown the association of ideas is also used to explain differences in taste between several nations. In his *Dissertation on the Rise, Union, and Power, the Progressions, Separation, and Corruptions of Poetry and Music* (1763), Brown states that the power of music to raise certain passions is due to "early Association and continued Habit".[44] Different associations produce various effects.

Thus certain Sounds being appropriated by Use, and having become the common indications of Grief, Terror, Joy, Pity, Rage, or any other Passion, will naturally excite their respective Affections among those who have adopted them; while a Hearer from another Country, whose Associations and Habits are different, will be little, or if at all, perhaps very differently affected by them.[45]

Civilized Europeans thus find it difficult to appreciate the music of the savage American Indians; and the native music of one country (a Swiss air, the sound of Scotch bagpipe, the musical effect of English fife and trumpet) is disliked in another because of the different ideas that are associated.

Melody therefore is to be considered as a relative thing, founded in the particular Associations and Habits of each People; and by

[44] P. 92; cf. also pp. 27, 39. I use the first edition (London, 1763). This statement on the role of habit and association in forming an ear for music is attacked by Daniel Webb, *Observations on the Correspondence between Poetry and Music* (London, 1769), pp. 2-3 and *passim:* "Some have thought to elude this difficulty, by supposing, that the influence of sound on passion may arise from the habit of associating certain ideas with certain sounds. It cannot be necessary to enter into a formal examination of such a principle as this, since it must fall of course on the discovery of a better." Webb's view is that the movement of sounds corresponds to that of the nerves or animal spirits and, consequently, of the emotions. The correspondence accounts for musical effects independently of any possible association of ideas. See Beattie, below, pp. 241-2.

[45] Pp. 74-5.

Custom (like Language) annexed to their Sentiments and Passions: Thus it becomes the natural Vehicle of these Sentiments and Passions; but a Vehicle, which can never extend farther than to Those, upon whom such particular Impressions have been made.[46]

In Sir Joshua Reynolds and Adam Smith, however, a compromise is found between neoclassic and romantic attitudes, between uniformity and diversity or relativity of taste. Reynolds firmly believes that the taste for beauty originates only in habit and custom. But like Hartley and others who adhere to the neoclassic *consensus gentium,* he also believes that "general habits" – those habits that everyone has – are best and furnish the most enduring standards of taste. In *Idler 82* (Nov. 10, 1759) Reynolds, following Shenstone and Spence, states that habit and custom are "the most general" sources of the standards of taste.[47] And like them, writing for non-philosophical readers, he often neglects to attribute habit formation to the constant association of ideas – a common eighteenth-century belief. Reynolds seems also to have his own system in mind. In a letter to Beattie in 1782, for example, he refers to his early *Idler* paper and reverses Hartley's method of defining the popular words, habit and custom, in terms of (what Hartley thought was) the more exact philosophic concept, association of ideas. Reynolds would rather have associations subordinated to what he thinks are the more inclusive habits: "May not all beauty proceeding from association of ideas be reduced to the principle of habit or experience? You see I am bringing everything into my old principle [i.e. habit]".[48] Despite the ignorance of the dominant eighteenth-century philosophy implied in this statement, Reynolds is certainly aware of the significance of association as an element in taste either independent of habit or equivalent to it. General and stable habits and associations, he states in one of the discourses, for example, form that

[46] P. 75.

[47] *The Literary Works of Sir Joshua Reynolds* (London, 1851-2), II, 134.

[48] *Letters of Sir Joshua Reynolds*, ed. F. W. Hilles (Cambridge, 1929), p. 93.

universal second nature which artists must use as a model.

In *Idler 82* Reynolds writes that custom can be the only cause for taste preferences. It is impossible to fix on any "general criterion" such as the objective quality of form or line, he believes, because nature is far too various and "will not be subjected to such narrow rules". We have, therefore, "no criterion of form by which to determine our judgment", except that of mere preference or association of ideas. "This position is", E. N. Hooker points out, "a direct contradiction of Burke's arguments in Part III, Sections iv and v."[49]

He who says a swan is more beautiful than a dove, means little more than that he has more pleasure in seeing a swan than a dove, either from the stateliness of its motions, or its being a more rare bird; and he who gives the preference to the dove, does it from some association of ideas of innocence which he always annexes to the dove.[50]

Once the taste for a species of beauty is established by custom, then, he goes on to say, the most beautiful object (swan or dove, white European or black Ethiopian) is that which inclines to the average or the most central form of the species, which he calls "the most general form of nature".

From what has been said, it may be inferred, that the works of Nature, if we compare one species with another, are all equally beautiful, and that preference is given from custom or some association of ideas; and that in creatures of the same species, beauty is the medium or centre of all its various forms.[51]

This average form is "the invariable general form which Nature most frequently produces, and always seems to intend in her productions". Moreover, it is, Reynolds writes in the

[49] *PMLA,* XLIX (1934), 584. But Reynolds *(Idler 82,* II, 135) follows Burke in opposing fitness as a source of beauty. His argument that "we always determine concerning its beauty [an animal's], before we exert our understanding to judge of its fitness" corresponds almost exactly with Burke's reasoning.

[50] Reynolds, *Works,* II, 133.

[51] II, 135.

fourth note to Du Fresnoy's *Art of Painting*, "by generalising his ideas" that the painter "arrives at the only true criterion of judgment".[52] Clearly, in the *Idler* essay, Reynolds regards the formation of taste for one among several species as due in part to subjective associations of ideas, although he believes that standards of perfection within one species are arrived at by neoclassic simplifying or purifying, "generalising". The associationist part of this doctrine is subsequently expanded in the *Discourses*, where it aids Reynolds in establishing a standard for artists.

It is interesting to observe that Reynolds is not far behind the neoclassicists, Hurd, Kames, Gerard, who defend the notion of universal reactions and common sense by means of the general associations of human nature, when he urges artists to use "general habits which are everywhere and always the same" or "habits of nature" as standards for achievement. The painter "must divest himself of all prejudices in favour of his age or country; he must disregard all local and temporary ornaments, and look only on those general habits which are every where and always the same".[53] Reynolds thus reflects the ways in which the new psychology of human nature was used for criticism and uses it himself particularly for the generalized beauty of the "grand style" of painting. Evidence of this union of neoclassicism and associationism appears in the "Seventh Discourse" presented before the Royal Academy.

In the "Seventh Discourse" (1776), Reynolds distinguishes between two types of nature or truth. Although the types seem to differ only in degree, Reynolds insists that the one is real and proceeds from "the general habits of nature", and that the standard of taste founded on this general nature is fixed and immutable; the other, however, is apparent or secondary truth and proceeds "from local temporary prejudices, fancies, fashions or accidental connections of ideas".[54] As the stan-

[52] II, 132, 301. "The Third Discourse" also has some discussion on nature's general form, the true standard of the arts.

[53] "The Third Discourse" (1770), I, 338.

[54] I, 413, 435.

dard of taste resulting from this secondary type of truth is variable, taste should conform to the former, or "universal opinion", because "whilst these opinions and prejudices, on which it is founded, continue, they operate as [invariable] truth".[55] That is to say, because certain associations and habits are stable and enduring and their influence extensive, they must be observed as standards by the artist, while other and more local associations must be avoided. It is precisely at this point that Reynolds, like Hurd and Hartley, employs associationism to support the neoclassic *consensus gentium.*

In proportion as these prejudices are known to be generally diffused, or long received, the taste which conforms to them approaches nearer to certainty, and to a sort of resemblance to real science [i.e. fixed truth], even where opinions are found to be no better than prejudices. And since they deserve, on account of their duration and extent, to be considered as really true, they become capable of no small degree of stability and determination, by their permanent and uniform nature.[56]

Having laid down this principle of truth, Reynolds proceeds to apply it to specific problems of art. He first re-defines the term nature. By nature he means both "the external form of things" and the "nature and internal fabric and organization, as I may call it, of the human mind and imagination". The first comprises "the general idea of nature" – the objective central form, the basis of the grand style, about which he is so much concerned throughout the discourses. The second, however, is subjective; it "is addressed to the mind, and depends on its original frame".[57] The latter, or the principles of the mind, is particularly interesting inasmuch as it shows again how Reynolds emphasized the neoclassic conception of a common and uniform sense.

The principles of these are as invariable as the former, and are to be known and reasoned upon in the same manner, by an appeal

55 I, 413.
56 I, 413, 436.
57 I, 423.

to common sense, deciding upon the common feelings of mankind. This sense, and these feelings appear to me of equal authority, and equally conclusive. Now this appeal implies a general uniformity and agreement in the minds of men. It would be else an idle and vain endeavour to establish rules of art.[58]

In the manner of Hutcheson and adherents of the internal sense doctrine, Reynolds states that the imagination is uniformly pleased by certain regular and fixed causes; and, again like Hutcheson, he refers to "accidental" associations of ideas as contrary to "what is fixed in the nature of things". For example, "that picture which pleases only one age or one nation, owes its reception to some local or accidental association of ideas".[59]

But Reynolds does not employ the association of ideas only to explain random divergencies from secondary nature or customary and universal taste. Like his immediate predecessors, Hume, Hurd, and Hartley, he also used associationism for the explanation of the custom favorable to universal taste. In particular, he uses it to explain the taste for classic drapery on statues. He states that by an association of ideas the veneration for the artistic excellence of Greece and Rome affects our approval "of every ornament and every custom that belonged to them, even to the fashion of their dress".

The figures of the great men of those nations have come down to us in sculpture. In sculpture remain almost all the excellent specimens of ancient art. We have so far associated personal dignity to the persons thus represented, and the truth of art to their manner of representation, that it is not in our power any longer to separate them.[60]

This special association, Reynolds continues, is not made in painting because no ancient paintings are extant: "This is not so in painting; because having no excellent portraits, that connection was never formed". However, another association has been the source of the dress used by certain portrait painters.

58 I, 423-4.
59 I, 426-7.
60 I, 431-2.

At one time, Reynolds points out, the clothes of portraits were painted in the style of Vandyke because of the dignity associated with it; but the effect was limited "to those only who had the means of making this association; and when made, it was irresistible". This type of association with the style of dress is not merely whimsical, Reynolds explains; it is the result of common feelings or second nature: "But this association is nature, and refers to that secondary truth and comes from conformity to general prejudice and opinion; it is therefore not merely fantastical". Thus Reynolds is able to turn from the limited and less enduring associations with Vandyke apparel and to advocate in its stead the use in modern painting of the more enduring associations with the classic drapery. That is to say, he believes dignity is more generally associated with the classic style and is a "more durable and lasting" prejudice.

> He, therefore, who in his practice of portrait-painting, wishes to dignify his subject, which we will suppose to be a lady, will not paint her in modern dress, the familiarity of which alone is sufficient to destroy all dignity. He takes care that his work shall correspond to those ideas and that imagination which he knows will regulate the judgment of others; and therefore, dresses his figure something with the general air of the antique for the sake of dignity, and preserves something of the modern for the sake of likeness. By this conduct his works correspond with those prejudices which we have in favour of what we continually see; and the relish of the antique simplicity corresponds with what we may call the more learned and scientific prejudice.[61]

Not only is a generally widespread association of ideas the source of the standard of taste for drapery in painting and sculpture, but it also is the source of the practice of introducing gothic touches to modern canvases. The discussion of this gothic association of ideas in the "Thirteenth Discourse" (1786) corresponds to the application of associationism in the seventh and to Shenstone's application of the psychology to the practice of building ruins in gardens. Reynolds describes the imagina-

[61] I, 432, 434.

tive effects of old, especially medieval, architectural forms in terms of a delightful association of ideas with the past.

To pass over the effect produced by that general symmetry and proportion, by which the eye is delighted, as the ear is with music, Architecture certainly possesses many principles in common with Poetry and Painting. Among those which may be reckoned as the first, is, that of affecting the imagination by means of association of ideas. Thus, for instance, as we have naturally a veneration for antiquity, whatever building brings to our remembrance ancient customs and manners, such as the castles of the Barons of ancient Chivalry, is sure to give this delight. Hence it is that towers and battlements are so often selected by the Painter and the Poet to make a part of the composition of their ideal landscape.

This association of ideas with gothic architecture, continues Reynolds, "is the ground of the effect we feel in many of . . . [Vanbrugh's] works".

And it is from hence, in a great degree, that, in the buildings of Vanbrugh, who was a Poet as well as an Architect, there is a greater display of imagination, than we shall find perhaps in any other, and this is the ground of the effect we feel in many of his works.[62]

The very same idea concerning the esthetic pleasure felt at the sight of an old castle is expressed in a criticism (written in 1776) of Gilpin's theory of the picturesque.[63] Reynolds disagrees with Gilpin and states that a castle is pleasing not because of its objective qualities – those qualities of roughness and irregularity claimed by Gilpin as sources of the picturesque effect – but partly because of a pleasing association of ideas with the past:

The pleasing effect of a castle in a landscape, proceeds from an association of ideas by sending the mind backwards into antiquity and producing some new sentiment – or by being marked by time, and made a sort of natural object; but in a new tower both those

[62] II, 75.

[63] The date of the essay's composition has been ascertained by W. D. Templeman, "Sir Joshua Reynolds on the Picturesque", *MLN*, XLVII (1932), 446-8.

ideas are destroyed, and consequently it is not considered as a picturesque object.[64]

Like almost all other important writers on critical problems in the middle of the century, Reynolds uses the theory of association to supplement his theory of art, especially his theory of general ideas and the grand style. Following Hartley, Hume, Spence, and Hutcheson, he shows how tastes are formed by custom and random associations of ideas. This notion of the origin of taste preferences is certainly liberal, for it readily subverts objective and uniform criteria and upholds diversity and relativity. Anything can become an object of beauty and admiration. But Reynolds is not entirely willing to go to such extremes. In *Idler 82* and the *Discourses*, he provides a compromise between these conflicting points of view: uniformity and diversity. Although the taste for a species is the product of subjective association, habitual observation, and experience, the most beautiful object of the species, he says clearly, is a fixed and invariable central form, the identical "general idea" of nature that Johnson, in the tenth chapter of *Rasselas* (1759), raises as a standard at which poets should aim. Furthermore, in the "Seventh Discourse" (1776), Reynolds used the association of ideas in accordance with the neoclassic concept of the *consensus gentium*. Because certain associations, especially the association of dignity with classic drapery, have pleased everyone since antiquity and are therefore stable and enduring effects of human nature, they can with good reason, Reynolds deduces, be imitated by artists as the fixed and general standards of nature. In explaining this critical standard, nature, as the secondary nature of habit and association, Reynolds merely follows the general trend among the associationist critics to reinterpret human nature and to furnish criticism with a new standard of taste. In a critical essay on Gilpin's picturesque and in the later "Thirteenth Discourse" (1786),

[64] "Considerations on Gilpin's Essay on the Picturesque", in C. R. Leslie and Tom Taylor, *Life and Times of Sir Joshua Reynolds* (London, 1865), II, 608.

Reynolds uses associations to explain the fashionable and romantic taste for gothic ornaments. Together with Shenstone's analysis of the effect of ruins, this new application is significant as being among the first attempts at an associationist explanation of the new esthetic feeling, the picturesque. [65] Reynolds is, of course, almost wholly unoriginal; but he is chiefly interesting as a distinguished practitioner who reflects the current philosophic approach to critical theory, relates it in practical fashion to his art, and passes it on with the weight of authority to large and learned audiences.

No doubt influenced by the writings of his good friend Hume, Adam Smith not only accepts the view that utility and fitness are among the principal sources of beauty, but also, like Reynolds, he describes how custom and fashion, operating through associations of ideas, are responsible for the various notions and judgments of beauty. Smith considers the beauty of utility, however, as independent of custom; therefore, fitness is not to be thought of as an association of ideas, which he defines as follows:

> When two objects have frequently been seen together, the imagination acquires a habit of passing easily from the one to the other. If the first appear, we lay our account that the second is to follow. Of their own accord they put us in mind of one another, and the attention glides easily along them. Though, independent of custom, there should be no real beauty in their union, yet when custom has thus connected them together, we feel an impropriety in their separation. The one we think is awkward when it appears without its usual companion. We miss something which we expected to find, and the habitual arrangement of our ideas is disturbed by the disappointment.[66]

[65] Cf. C. Hussey, *The Picturesque* (London, 1927), p. 60: "The *Discourses* show a progressive trend away from the Grand Style of vision towards the looser emotionalism that animated the Picturesque point of view, and flooded art and criticism as the Theory of Association."

[66] Adam Smith, *The Theory of Moral Sentiments* (London, [1759], 1892), Pt. V, Ch. i, pp. 281, 289. Cf. also Pt. IV, Ch. i. "Of the Beauty which the Appearance of Utility Bestows upon all the Productions of Art, and of the extensive Influence of this Species of Beauty."

The association of ideas, Smith notes, affects the trivial fashions in dress and furniture as well as the taste for music, poetry, and architecture. For example, the association of ideas with verse measures differs in France and England:

Custom has made the one nation associate the ideas of gravity, sublimity, and seriousness, to that measure which the other has connected with whatever is gay, flippant, and ludicrous. Nothing would appear more absurd in English than a tragedy written in the Alexandrine verses of the French; or in French, than a work of the same kind in verses of ten syllables.[67]

Furthermore, even the taste for "natural objects" is affected by custom. Like Reynolds, Smith believes that taste for a species of beauty is established by custom. Because customs differ, this view allows for a diversity of tastes: "What various and opposite forms are deemed beautiful in different species of things! The proportions which are admired in one animal are altogether different from those which are esteemed in another". And making the very same compromise with the neoclassic ideal of common nature as Reynolds, he writes of the "general character" that is the most beautiful object in the species. Incidentally, here Smith suggests a source for Reynolds's analysis of the general form.

It is upon this account that a learned Jesuit, Father Buffier, has determined that the beauty of every object consists in that form and colour, which is most usual among things of that particular sort to which it belongs. Thus in the human form the beauty of each feature lies in a certain middle, equally removed from a variety of other forms that are ugly.... It is the form which Nature seems to have aimed at in them all.... In the same manner, in each species of creatures, what is most beautiful bears the strongest characters of the general fabric of the species.

Smith can thus deduce that "the most customary form therefore is, in each species of things ... the most beautiful".[68]

[67] P. 285.

[68] P. 287. The relationship between Claude Buffier's *Traité des Premières Vérités* and Reynolds' *Idler 82* is discussed by E. S. Thompson, "The *Discourses* of Sir Joshua Reynolds", *PMLA*, XXXII (1917), 361-2.

But Smith is unwilling to admit custom and associations of ideas as the only source of the taste for beauty. Like Burke, he also states that certain colors, smooth surfaces, and orderly arrangements of varied parts please the sense of beauty without the intervention of associated ideas.[69] In Smith, therefore, is to be found the usual dichotomy: his belief that regularity of form and structure is a uniform taste among men is in the neoclassic tradition, while, at the same time, his admission of diversity of taste contributes to the forces that weaken the neoclassic system. And as others have done before him from the time of Hutcheson, Smith explains diversity by the theory of association. Yet it is interesting to notice that Smith himself supplies the compromise between uniformity and diversity of taste. In the final analysis, then, it may be said that Smith does not relax his neoclassicism, but rather that he tries to strengthen and deepen it with the acceptable philosophy of the time. In the latter respect, he presages the significant neoclassic associationism of Gerard and Kames.

In *An Essay on Taste* (1759), Alexander Gerard reconciles the conflicting critical theories of Hutcheson and Hume. Like Hutcheson, from whom he readily admits borrowing, he equates the philosophic conception, the pleasures of the internal sense, with that of the popular Addisonian pleasures of the imagination, and alleges that these pleasures are the foundation of taste in the arts. But he enlarges the number of Hutcheson's internal senses into seven, each answering to some esthetic taste – novelty, sublimity, beauty, imitation, harmony, wit, and virtue. From Hume, another admitted source, Gerard has taken his conception of the influence of associations upon the activity of the imagination or its equivalent, the internal senses. Unlike Hutcheson who, as we have seen, generally regards association as a corrupting agent, Gerard subscribes to Hume's conviction concerning the important positive influence of associations upon the imagination and affirms that the association of ideas

[69] P. 289.

is one of the principal sources of the taste for sublimity and beauty and a partial or minor source of the imaginative senses of imitation and harmony.

Gerard's characteristic application of the theory of association may be seen best in the section on the imaginative power or sense of grandeur and sublimity, the section in which the association of ideas receives its most extended discussion in the *Essay on Taste*. For his analysis of the associationist sublime, Gerard leans heavily, he confesses, upon Baillie's *Essay on the Sublime* (1747) and Hume's *Treatise on Human Nature* (1739).[70] "Objects are sublime", writes Gerard, "which possess quantity, or amplitude, and simplicity, in conjunction". The mind is filled with this natural object and expands, as Baillie had described before, in "one grand sensation, . . . deep silent wonder and admiration".[71] An association of cause with effect may intensify the emotion produced by large objects, since it joins two closely related sublime ideas:

> There being in the mind a natural proneness to admire a great degree of mental qualities, the admiration bestowed on them will be likewise extended to whatever we consider as an effect of them. . . . The greatness, for instance, of the works of nature, is considered as a striking indication of the omnipotence of their author. A vast fleet or army suggests an high opinion of the sovereign or the nation by whom they are provided or employed. In such cases, our admiration of the cause is excited by the view of the effect, and, being reflected back on the effect, heightens the sentiments of sublimity which it inspires, by means of the principles of the mind already pointed out.[72]

[70] *An Essay on Taste* (Edinburgh, 1780) I, ii, 11n., 19n. Part, section, and page of the third edition are given. The work was submitted in 1756 to the Edinburgh Philosophical Society, and was awarded a prize. It was first published in 1759 in enlarged form. A second edition, "with corrections and additions", was published in 1764. The most important addition was that of Part IV, "Of the Standard of Taste". This chronology explains the references in Part IV, ii, 218n., iii, 221n. to Kames's *Elements of Criticism* (1762) and to Burke's essay "On Taste" (1759).

[71] I, ii, 11-2.

[72] I, ii, 17-8.

The role of the association of ideas in enriching and deepening the sublimity of objects originally or naturally grand is not, however, so significant as that of ideas or objects which do not have "quantity, or amplitude". All objects lacking mass or grandeur, Gerard avers, can only receive their sublimity through association with ideas originally sublime. It is obvious that this view is an eighteenth-century addition to the classical source of the sublime. Certainly Longinus is not responsible for the following statement: "But in order to comprehend the whole extent of the sublime, it is proper to take notice, that objects which do not themselves possess that quality, may nevertheless acquire it by *association* with such as do. It is the nature of association, to unite different ideas so closely, that they become in a manner one".[73] By this process, continues Gerard, an association with an already sublime idea can become the source of the sublimity of style, elevation, distance, and remoteness.

At least, association renders the transition of the mind from one idea to another so quick and easy, that we contemplate both with the same disposition; and are therefore similarly affected by both. Whenever, then, any object uniformly and constantly introduces into the mind the idea of another that is grand, it will, by its connection with the latter, be itself rendered grand. Hence words and phrases are denominated lofty and majestic. Sublimity of style arises, not so much from the sound of the words, though that doubtless may have some influence, as from the nature of the ideas which we are accustomed to annex to them, and the character of the persons among whom they are in most common use. This too is the origin of the grandeur which we ascribe to objects high and elevated in place; of the veneration with which we regard things in any direction distant; and of the superior admiration which is excited by things remote in time; especially in antiquity, or past duration.[74]

"But", Gerard proceeds, reasoning rather loosely, "the fine arts present the most numerous examples of grandeur produced by association". The artist excites ideas of sublime objects and leads us by his imitation "to form ideas and conceive

[73] I, ii, 18.
[74] I, ii, 19.

images of sublime originals". Similar sublime feelings, although less intense than those produced by originally grand ideas, are thus aroused by mimic arts through these associations with the ideas of sublime nature. This effect is seen in architecture (as Baillie had written); for "the principal source of grandeur in architecture is association, by which the columns suggest ideas of strength and durableness, and the whole structure introduces the sublime ideas of the riches and magnificence of the owner". In painting, as in poetry, the landscapist has the power of suggesting ideas of "sublime natural objects"; and so, by means of this associational power his art may produce the sublime effect. This concept of association is so sweeping that it can make anything sublime, even miniatures. "And so complete is the power of association, that a skilful painter can express any degree of sublimity in the smallest as well as in the largest compass. It appears in the miniatures of Julio Clovio, as really as in the paintings of Titian or Michael Angelo". [75]

Moreover, similar associations with grand ideas are normally responsible for sublimity of language, and, consequently, of poetry: "The sublime of those arts in which the instrument of imitation is language, must evidently arise entirely from association; because it is the only principle from which words derive their force and meaning". [76] Comparisons and figures of speech, especially "those which have a relation to the gods" or to large ideas, turn on this principle: "If an author's main subject, is destitute of innate grandeur, it may be rendered grand, by comparing, or some way associating it with objects naturally such". [77] Lastly, the opposite of sublimity, meanness, "arises often likewise from association, when low and groveling ideas are suggested .... Thus, also, words and phrases become mean, when they excite mean ideas, either by their proper

[75] I, ii, 21-3.

[76] I, ii, 23; cf. p. 26: "The power of imparting sublimity to objects which naturally have it not, by giving them a relation to others, is an advantage peculiar to the arts which imitate by language."

[77] I, ii, 25.

signification, or by their being used only by those of inferior rank".[78]

Monk's study of the eighteenth-century sublime leaves us with the mistaken impression that Gerard applies the psychology of association only to that esthetic response.[79] However, Gerard unequivocally declares that "the sense or taste of Beauty" is also determined in large part by associations. Although the "soft and tender sensation" of beauty is often excited in accordance with other principles of human nature than those of the association of ideas, – the blending and balancing of uniformity, variety, and proportion, – yet to association, Gerard believes, is due much credit for its production and modification. The vicissitudes of associationism are indeed curious; only two years before the publication of Gerard's essay, Burke was most successfully anti-associationist in his analysis of beauty. But now, Gerard, more thoroughly imbued with the associationist philosophy of his fellow-Scotchman Hume, lays stress on the connection between the association of certain ideas and the taste for beauty.

The suggestion of design, Gerard first writes, increases the pleasure in beauty. When uniformity and variety are so combined that they produce great delight and are also "indications of design, wisdom, and contrivance; qualities of mind which we never fail to survey with pleasure, ... we take pleasure in conceiving the excellency of the cause, and by this the delight is heightened which we find in beholding the effect that suggests that excellence".[80] The association of design and wisdom, later used by Alison, as a source of extra esthetic delight, is perhaps original with Gerard. It is, however, only another association that has some kinship with the Humean principle

[78] I, ii, 28.

[79] Monk, *The Sublime,* p. 112; "... leaving association to be completely theorized into aesthetic by his fellow-countryman, Archibald Alison". Similarly, the DNB article on Gerard creates a false impression by noting only the connection in Gerard's essay between association and beauty: "Under the sense of beauty Gerard gave a prominent place to the principle of association, in which he has been followed by Alison."

[80] I, iii, 36.

of causality. Another species of association also closely related to this principle is fitness: "When ... we see a work, it leads us by a natural association to conceive its end; prone to comparison, we examine the propriety of the parts in relation to this end". The satisfaction on perceiving the proper application of means to an end "communicates itself to the effect so closely connected with it by causation". Thus, unlike Burke, Gerard agrees with the many claimants of utility, with those who believe that the association of use may enrich the feeling of beauty. [81]

Without transition Gerard next analyzes the source of the beauty of color. A simple association with agreeable ideas is almost the only source of this beauty, Gerard suggests.

> The beauty of colours is, in most instances, resolveable into association; those being approved, which, either by a natural resemblance, or by custom, or opinion, introduce and are connected with agreeable ideas of any sort; and those being disapproved which have any way become related to disagreeable ones. The verdure of the fields is delightful, not only by being inoffensive to the eye, but chiefly by its suggesting the pleasant idea of fertility.[82]

Furthermore, the beauty of color in clothes depends entirely upon the association with the wearer, his sentiments, character, and station in life. It is interesting to observe how Gerard adapts Hurd's and Hartley's concept of uniform or similar association, the concept of the *consensus gentium*, for the trivial subject of dress. This significant neoclassic concept in associationist critical theory will also be used by Kames to found stable standards of taste.

> In some cases, a particular dress, in consequence of established manners, suggests to the generality nearly the same idea. Wherever this general connection takes place, it forms a kind of standard in dress, for persons in certain stations or professions. We come to perceive a propriety in conforming to it; and we are displeased with the indecency of deviating remarkably from it.[83]

[81] I, iii, 40-1.
[82] I, iii, 41-2.
[83] I, iii, 42.

But Gerard is also aware of the difficulty of ever fixing standards of taste, for he freely recognizes that because associations may differ in different persons, "relish" may vary: "When the idea suggested by dress is different in different persons, so also is the relish for the colour; what suggests to one a liveliness and vivacity of turn, gives another the idea of gaudiness and levity".

The last point made by Gerard concerning the influence of associations upon the sense of beauty considerably weakens the neoclassic belief in an objective, pure or intrinsic type of beauty which is determined by the proper balance of uniformity and variety. According to the psychological view, beauty, as well as every other esthetic effect, is or should be entirely subjective and merely a matter of individual response, and Gerard seems often to examine art from this romantic point of view. To him, art must in part be suggestive, that is to say, it must move the internal senses or the imagination. Thus, after stating that beauty is applied to "every pleasure which is conveyed to the eye", he also agrees that it equally applies

> to the pleasure we receive, either when an object of sight suggests pleasant ideas of other senses, or when the ideas suggested are agreeable ones formed from the sensations of sight, or when both these circumstances concur. In all these cases, beauty is, at least in part, resolveable into association.

Beauty may, for example, be caused by an association of ideas from two senses: the suggestion of virtue in a face may diffuse beauty over it by its agreeable association. In the second place, Gerard conceives that ideas in descriptive poetry receive their beauty by association with visions of nature to which agreeable emotions are already attached, flowers, fields, meadows, or groves: "This is one great part of the beauty of pastoral", he writes, "and enters in some degree into every kind of poetry".

The internal sense of imitation, another "power of imagination", delights in what Gerard calls "designed resemblance". Resemblance or "similitude is a very powerful principle of association, which, by continually connecting the ideas in which it is found, and leading our thoughts from one of them to the other, produces in mankind a strong tendency to comparison". [84] According to Gerard, this association of ideas basically works as follows: the recognition of resemblance mildly exerts the mind and so produces pleasure, even when the original object may not in itself be agreeable; moreover, the mind, wishing to gratify its curiosity, is led to compare or associate the original with the copy. When the association between these resembling ideas is recognized as the actual design and intention of the artist, the pleasure is greatly augmented and a more effective esthetic response is thus produced.

As in all eighteenth-century critical thought art is thought to be imitation, Gerard has thereby reinterpreted the chief neoclassic or Aristotelian principle in accordance with a psychological law of association – resemblance. Thus the classical concept of imitation is examined through the new lens of the current psychology. But the meaning remains nearly the same, for instead of using the concept of *imitation* of nature, Gerard merely uses *resemblance* to nature. This psychology, therefore, does not entirely subvert neoclassic norms; on the contrary, it may often reinforce them, as we have seen in the writings of Hume, Hurd, Hartley. In Gerard, such also is the case. For example, a doctrine closely related to imitation, verisimilitude – the doctrine which upholds truth to nature as a standard for the arts – is upheld by means of the principle of resemblance: "Improbability, which is want of resemblance to natural things, always renders a fable or story less entertaining; and if the improbability be very great, or extended to the material parts, it often makes it wholly nauseous". [85] We may infer from this critical statement that when the mind fails to perceive an association or resemblance to nature, no

[84] I, iv, 47. Cf. *Essay on Genius* (London, 1774), III, ii, 334-5 on imitation and resemblance.
[85] I, iv, 49.

esthetic pleasure is felt; or that when improbability spoils the association of the imitation with nature, taste is adversely affected.

Ordinarily, the associational law of resemblance is used to explain the operations of the active or shaping imagination of the artist. Hume, as we have showed, is the first to show how this law helps govern the shaping imagination; and Gerard himself, in his later *Essay on Genius*, also explains how resemblance helps the imagination form regular works of art.

In genius for the arts, resemblance, the predominant principle of association, continually operates along with the other principles, and by uniting its force to theirs, causes them to suggest only, and suggest quickly, such ideas as are conducive to the imitation or representation which the artist has in view. The attributes, qualities, and circumstances of any subject, are connected with it by co-existence, and are naturally suggested to the imagination by this relation: the predominance of resemblance as an associating principle in the poet or painter, will make these to be suggested, whenever they are necessary for marking distinctly the object which he describes or represents; and it will make those of them to occur most readily which are properest for this purpose, even though they be in themselves remote.... In every good picture, in every good poetical description, we perceive the influence of co-existence operating on the imagination, under the direction of resemblance.... A defect in the former respect, produces poverty of genius; a defect in the latter respect, irregularity.[86]

But in the *Essay on Taste*, Gerard gives a novel and unusual interpretation to this law by explaining the manner in which it affects the passive imagination of the observer. He uses it, in short, to supplement the neoclassic norms, imitation of nature, and its corollary, verisimilitude. Herein, Gerard paves the way for Kames's more thoroughgoing neoclassic associationism in the *Elements of Criticism.* In the latter influential work, not only the neoclassic doctrine of verisimilitude, but also the doctrines of decorum and the distinction of the genres are reinforced by the appeal to the associationist conception of nature.

[86] *Essay on Genius* (London, 1774), pp. 339-41.

Imagination or taste, then, according to Gerard's system, functions through the principle of association wholly in sublime and to some extent in beautiful imitations of nature. But the application of the theory of association in Gerard's essay does not cease here. The power of the imagination in harmony, which enables us to perceive beauty in sound, also includes the associationist concept. In addition to the several neoclassic methods of producing delight, there is also the association of ideas; that is to say, music or harmony may produce beautiful effects by means of regularity, proportion, variety, not to mention the association of cause and effect.

By the natural fitness of sounds for accomplishing an imitation of, or association with, their objects and natural expressions, it infuses into the breast passions correspondent; settles into calm serenity, melts into tenderness or pity, sinks into sorrow, soothes into melancholy, agitates with terror, elevates with joy, excites to courage, or enraptures with devotion; and thus inexpressibly delights the soul.

Indeed, the associationism in Gerard's *Essay on Taste* has a much wider influence upon the imaginative powers of human nature than historians of taste and critical theory have generally credited it with. It is best used in the taste for the sublime, as Monk contends; but it is also significantly employed with beauty and imitation, and, to a certain extent, with harmony. Furthermore, it should be noted that Gerard's applications of the psychology are not entirely inconsistent with his neoclassic approach to criticism; and, as we shall now see, his associationism generally supplements a neoclassic belief in standards of taste. But before standards of taste can be discussed, it is important to understand the way in which Gerard believes that taste itself is formed.

A good or true taste, Gerard states, "consists in certain excellences of our original powers of judgment and imagination combined".[87] He thinks of the imagination that helps form this good taste as a composite faculty; for when the various internal powers of imagination or senses join, the greater

[87] II, iii, 95.

will be the esthetic "complicated pleasure". [88] Following Hume, Gerard therefore seriously exploits the possibility of association between the several internal senses so that a "compound pleasure" more intense than any single one can be produced: "Taste is not one simple power, but an aggregate of many, which, by the resemblance of their energies, and the analogy of their subjects, and causes, readily associate, and are combined". [89] Furthermore, "sensibility and delicacy of taste" often depend upon habits and associations:

The sentiments of taste depend very much on association. So far as they proceed from this, custom must augment them; as custom, by adding a new principle of union, renders the connexion more intimate, and introduces the related ideas more quickly and forcibly. Custom likewise begets new associations, and enables works of taste to suggest ideas which were not originally connected with them: and what a surprising intenseness the association of ideas, originally foreign, bestows on our perceptions, both pleasurable and painful, is obvious in too many instances to require being enlarged on.[90]

That associations strengthen and enlarge taste or the esthetic response is the mature opinion held by Gerard – the very same that is more elaborately expounded in the later *Essay on Genius*. And in these two essays, Gerard has recourse to Hume's analysis of the regular imagination operating in conformity with the laws of association: in the one to show how the associationist and active imagination of genius creates a work of art, in the other to show how taste is in large part dependent on the regular associations of the receptive imagination. Consequently, any explanation of Gerard's theory of the formation of taste cannot be accurate or complete without knowledge of the way the imagination works by means of associations.

Gerard cannot omit anything from his theory of taste. Judgment and sensibility (which are generally held to be mutually exclusive), and associations in the imagination, all must have

[88] II, ii, 82.
[89] II, vii, 133.
[90] II, iv, 101-2.

a place in his eclectic theory. Excepting the inclusion of judgment, Gerard more or less adopts Hume's view of the imagination and repeats the statement on its regular functioning. His point is that the imagination takes the place of memory which is tied down to "original sensation", that is to say, contiguity, and "by its associating power, confers upon them [ideas] new ties, that they may not lie perfectly loose; and it can range them in an endless variety of forms". Although the imagination may be "wild", it still conforms to regular rules or formulae:

But wild and lawless as this faculty appears to be, it commonly observes certain general rules, associating chiefly ideas of such objects as are connected by the simple relations of resemblance, contrariety, or vicinity; or by the more complex ties of custom, co-existence, causation, or order. . . . Ideas to which they belong, are often so strongly connected by the imagination, that they become almost inseparable, and generally appear together. When one of them is conceived, no force can prevent the other from rushing into the mind. Many instances of this are observable every day; particularly in the prejudices, the attachments, and the antipathies of men; and there have occurred, in the former parts of this essay, many instances of objects which please, or displease taste, only, or chiefly, by means of ideas which are associated with them, and suggested by them; as in the sublimity of works of art, and in several kinds of beauty.[91]

This "easy transition from one perception to others associated with it" in the imagination profoundly influences the pleasures of taste; for if the mind must exert itself and strain to perceive a connection, "it would disturb the operations of the soul, and destroy all our pleasure". It is this smooth operation of associating ideas in the fancy that is the source of the unity of a work of art as well as of the esthetic pleasure in perceiving unity.

It is fancy which thus bestows unity on number, and unites things into one image, which, in themselves, and in their appearances to the senses, are distinct and separate. By this operation too, fancy

[91] III, i, 153, 154-5.

has great influence on taste: for all the objects that affect taste, and excite its sentiments, are certain forms or pictures made by fancy, certain parts or qualities of things which it combined into complex modes.[92]

Again, following Hume's conception of double associations of ideas and emotions, Gerard also notes how "the mixture of concomitant emotions" – which is Gerard's version of the association of ideas and emotions – helps produce "a vigorous and lively taste".[93]

Although Gerard's emphasis on the correcting judgment must not be overlooked in the final evaluation of his neoclassicism, it must also be remembered that his conception of the imagination as being under the control of regular associations and as producing a unified work of art, is also indicative of a neoclassic attitude which he shares with his predecessors, Hume, Hurd, and Hartley. With all these writers, taste and imagination are in part or in their entirety understood with relation to an associationist conception of human nature. Thus Gerard writes similarly of the universal activity of these associations in the imagination:

That these sentiments [of taste] arise from imagination, does by no means imply, that they are fantastical, imaginary, or unsubstantial. They are universally produced by the energies of fancy, which are indeed of the utmost consequence, and have the most extensive influence on the operations of the mind.[94]

If he wished, Gerard might have ignored judgment and might have permitted, like Hume, this conception of universal association in the imagination to stand alone as the source and basis of taste.

92 III, i, 156-7.
93 III, i, 161; vi, 184-5. Like Hume, Gerard also compares the activity of associations in the imagination to physical laws: (III, ii, 163-4) "As the magnet selects, from a quantity of matter, the ferruginous particles which happen to be scattered through it, without making an impression on other substances, so imagination, by a similar sympathy equally inexplicable, draws out from the whole compass of nature such ideas as we have occasion for, without attending to others."
94 III, i, 162.

The last characteristic of Gerard's thoroughgoing associationist approach to critical theory is an anticipation of his later study on genius. In the *Essay on Taste*, he writes of the connection of taste with genius: "The first and leading quality of genius, is invention, which consists in a great extent and comprehensiveness of imagination, in a readiness of associating the remotest ideas that are any way related". A man of genius, he continues, possesses vigorous principles and has quick associations; he arranges natural order out of rude chaos by "the same associating power" and "designs a regular and well-proportioned whole".[95] The relationship between genius and associations in the imagination is exhaustively described in the later work on genius; in this essay, the dependence of taste upon the associationist genius is merely summarily stated.

To sum up, the principle of association is of enormous significance in Gerard's critical theory. Without first understanding the influence of the association of ideas, neither Gerard's conception of the imagination nor his conception of taste can be accurately evaluated. With Gerard, taste is a passive faculty comprising several internal senses or powers of imagination operating in part by regular associations of ideas. Likewise, Gerard suggests in passing how the plastic imagination of a genius does not act at random but compounds or invents a regular and unified work of art by using regular laws of association. But in addition to these applications of the theory of association, there is one more critical problem related to taste to which Gerard applies the theory – the problem of single and diverse standards of taste. Here, since he perceives that associations are sometimes the sources of wide diversity in taste, he is driven by his neoclassic temper, in order that uniform standards may be set up, to accept the checks of judgment.

Gerard recognizes, as we have seen, that associations are

[95] III, ii, 163-4. To "this operation of genius" Gerard footnotes Akenside's associationist passages in *The Pleasures of Imagination,* III, 348-410.

responsible for wide diversity of taste in color; he also shows the effects of association upon standards in Part IV, Section i, entitled "That differences of taste are unavoidable". "The constitution of human nature", declares Gerard, "renders this variety of tastes inevitable". Not only are these differences due to original differences of the internal senses, of emotional sensibility, and of intellect, but they are also due to the variety of modifying associations.

All the sentiments of taste have a great dependence on association; and must derive immense variety from the endless diversity which takes place, in the strength of the associating principles, in their particular modifications and combinations, in the tracks to which they have been most accustomed, in the nature and the number of accessory ideas which they connect with the objects of taste.[96]

Notwithstanding the inevitability of diversity of taste, the neo-classicist Gerard contends strongly for a regular and uniform standard of taste based on the sentiments of all men, based, so to speak, on the "general principles" determining their approbation – those principles that control the activity of the imagination. The imagination, he repeats, must not be deemed a merely fanciful, lawless, wild, and irregular faculty. The imagination operates according to fixed and regular principles of human nature. And among the most important of these principles, we have seen, are those of the associationist psychology:

In the genuine province of taste, in the sublime field of nature and the fine arts, though it be certain, and though it has been a great part of our business to prove, that almost all the sentiments of taste

[96] IV, i, 200, 202. The same idea reappears, of course, in the *Essay on Genius,* p. 349: "When we consider how many and how dissimilar modifications every associating principle admits, we must be sensible that the power of the predominant principle [of association, resemblance,] to modify the others suitably to its own designs, will introduce great variety into their effects, and give birth to very different kinds of genius." It is also true that diversity is accepted because of the differences in temper and nationality. These differences affect emotion. Cf. II, i, 80: "This diversity in the formation of the heart will produce a considerable diversity, in the sentiments which men receive from works of taste, and in the judgment which they form concerning them."

are derived from certain exertions of the imagination, it is equally certain, and has been proved with the clearest evidence, that these exertions are as little capricious, as regular, as universal, and subject to as fixed laws, as the exertions of any other principle in the human constitution.[97]

Not content, however, to rely only on the general principles of association in the imagination, Gerard buckles under the pressure of a neoclassic temper and gives to the judicious intellect the functions of estimating beauties and defects and of deducing from common principles of the imagination the standard of true and good taste for the arts.[98] Judgment, moreover, can discern that "a groundless association" may be the source of an object's disgusting quality; and, therefore, it may deduce that the object ought not be disliked. Thus Gerard agrees with Kames, whom he quotes, that "a man *ought not* to be pleased when he is, or *ought to be* pleased when he is not". And he can conclude that "men ... who are *affected* differently, may notwithstanding *judge* alike".[99] But unlike Kames, Gerard does not clearly indicate how judgment establishes the criteria of art upon permanent, rational, or natural associations uniform in all men. He still actively believes in the old neoclassic dichotomy between reason and imagination.

But in effect, Gerard's use of judgment only makes certain that the associationist imagination will be regular and classical. Although the powers of imagination are in large part governed by regular principles of association uniform in all men, he still considers it necessary to add that a *true* criticism and a *good*

[97] IV, ii, 212.

[98] IV, ii, 214: "Taste implies judgment, as well as sentiment: and therefore, it must, in some respects at least, refer to something beyond ourselves, and be either right or wrong, according as it is conformable or not conformable to that external standard." Also IV, v, 266-7: "In the fine arts it is not the several sentiments of individuals, but just conclusions deduced from them, concerning the qualities in objects which gratify taste, and the simple mental principles from whose operation the gratification is derived, that serve immediately for estimating excellence or faultiness."

[99] IV, ii, 216-9. This part was added after 1762. See *post,* p. 214.

taste must be refined by reason and judgment. Gerard is apparently more conservative than the conservatives, as he suggests that he is unwilling to trust the *consensus gentium* based on the uniform and habitual associations of human nature. In this respect, his associationism differs from that of Hume and harks back to the more narrow psychological neoclassicism of Hobbes. Except for this emphasis on judgment, Gerard's use of the theory of association in discovering the origin of taste and in clarifying critical problems is more complete and more significant than that of any other writer from the time of Hume's *Treatise of Human Nature* (1739) to that of this *Essay on Taste* (1759).[100]

Gerard emphatically acknowledges the influence of the association of ideas in critical theory. He differs with Burke, who applies it only to sublime ideas of nature and generally minimizes the importance of the associationist psychology, and he makes it the chief source of much of the taste for the sublimity of art and for the beautiful. His dependence on the subjective aspects of his psychology for the explanation of sublimity and beauty makes Gerard a far more complex figure than his neoclassic stress on reason and judgment superficially suggests. Certainly, his analysis of these two important senses in terms of associational suggestion proves that eighteenth-century critical theorists do not invariably hold with Shaftesbury and Hutcheson that esthetic effects are best produced by uniform structures and simple forms. On the contrary, Gerard very clearly shows that the taste for art is excited and enriched by emotional suggestion. This subjectivism, which goes beyond the mere form of the object, is undoubtedly a romantic point of view. But Gerard's critical position with respect to the concept of the imagination conforms, on the other hand, to the neoclassic tradition. His concept of the inventive (plastic) imagination and of the perceptive imagination or internal senses is infused with

[100] Saintsbury's opinion of Gerard is not very flattering. Cf. *A History of English Criticism* (New York, 1911), p. 289n: "Gerard, however, though habitually dull, is less absurd than Alison, whom he undoubtedly supplied with his principle of Association."

the Humean principles of regular association. And although he is aware of the subjective and diversitarian capabilities of associations in the imagination, he prefers to lay stress on its uniformitarian tendency, supported by the rational judgment, to follow laws of order and regularity. In this last respect, Gerard's associationism is at one with the tenets of neoclassicism and prepares the ground for the neoclassic associationism in Lord Kames's *Elements of Criticism* and his own *Essay on Genius*.

Gerard's *Essay on Genius* (1774), the complement of his former work on taste, grew out of a series of lectures read from 1758 to 1771 to the Aberdeen Philosophical Society, a small club which numbered among its members many eminent literary Scotsmen, James Beattie, Thomas Reid, John Gregory, and George Campbell.[101] The subjects of these lectures were genius and the influence of habit and passion on the association of ideas. As we have seen, Gerard had already attempted, when relating taste to genius in the *Essay on Taste*, to analyze philosophically the process in which genius originates. In that essay, he pointed out only in passing that taste is dependent in part on genius, – his major point being the dependence of taste on the associational powers of the *perceptive* or passive imagination. In the *Essay on Genius*, however, Gerard describes the ways in which genius originates in the associational power of the *inventive* or plastic imagination. In both essays, it is true, he describes the ways in which the regular laws of association govern the activity of the imagination. But the difference between them remains clear: in the present essay invention or the plastic imagination is the main subject, while in the earlier work the chief subject is the perceptive imagination or taste.

Gerard's long-winded treatise on genius is, in effect, an essay on the state of psychological esthetics in the third quarter of the century. As one of his severe critics, William Belsham,

[101] See McCosh, *The Scottish Philosophy*, p. 228; Margaret Lee Wiley, "Gerard and the Scots Societies", *Texas University Studies in English* (Austin, 1940), p. 134.

has unkindly insinuated, the essay explains the associationist psychology more than its putative subject, genius.[102] Although it cannot be denied that the essay is heavily weighted with psychology, we are nevertheless more than fortunate in having Gerard's comprehensive speculations on associationism because they are such a well-shaped and strong link in the chain of associationist thought in later eighteenth-century critical theory.

The concepts employed by Gerard, as Belsham remarks in disgust, are not unlike those used by Locke, Hume, or Hartley. Gerard, it is true, is unoriginal and borrows much from previous studies, especially in Part II, in which the following subjects are discussed: "Of the Source of the Varieties of Genius in the Imagination; particularly of the Qualities of Ideas which produce Association", – "Of the Influence of Habit on Association", – "Of the Influence of the Passions on Association", – "Reflections on the Principles of Association". "Ideas suggested, either by Sensations, or by other Ideas", – "Of the Combination of the associating Principles", – "Of the Modifications of the associating Principles". These analyses show a definite development in Gerard's thinking. Compared with the analyses and applications of associationism in this work, those in the earlier essay on taste appear to be fragmentary and shoddy, and to be included in the text merely as sops to the contemporary enthusiasm for a new philosophy of art. In the *Essay on Genius* are Gerard's matured and carefully considered opinions on the manner in which associations of ideas make themselves felt in art and life. In this essay, the theory of association is carefully elucidated and studied with respect to the imagination and genius; furthermore, the theory is profitably applied to art, especially to the plays of Shakespeare.

Gerard is very definite about the constituent parts of genius: "Genius", he makes explicit at the start, "is properly the faculty of *invention*; by means of which a man is qualified

[102] *Essays, Philosophical, Historical, and Literary* (London, 1789), I, 383-4.

for making new discoveries in science, or for producing original works of art". Invention originates in the imagination; but no matter how lawless or injudicious the product of the imagination may be, Gerard declares, invention is decisive as a mark of genius: "His invention may be irregular, wild, undisciplined; but still it is regarded as an infallible mark of real natural genius and the degree of this faculty, that we ascribe to him, is always in proportion to our estimate of the novelty, the difficulty, or the dignity of his inventions".[103] "It is imagination that produces genius", he states in one place; and in another he writes, "If none of the associating principles be strong, there can be no genius".[104] But although these are undoubted facts, judgment is also a requirement of a perfect genius and must control the imagination and its principles of association. Again and again in this essay, judgment bridles the imagination whenever it becomes, in the opinion of our rational and neoclassic critic, extravagant, or is misled by "an accidental or trifling association". In Gerard's opinion, judgment must almost always regulate the operations of the inventive imagination. Only in exceptional cases is the artist's imagination allowed to transgress the rules:

In all the arts, invention has always been regarded as the only criterion of genius. Even wildness and extravagance of invention sometimes procures higher praise, than the utmost nicety and correctness. We ascribe so great merit to invention, that on account of it, we allow the artist who excels in it, the privilege of transgressing established rules.[105]

Judgment, however, is generally a necessary ingredient of art:

Genius of every kind derives its immediate origin from the imagination. Mere imagination, it is true, will not constitute genius. If fancy were left entirely to itself, it would run into wild caprice and extravagance, unworthy to be called invention. . . . When it [fancy] exerts itself in the way of genius, it has an immediate connexion

[103] I, i, 8, 9. I use the first edition, London, 1774.
[104] I, ii, 37; II, viii, 242.
[105] I, i, 14.

with judgment, which must constantly attend it, and correct and regulate its suggestions.[106]

This is the type of nice qualifications and compromises that enervate Gerard's lively analysis of genius. "Without judgment, imagination would be extravagant; but without imagination, judgment could do nothing". But he adds, after all, it is imagination that is the source of genius. "It is the imagination, therefore, with its operations and laws, that we must especially examine, in order to explain the nature of Genius". [107]

For the most part, these operations and laws of the imagination are, as we should expect from Gerard, those of the associations of ideas. According to the neoclassical psychology of the imagination, about which D. F. Bond has written, the imagination is explained as thoroughly libertine and unlimited in its power to form fantastic ideas not found in nature. [108] It can compound ideas of sense, re-assemble them, or transpose them, and so can produce wholly new combinations. This notion of the random and uncontrolled activity of the imagination was generally accepted until Hume introduced into criticism the regularizing principles of association. With Hume associationism invaded this psychology of the imagination, so altering it that it became entirely acceptable to neoclassic rationalism. After Hume, no longer can the imagination be considered as absolutely free to form new combinations; for, according to associationism, it is apparently free, while in reality it is subject to the principles of association, those principles which support the rules. Gerard accepts the Humean analysis of the imagination.

Gerard begins his analysis of the principles of association by first showing how the imagination is dependent on sensations and then stating how it differs from the memory. Although the source of ideas in the imagination is in sensations, the imag-

[106] I, ii, 36-7.

[107] Pt. I, Sec. ii, p. 38.

[108] *ELH,* IV (1937), 245-64. See also " 'Distrust' of the Imagination in English Neoclassicism", *PQ,* XIV (1935), 54-69.

ination can, Gerard declares with Hume, "connect ideas by new relations". And these connections displace those of the memory: "In this operation, it is far from being capricious or irregular, but for the most part observes general and established rules". Continuing in the Humean tradition, he implies the existence of laws, although he does not list them here.

There are certain qualities which either really belong, or at least are supposed to belong to all the ideas that are associated by the imagination. *These qualities must be considered as, by the constitution of our nature, rendering ideas fit to be associated.* It is impossible to give a reason, why these qualities unite ideas. ... Experience informs us, that the influence of association is very great. By means of it, multitudes of ideas originally distinct and unconnected, rise always in company, so that one of them cannot make its appearance, without introducing all the rest.

It is this power of association in the imagination that is the ultimate source of genius.

Association is often so strong, that it bestows a sort of cohesion on several separate ideas, and makes them start up in numberless combinations, many of them different from every form which the senses have perceived; and thus produce a new creation. In this operation of the imagination, its associating power, we shall, on a careful examination, discover the origin of genius.[109]

But Gerard does not think of genius as a wild and lawless faculty in conflict with the rules, as in the early eighteenth-century dichotomy. Nor does he consider it as the rude, irregular genius of nature so much praised by Edward Young. The artistic and inventive genius, according to Gerard, must be regular; it "requires a peculiar vigour of association. In order to produce it, the imagination must be comprehensive, *regular*, and active". By the first quality, Gerard means that there must be "vigorous associating principles" guiding a fertile imagination as it collects ideas. That is to say, "in a man of genius, the power of association is so great, that when any idea is present to his mind, it immediately leads him

[109] I, iii, 39, 40, 41.

to the conception of those that are connected with it".[110] By the third quality, Gerard means the Hobbesian ability of the imagination to range quickly over the proper ideas; and this ability "arises from the same perfection of the associating principles, which produces the other qualities of genius". And concerning the second quality, Gerard argues, "Genius implies *regularity,* as well as comprehensiveness [and swift ranging] of imagination". Regularity is defined in terms of Hume's associationist understanding of the Aristotelian rule, unity of action.

> Regularity arises in a great measure from such a turn of imagination as enables the associating principles, not only to introduce proper ideas, but also to connect the design of the whole with every idea that is introduced. When the design is steddily (sic) kept in view, and the mind so formed as to be strongly affected by that associating quality by which the design is related to the means of executing it, the imagination can scarce fail of being regular and correct.

The *artist's* imagination must, therefore, be ordered and regular; and the parts of a work of art must always be associated with the main design. Gerard applies this critical standard, the unity of associated ideas, to literature. The unity in Homer's *Iliad,* for example, exhibits the operations of regular imagination; Homer's "correct imagination admits no detail inconsistent with the unity of the fable". His is, thus, the sort of imagination that produces genius.[111] Without this unity of associated ideas "organized into one whole", a design "can be regarded only as an abortion of fancy". Like Hume and Kames, Gerard opposes the insertion of digressions with slight connection, and again applying this rule to literature, charges Ariosto and Spenser with this fault of irregularity. No doubt Sterne is implied in Gerard's attack on those inartistic writers who yield up "the mind to follow passively whatever associations chance to affect it". True genius, in contrast with this irregular type of genius, is a combination of fertility

[110] I, iii, 41, 43.
[111] I, iii, 46, 48.

and regularity of association, and can be found in Shakespeare and Thomson.[112]

Although Gerard is insistent upon the importance of judgment in correcting and perfecting the associated ideas and in keeping the associations of the imagination within the bounds of truth and probability, he does suggest how superfluous judgment may be when the principles of association themselves form a regular work of art. In effect, such an exposition scarcely differs from Hume's description of these principles gently guiding the activity of the plastic imagination. Gerard here implies that if the artist were to allow nature to take its course, associations will fall into their proper place and form a regular work of art. Indeed, as this view of the associationist imagination is the same as Hume's, judgment appears to be entirely unnecessary; for imagination itself, "by means of its associating power, after repeated attempts and transpositions, designs a regular and well-proportioned edifice". This is the very same view of associations operating in a passive imagination with which Coleridge and Hazlitt were to find fault.

> The same force of association [writes Gerard] which makes us perceive the connexion of all the ideas with the subject, leads us soon to perceive also the various degrees of that connexion. By means of it, these ideas, like a well-disciplined army, fall of their own accord, into rank and order, and divide themselves into different classes, according to their different relations. The most strongly related unite of course in the same member, and all the members are set *in that position which association leads us to assign to them, as the most natural.* If the principles of association should not at first lead readily to any disposition, or should lead to one which is disapproved on examination, they continue to exert themselves, labour in searching for some other method, project new ones, throw out the unapposite ideas which perplex the mind and impede its operations, and thus by their continued efforts and unremitted activity, conduct us at length to a regular form, in which reason can find scarce any idea that is misplaced.[113]

Here, as in Hume, nature and regularity of association and neoclassicism are once again allied.

[112] I, iii, 49, 51-2, 52-3, 55-6.

[113] I, iii, 63, 64, 65. By natural and regular association, Gerard means the

Gerard's conception of the imagination is, therefore, thoroughly associationist. Following Hume closely, he accounts for the regular operations of the imagination, as it forms unified and well-formed wholes, by means of the governing principles of association. It now remains to inquire into the nature of these established laws or principles of association to which the faculty of imagination is subject. As Gerard himself admits, Hume and Kames "have observed imagination does not act at random in associating ideas, and have, with considerable success, traced out the laws by which it is governed". [114] Except for the fact that he provides copious literary illustrations, Gerard merely repeats the analyses made in Hume's *Treatise of Human Nature* and Kames's *Elements of Criticism.*

In the second part of the *Essay on Genius*, the three laws which Hume "discovered" are summarized: "The simple principles of association may be reduced to three, resemblance, contrariety, and vicinity". Each of these laws, excepting vicinity, is illustrated with reference to literature. Suggestive of the sort of associationist criticism of Shakespeare that Alison will later indulge in is the following application of associationist nature through the law of resemblance. This law, as has been noted so often before, "suggests similitudes and images".

> Shakespeare represents Northumberland as guided by this associating quality, when he saw Morton, come in haste from the battle where his son had been engaged, pale, trembling, agitated, at a loss what to say; and represents him very naturally as led by this occasion to think of a like event.

He quotes a passage from *2 Henry IV* (I, iii) to illustrate this detail of Shakespeare's accurate and "natural" use of figure. [115]

---

aptness of closely related ideas to be brought together or associated: "As related ideas are apt to be associated, so, by the very same constitution of our nature, those that are most nearly related will be most strongly and intimately associated together."

[114] II, i, 108.

[115] II, i, 110-1.

Contrariety, a law that Hume failed to use in critical theory, but that Kames used well, is also illustrated in Gerard's essay. When "a perception does suggest another which is in some sense contrary to it", the source of this association is that activity of human nature identified as contrariety. Among the illustrations given by Gerard are very many selected from Shakespeare's plays. I take only one, from *2 Henry IV*, as an interesting example of what Gerard believes is Shakespeare's adherence to the ways of associationist human nature. "A monarch groaning under the cares of government, and kept awake by his disquietude, *will readily think*", states Gerard, "on the ease of the peasant, and reflect, 'How many thousands of my poorest subjects Are at this hour asleep!' " [116]

Vicinity, likewise a principle of association, is merely Hume's contiguity in time and place. "The conception of any object naturally carries the thought to the idea of another object which was connected with it either in place or in time". But because this principle apparently applies more to recollection and memory than to imagination, Gerard gives no illustration of its effect on the plastic imagination.

Gerard also lists and describes additional laws of association. These are co-existence, which Hartley had used to explain the formation of complex ideas; cause and effect, which is Hume's contribution; and a new law, order, which is Kames's contribution. The first of these is given no literary application by Gerard. The second, or causality, however, is very important for literary theory; and it is hardly distinguishable from the third, the order of connected ideas, as a reading of the first chapter of Kames's *Elements* proves.

Causality, writes Gerard, is one of the laws or "qualities which form natural relations among the parts of a work, affecting the imagination".

For instance, in a fable fit for tragedy, there are some incidents which are properly causes, and others which are their effects or consequences: causation operating on the fancy as an associating

[116] II, i, 112-6.

quality, will lead imagination, in the most rapid career of invention, even though it should outrun judgment, to place these incidents for the most part in their natural situation, according to the relation which subsists between them.[117]

The importance of this principle cannot be overestimated because, as Gerard says, it "produces regularity of imagination" or a unified design:

> this connexion which subsists between the parts and the design, and in general the connexion between all means and their end, is a species of the relation of cause and effect. Every part of a regular work, both in science and in the arts, either immediately promotes the design or is subservient to some other part which promotes it.

Governed by this principle, the imagination can, without reflection or rational judgment, supply "the natural means of promoting" the design in view. Again, Gerard implies that judgment is uncalled for in the associationist system; for these associationist principles (including especially that of causation), "relations or qualities of ideas operate upon the imagination in an instinctive or mechanical way, that is, without our reflecting that they belong to the ideas".[118] These principles, descriptive of the way human nature operates, are indeed in themselves almost sufficient to form a regular work of art. And we may safely assume that of these principles causality is perhaps the chief shaping principle of the imagination:

> The plan of a poem or a picture may be conceived by the sole power of fancy. The associating principles may suggest abundance of materials suited to the design. The same principles will naturally give these materials different degrees of attraction, proportioned to their several degrees of relation to one another, by means of which the most clearly related will fall regularly into the same member, and the whole will acquire, in a good measure, a proper order and arrangement. The exertion of judgment will no doubt contribute much to render the work more complete; it will cut off redundancies,

117 I, iv, 85.
118 II, i, 120, 121, 123.

rectify disorders, and even supply defects: *but still without it, a picture or a poem may acquire some degree of form.*[119]

Following the traditional discussion, Gerard next inquires into the influence of habit and passion upon the associations of ideas. Habit or custom "gives great assistance to any of the associating qualities with which it happens to co-operate, and makes them introduce an idea that is familiar to us rather than another less familiar, though to this latter these qualities equally belong". [120] Here, the discussion becomes too involved with psychology and has little of immediate significance for literary theory. It is interesting to notice, however, that Gerard again draws from Shakespeare for all illustrations of the influence of passions on the succession of associated ideas in the imagination. He suggests by his many detailed selections how close Shakespeare is to nature. With similar remarks by Kames on Shakespeare as a close observer of human nature, Gerard's examples initiate the associationist approach to the psychological study of Shakespeare.

In reopening discussion of a problem thoroughly examined at the end of the seventeenth century by Dryden and others – the place of figures of speech in states of passion, – Gerard shows, for example, how searchingly minute this associationist criticism can be. Shakespeare can be blamed as well as praised, therefore, in accordance with the principles of associationist human nature. A train of resembling ideas simultaneously represented with passion, Gerard proves, is faulty and unnatural. An instance of this fault in Shakespeare's *Richard II* (V, x) provokes him to the following criticism. Nature, it will be noted, is his norm, that is to say, associationist human nature.

A passion occupies the mind too much, to leave it leisure or inclination of hunting after similitudes. One resembling idea is often suitable to the passion, and fit to influence it; but by conceiving another idea resembling that, much more by going through several

[119] IV, v, 378-9.
[120] II, ii, 132.

ideas, each of which is suggested by its resemblance to the preceding, we must come to such as are by no ways related to the passion, as are wholly unfit for influencing it, and as bear no likeness to any of the objects closely connected with it. But the nature of passion permits us not to indulge ourselves in the conception of such ideas. Richard giving vent to his grief in prison, might naturally say, on hearing time broke in music,

> And here have I the daintiness of ear,
> To check time broke in a disorder'd string;
> But for the concord of my state and time,
> Had not an ear to bear my true time broke:
> I waste time, and now doth time waste me.

But he could scarce naturally add,

> For now hath time made me his numb'ring clock:
> My thoughts are minutes; and with sighs they jar
> Their watches to mine eyes the outward watch;
> Whereto my finger, like a dial's point,
> Is pointing still, in cleansing them from tears.[121]

The problem of diversity, popular among the associationist critics, is also dealt with by Gerard in conjunction with his special thesis on genius. Of course, the exposition of diversity, as grounded on varied associations of ideas that are, in turn, under the influence of a variety of habits and passions, is not new; yet the special application of associationist diversity to genius is, to some extent, original with Gerard.

Genius has, in some men, great force and compass [he writes]: but a vigorous construction of the associating principles is sufficient to account for it, however great it be; for if they be vigorous, any one perception may introduce a great multitude of others, and that by means of many different relations. The principles of association likewise being so various, cannot but admit many distinct combinations and modifications, by which genius will be moulded into a great diversity of forms.[122]

For example, because the principles of association are so numerous, Gerard believes that they can join in "an almost infinite number of combinations". This fact, together with the possibility of varied associational effects in different persons,

[121] II, iii, 179-80.
[122] II, iv, 185.

"all produce a correspondent diversity both in the substance and structure of their works". [123]

A large part of the second and third divisions of the essay is devoted to a purely psychological examination of this theme, the diversity of genius. Gerard shows at great length how diversity is produced by the variety of associations, by the variety of associationist principles, by the combination of these principles, and by the influences of habits and passions on the associations of ideas. This discussion is positive proof of the importance of the psychology in Gerard's estimation. But it is impractical to follow his complex arguments simply because it will mean only an excursion into pure psychology with no fruitful literary or critical digressions.

Beyond what has been indicated, there are few additional significant applications of the principle of associations to critical theory in Gerard's *Essay on Genius*. By and large, in this essay Gerard, along with Kames, reflects the tendency to judge literary works, especially the plays of Shakespeare, according to norms drawn from an associationist understanding of nature. He believes that "regularity of imagination is an essential constituent of genius", and that this regularity is effected by principles of association, those principles of human nature that constantly govern the imagination in its plastic operations. Unlike Hume, Gerard is unwilling to believe that the regular operations of these principles can alone produce a well-turned work of art, or a well-formed genius or taste. Gerard is unwilling to forego the rational judgment; and as in his earlier work on taste, he still urges the use of judgment to correct and perfect the associations of the imagination. [124] That Gerard is obviously neoclassical is proved by the presence of these two chief elements in his creed: a belief in the regular operations of the imagination that shape an orderly work of art and an emphasis upon the determinations of reason and judgment in artistic matters. This neoclassic attitude is

[123] II, iv, 196.

[124] See esp. *Essay on Genius,* II, x, "Of the Varieties of Judgment, and their Influence on Genius".

balanced by a complete acceptance of the diversitarian position, especially as it is related to genius. And one of the important corollaries of this diversitarian point of view is that imaginations of different people vary as a result of the complex activities of associationist principles. Also implicit in such a belief, but never made explicit by the conservative neoclassicist Gerard, is an undermining of fixed Aristotelian standards for taste and judgment.

Along with Hume, Hurd, and Kames, therefore, Gerard for the most part shows the tendency to reinforce neoclassic critical theory and at the same time to make the basis of this theory the conception of the associationist psychology – that conception, in short, of a regular and orderly human nature regulated by general principles of association. Despite his unoriginality in associationist thinking, Gerard is significant for being the first important critic to expound systematically the relationship between genius and associationism,[125] and together with Kames, to apply the principles of association to an appreciation of Shakespeare's art. In his associationist approach to Shakespeare's characters, Gerard anticipates the applications of the theory by the three most significant "psychologizers" of Shakespeare in the later eighteenth century, William Richardson, Maurice Morgann, and Walter Whiter.[126]

[125] But he is not the first to analyze genius in terms of associationism, as Paul Kaufman believes ["Heralds of Original Genius", *Essays in Memory of Barrett Wendell* (Cambridge, Mass., 1926), p. 205]. William Sharpe, *A Dissertation on Genius* (London, 1755), pp. 97-8, anticipates Gerard by noting how "the necessary differences in the accidental association of ideas" is one of the chief causes of variety in genius. Indeed, Sharpe's thesis, that genius is an acquired second nature established by habit, propensity, and environmental conditions, generally foreshadows Gerard's associationist analysis. A similar but very short anticipation of Gerard's explanation of genius is to be found in Abraham Tucker's *Light of Nature Pursued* [1768], (London, 1805), Vol. II, ch. xxii, Art. 3, pp. 145-7; Vol. VII, ch. xxxi, Art. 1, pp. 332-3. Another anticipation may be found in William Duff, who, in *An Essay on Original Genius and its various Modes of exertion in Philosophy and the Fine Arts, particularly in Poetry* (London, 1767), writes of the associating power of imagination. See pp. 6-7, 33, 48-9, 88, 89, 93-4, 127, 127n.

[126] Cf. R. W. Babcock, *The Genesis of Shakespeare Idolatry 1766-1799*

Contrary to Edward Young's romantic effusions on original genius – that genius which is untaught by classic rules, precedents, or models, – is Gerard's rational analysis of genius in terms of the current psychology of association. Genius, according to Gerard, is a product of the imagination; and imagination is controlled and regulated by the shaping principles of association. As a result, he conceives of artistic genius as regular, orderly, disciplined. Gerard is, then, thoroughly neoclassic and conservative in his attitudes.

The chief literary work of the versatile legal expert, Henry Home, Lord Kames, is the influential *Elements of Criticism* (1762). This critical work was tremendously popular and its ideas were given a much wider currency than can be deduced from the appearance of eight British editions from 1762 to

---

(Chapel Hill, 1931), pp. 176-82. Babcock ignores Gerard. Babcock seems to exaggerate the presence of associationism in Morgann and Richardson. In reality, neither has the associationist point of view. Of the two references to the psychology in Morgann's *Essay on the Dramatic Character of Sir John Falstaff* (1777) [ed. W. A. Gill (London, 1921), pp. 46-7, 60n.], only one is significant. In proof of his contention that the dramatic impression made by Shakespeare's characterization of Falstaff is not that of cowardice, Morgann adduces the evidence of an association of ideas between courage and high birth. It cannot be denied that the associationist psychology is also evident in Richardson's *Essays on Some of Shakespeare's Dramatic Characters* (1774). But here again the psychology is only of minor importance, while in the works of Gerard, Kames, and Priestley it has a central position. Richardson's stress falls entirely on the ruling passions and their effects on character and action, despite the fact that he admits in his "Introduction" (pp. 14-5 of the 1797 edition) the need of understanding the influences of associations upon the passions. However, three very interesting references to associationism do appear: (1) The association or suggestion of images in the mind heightens esthetic response (pp. 29-30). (2) A habit of uttering our passions aloud whenever we are emotionally excited, is contracted during childhood; hence, emotional stress in maturity provokes similar utterances or soliloquies "by force of association and habit". Moreover, if the habit or association and the restraints of reason "are of equal energy, our emotions are uttered in broken and incoherent sentences" (pp. 49-50). This effect of an association of ideas is illustrated with Macbeth. (3) An association with real objects makes passion stronger (pp. 173-8). A sentiment uttered by Imogen is explained in this manner. Two other references to associationism by Richardson have no significance (pp. 243, 295). For Whiter, see below, pp. 274-5.

1807 and the more than twenty-five English and American editions and abridgments from 1816 to 1883, because many chapters (architecture, gardening, beauty) were also reprinted in the famous *Encyclopaedia Britannica* (1771) edited by the Edinburgh professors. The influence that its associationism might have had on its many readers is interestingly attested by the suggestive evidence of Miss Elizabeth Hamilton. In her *Letters on the Elementary Principles of Education* (1801), Miss Hamilton recognizes the importance of the principles of association in the education of youth: "The first book in which I found a hint upon the subject", she states, "was Lord Kaime's (sic) *Elements of Criticism*".[127] Then, she adds, she found Locke and Hartley.

From the very first chapter of the *Elements*, it is obvious how much Kames owes to the associationism of Hume for his fundamental conception of human nature; and, like Hume, he asserts that his critical principles and conception of taste are "rooted in human nature, and governed by principles common to all men". These psychological principles are, in large part, as we expect them to be in a Scottish critic, those of the association of ideas. Although Kames gives willing obedience to the neoclassic discipline, again echoing his good friend Hume, he reserves the right to think for himself and to show how rules agree with human nature. He is opposed to the common critical method of founding rules on the practice of the ancients, Homer and Virgil, supported by the authority of Aristotle.[128] Nevertheless, despite the freedom implied in this statement, he winds up in the same pigeonhole as the neoclassic critics. As we shall soon see, he merely gives psychological justification to the tenets of the neoclassic creed, verisimilitude or close imitation of nature, distinction of the genres, decorum, and strict unity of action. He also accepts other critical principles, such as contrast and utility, that accord with the associationist psychology. It must be agreed,

[127] *New Annual Register of 1801*, p. 131.
[128] *Elements of Criticism* (Edinburgh, 1769), I, 6, 12-3.

then, that although his taste and creed remain for the most part conventionally neoclassical, Kames's psychological method is fashionably modern.

The principles of human nature furnish the new norms for criticism and are, Kames declares, "the true source of criticism". That is to say, they are the *elements* in the title of the book. In the first chapter, entitled "Perceptions and Ideas in a Train", Kames describes these important principles of nature. As Hobbes and Locke had long ago pointed out, the ideas in the mind are quite often linked together in a continuous chain. But Kames does not entirely follow Locke. He accepts instead the views of Hobbes and Hume and believes that the "train of our thoughts is not regulated by chance", but is connected "in a great measure" by the laws of association, those laws that explain why certain qualities in objects fit them for association or connection:

> one thing, perceived to be a cause, is connected with its several effects; some things are connected by contiguity in time, others by contiguity in space; some are connected by resemblance, some by contrast; some go before, and some follow [order]: not a single thing appears solitary and altogether devoid of connection; the only difference is, that some are intimately connected, some more slightly; some near, some at a distance.[129]

To be sure, Kames substitutes "succession of ideas" for Locke's "association of ideas"; but the essential associationism of ideas in succession is unmistakeable. "An external object is no sooner presented to us in idea", he writes, "than it suggests to the mind other objects with which it is connected; and in this manner is a train of thoughts composed. Such is the law of succession". Kames admits that the will may select some and reject other associated ideas but affirms that, although the order of the connected ideas may be varied, it will still remain "within the limits of connected objects". He suggests in this way the basic view of Hartley and Hume that if the natural or passive operation of associations in the mind is

[129] I, 18.

left to itself, the best connections will then be produced: "Where ideas are left to their natural course, they are generally continued through the strictest connections: the mind extends its view to a son more readily than to a servant, and more readily to a neighbour than to one living at a distance".[130]

In addition to the laws of connection listed by Hume, Kames also mentions the principle of order. The order of our ideas, he observes, is also determined for us by nature, for "our tendency is, to view the principal subject before we descend to its accessories or ornaments, and the superior before the inferior or dependent". This principle of natural order is Kames's own addition to the number of laws that govern the movement of associated ideas in the mind. Gerard also uses it for critical purposes in his later *Essay on Genius*. But with Kames and Gerard it seems in effect to be little different from the order and regularity formed by Hume's important law of causality.[131]

The psychological law of order, together with that of causality, is important for critical theory, for it supports the neoclassic doctrine of verisimilitude. It is felt, for example, that because our minds proceed most easily along the natural course of ideas, they are esthetically pleased with the sense of logical order. Any other order will generally displease. Hence, the natural order is declared best because an agreeable artistic effect is best maintained by it. Thus, according to Kames's psychological reinterpretation of Aristotle, as soon as an improbable event disturbs the natural order, our interest disappears, or, as Kames picturesquely says, "farewell relish and concern". The esthetic transport, which Kames calls "ideal presence" or "waking dream", fades away and the work of art is consequently felt to be imperfect.

> Events that surprise by being unexpected, and yet are natural, [i.e. "strict imitations of nature",] enliven greatly an epic poem;

130 I, 19. See also Gordon McKenzie, "Lord Kames and the Mechanist Tradition", *University of California Publications in English*, XIV (1943), 110ff.

131 Cf. Kames, I, 23-5; Gerard, above, pp. 192-3.

> but in such a poem, if it pretend to copy human manners and actions, no improbable incident ought to be admitted; that is, no incident contrary to the order and course of nature. A chain of imagined incidents linked together according to the order of nature, finds easy admittance into the mind; and a lively narrative of such incidents, occasions complete images, including ideal presence: but our judgement revolts against an improbable incident; and if we once begin to doubt of its reality, farewell relish and concern.[132]

Such a psychological reinterpretation of nature and art is, of course, not original with Kames. Hume had used the same concept of nature as the critical norm of art and had arrived at neoclassic conclusions; and now Kames similarly employs the principle which explains what may today be called "psychological realism", but what was actually called, in the late seventeenth and in the eighteenth century, imitation of nature or verisimilitude.[133] It would be understatement to say that

[132] I, 102.

[133] McKenzie uses the modern term; *op. cit.*, p. 119. That this regular or "natural" or customary association of ideas is merely another expression for verisimilitude is suggested by George Campbell [*The Philosophy of Rhetoric* (1776) (New York, 1875), pp. 105-6]: "When I explained the nature of experience, I showed that it consisteth of all the general truths collected from particular facts remembered; the mind forming to itself often insensibly, and, as it were, mechanically, certain maxims, from comparing, or, rather, associating the similar circumstances of different incidents. Hence it is that when a number of ideas relating to any fact or event are successfully introduced into my mind by a speaker, if the train he deduceth coincide with the general current of my experience, if in nothing it thwart those conclusions and anticipations which are become habitual to me, my mind accompanies him with facility, glides along from one idea to another, and admits the whole with pleasure. If, on the contrary, the train he introduceth run counter to the current of my experience, if in many things it shock those conclusions and anticipations which are become habitual to me, my mind attends him with difficulty, suffers a sort of violence in passing from one idea to another, and rejects the whole with disdain.... In the former case I pronounce the narrative natural and credible; in the latter I say it is unnatural and incredible, if not impossible; and which is particularly expressive of the different appearances in respect of connexion made by the ideas in my mind, the one tale I call coherent, the other incoherent.... This [drawing upon experience], if properly employed, will prove a potent ally, by adding the grace of verisimilitude to the whole." For his definition of experience, Campbell refers his readers to another section (pp. 69-71). It is defined there as memory plus the customary association of ideas.

this application of the associationist psychology does not conflict with the order and regularity desirable in neoclassic taste, for Kames himself is very explicit about the orderliness, regularity, and uniformity of associationist "nature".

It now appears that we are framed by nature to relish order and connection. When an object is introduced by a proper connection, we are conscious of a certain pleasure arising from that circumstance. Among objects of equal rank, the pleasure is proportioned to the degree of connection: but among unequal objects, where we require a certain order, the pleasure arises chiefly from an orderly arrangement.[134]

More than once Kames assures his readers that the manner in which ideas fall into regular forms or orderly trains will be useful for art and criticism. He says, for example, that the laws regulating the trains of ideas "will be found of great importance in the fine arts", and that "the foregoing speculation leads to many important rules of criticism". "Taste and Judgment", he also makes explicit, are dependent upon this clearly defined norm, the "natural" trains of ideas in the mind. Again, in other words, art must imitate nature closely:

Every work of art that is conformable to the natural course of our ideas, is so far agreeable; and every work of art that reverses that course, is so far disagreeable. Hence it is required in every such work, that, like an organic system, its parts be orderly arranged and mutually connected, bearing each of them a relation to the whole, some more intimate, some less, according to their destination: when due regard is had to these particulars, we have a sense of just composition, and so far are pleased with the performance.[135]

By thus making nature and the regularizing laws of association equivalent to regularity of structure, Kames is of course merely ringing the changes on Hume's neoclassic associationism. And, like Hume, Kames applies the rule drawn from this psychology, the unity of natural and close connection of

[134] I, 25.
[135] I, 18, 27.

ideas, to literature by noting the defects "in order and connection" of Homer, Pindar, Horace, and Virgil. Finally, in the last part of the first chapter, he again follows Hume and suggests the connection of this psychology with Aristotle's chief rule, the unity of action: "Relations [the laws of association] make no capital figure in the mind, the bulk of them being transitory, and some extremely trivial: they are however the links that, by uniting our perceptions into one connected chain, produce connection of action".[136] As we shall soon see, this law of close connection is best applied to the unity of epic and dramatic action.

Kames also borrows from Hume the conception of emotions in association. As Kames applies it, this association between resembling emotions becomes a completely subjective notion: a pleasant emotion may make any object with which it happens to be associated equally pleasant.

> An agreeable object makes every thing connected with it appear agreeable; for the mind gliding sweetly and easily through related objects, carries along the agreeable properties it meets with in its passage, and blends them with those of the present object, which thereby appears more agreeable than when considered apart.[137]

In this way agreeable emotions are conveyed from the whole object to any of its parts, and so can change partial blemishes into beauties. For examples of the way in which this association of emotion can influence taste, Kames notes that "the wry neck of Alexander was imitated by his courtiers as a real beauty"; and he also notes that the admirable valor of Shakespeare's Percy turns all his defects into good points. Furthermore, he adds, "one passion may be generated by another", especially when resembling it or "similar in tone". Pity, for instance, may turn into admiration and then into love. This is illustrated from Shakespeare, – the story of Othello's courtship of Desdemona.[138] Finally, like Addison and Hume,

[136] I, 32.
[137] I, 66.
[138] I, 78-80. See Helen W. Randall, *The Critical Theory of Lord Kames* (Northampton, Mass., 1944), pp. 63-4.

Kames describes the union of various senses and emotions through resemblance, for the production of a complex and rich emotional effect.[139]

Resemblance may be important in the drama for the connection between ideas and between ideas and emotions; but in certain branches of the fine arts, writes Kames, resemblance is often too weak a bond. This psychological fact leads him to speculate on a new and important principle of art, the principle of contrast. Hume had recognized the significance of contrast as a principle of association but had failed to apply it to art. Kames shows how important it may be as a principle of art.

> The emotions raised by the fine arts, are generally too nearly related to make a figure by resemblance; and for that reason, their succession ought to be regulated as much as possible by contrast. This holds confessedly in epic and dramatic compositions; and the best writers, led perhaps by a good taste more than by reasoning, have generally aimed at this beauty. It holds equally in music: in the same cantata, all the variety of emotions that are within the power of music, may not only be indulged, but, to make the greatest figure, ought to be contrasted. In gardening there is an additional reason for the rule: the emotions raised by that art, are at best so faint, that every artifice should be employ'd to give them their utmost vigour: a field may be laid out in grand, sweet, gay, neat, wild, melancholy scenes; and when these are viewed in succession, grandeur ought to be contrasted with neatness, regularity with wildness, and gaiety with melancholy, so as that each emotion may succeed its opposite. . . .[140]

Thus Kames lays the associationist ground for this new and fashionable rule for art, a rule that Reynolds had satirized in *Idler 76* (1759), but was to discuss seriously in the "Eighth Discourse" (1778).

Burke, as we have already seen, divided esthetic effects into positive pleasure or beauty and relative pleasure or sublimity. The former is caused by the objective qualities of

[139] I, 127-9.
[140] II, 297-8.

things and our immediate emotional reactions to them; here associations exert no influence. The latter is caused for the most part by an association with danger. Kames borrows Burke's ideas on beauty and calls the objective beauty of things "intrinsic". But he further admits utility and fitness as associations that may affect the idea of beauty, and so allows what he calls a "relative beauty". Symmetry, for example, is intrinsic; but means to ends or use is relative. In direct opposition to Burke, Kames asserts that the latter, which are associations, may make homely objects beautiful:

The utility of a plough, for example, may make it an object of admiration or of desire; but why should utility make it appear beautiful?. ... The beauty of the effect, by an easy transition of ideas, is transferred to the cause, and is perceived as one of the qualities of the cause: thus a subject void of intrinsic beauty, appears beautiful from its utility.[141]

It is interesting to perceive the way in which this standard of the beautiful affects general standards of taste. Certainly a freeing from the restrictions of classic taste is to be observed in the following illustrations: "an old Gothic tower, that has no beauty in itself, appears beautiful, considered as proper to defend against an enemy; a dwelling-house void of all regularity, is however beautiful in the view of convenience". But these are exceptions; Kames rarely takes the romantic point of view.

Kames's concept of the sublime is altogether different from Burke's. He seems to believe that qualities of objects, such as magnitude, uniformity, regularity, order, and proportion are all necessary for the production of the "deep impression" known as the grand and sublime condition, in which the whole attention is occupied and the heart swells "into a vivid emotion". No association of ideas is to be found in Kames's analysis of the sublime. Nor can it be found in his examination of dignity, grace, ridicule, and wit. And, although he discusses the influence of habit and custom on the determination of taste,

141 I, 197.

he does not show their relation to constant and reiterated associations of ideas.

When he does rely on associationism, he almost always uses it to reinforce his neoclassic approach to art. As we have already mentioned, he states the case for one of the chief neoclassic doctrines, verisimilitude, by arguing against improbabilities in the natural train of our ideas. He is also clearly an advocate of decorum, and for exactly the same reason – that the pleasant train of perceptions is broken when the spectator is roused by violent action: "he wakes as from a pleasing dream, and gathering his senses about him, finds all to be a fiction". On this ground he opposes the horrible matricide committed by Orestes, even when it occurs offstage. In substance, the neoclassic argument against violence rests on the doctrine of decorum, the assumption that violence is barbarous and shocking to a polite audience. Kames's argument is clearly neoclassic, but his opposition to violent action is arrived at through the contemporary psychology.[142]

Similarly, the neoclassic doctrine of the distinction of genres is reinterpreted by Kames in accordance with the way the associations operate in the mind:

> In every work of art, it must be agreeable to find that degree of variety, *which corresponds to the natural course of our perceptions;* and that an excess in variety or uniformity must be disagreeable, by varying that natural course. For this reason, works of art admit more or less variety according to the nature of the subject.[143]

Different arts and different subjects have different needs: a greater variety of objects can be perceived in nature than in a picture, and in a picture than in a description or poem. This doctrine has as its corollary the rule of congruity or propriety, of which Kames makes so much in his tenth chapter. The assumption, for example, that a lofty style is "proper" for the epic, is sound, as the associational laws of nature prove:

[142] II, 398.
[143] I, 318-9. My emphasis. But Kames does admit that it is futile to establish absolute distinctions between the kinds. See II, 370-1n.

If things connected be the subject of congruity, it is reasonable beforehand to expect, that a degree of congruity should be required proportioned to the degree of connection. And upon examination, we find this to hold in fact: where the relation is intimate, as between a cause and its effect, a whole and its parts, we require the strictest congruity; but where the relation is slight, or accidental, as among things jumbled together in the same place, we require little or no congruity.... the relation between an edifice and the ground it stands upon, is the most intimate kind, and therefore the situation of a great house ought to be lofty.[144]

These and similar conclusions are always arrived at by first observing the normal course of perceptions or ideas in the mind, which are described in the first chapter. Thus, because human nature is his standard, Kames also reasons that the proper amounts of uniformity and variety can only be applied to art in terms of ideas in natural association: "It may surprise some readers", he observes, "to find variety treated as only contributing to make a train of perceptions pleasant, when it is commonly held to be a necessary ingredient in beauty of whatever kind; according to the definition, 'That beauty consists in uniformity amid variety' ".[145]

The natural course of associated ideas, as it is slow or rapid, or determined by temper, climate, age, and emotions, is, therefore, a very important over-all standard for critical judgment. For a literary illustration of the influence of emotions over the train of associated ideas, Kames goes to Shakespeare; and his appreciation of Shakespeare's accurate characterization of Hotspur's anger proves how well this new concept, the natural association of ideas in a state of emotion, may be used as a standard of criticism.

The mind ingrossed by any passion, love or hatred, hope or fear, broods over its object, and can bear no interruption; and in such a state, the train of perceptions must not only be slow, but extremely uniform. Anger newly inflamed eagerly grasps its object, and leaves not a cranny in the mind for another thought but of revenge. *In the*

144 I, 333.
145 I, 321.

character of Hotspur, this state of mind is represented to the life; a picture remarkable for high colouring as well as for strictness of imitation.[146]

The standard of a train of closely connected ideas is used best by Kames for the explanation of the unity of action. Hume's application of the associationist principle of causality was most successful with respect to this rule; and Kames follows suit by similarly re-examining epic and dramatic unity in relation to the causal chain of ideas. As McKenzie has observed, Kames leans heavily upon the principle of causality: "It is evident that, with the emphasis on cause and effect as a determining connection in experience, Kames will look upon the action of a play as a perfect example of such relationships".[147] But Kames is often not so specific as to mention the law of causal association that controls the orderly movement of ideas. More often than not, Kames writes merely of the *unity* necessary in all art. It is only by our being constantly aware of what he means by this term and the manner in which he defines it, that we can perceive the psychological roots of his neoclassicism.

Kames firmly believes that unity must be present in all art. A conviction of reality can only be sustained, he writes, by unity of tone or character;[148] this tone cannot be mixed, and all parts must be subsumed in the whole because of the requirements of our "natural" feelings. An agreeable effect may thus be produced, and it will be sustained by congruity and propriety. The test for congruity and propriety is the degree of the connection or association among a plurality of objects. In art, the epic and the drama, the connections between the part and the whole are so important that "even the slightest deviation is disgustful". To illustrate the importance of this rule of connection, Kames offers an almost ridiculous example: Homer, he observes, does not appear to understand this principle, because he places incongruous pictures of peace

146 I, 307.
147 *Op. cit.*, p. 118.
148 Kames, II, 417-8.

on Achilles' shield. Kames judges this to be incorrect, for "all the ornaments upon a shield ought to relate to war".[149] Certainly, this seriously expounded refinement is evidence of a painfully severe neoclassic conservatism, – what Reynolds called, in his *Idler* paper (No. 76), "a servile attention to minute exactness".

Kames also discusses the three dramatic unities, and tries to find rational and psychological justification for them. To be sure, he rejects the unities of time and place since they are not acceptable to modern dramatic conditions; but he firmly enjoins their use for the separate acts. It was psychologically correct, Kames believes, for the Greeks to observe these minor unities, because their dramatic performances were continuous. At present, however, act division prevents continuous presentation; nevertheless, we are obligated to retain them for the duration of the act, he concludes his argument, because nothing ought to interrupt the "impression of reality", that is to say, the train of ideas in causal relation must not be broken. In this way it is possible to maintain enthusiastic transport or "ideal presence", or "the waking dream" in which trains of "naturally" connected ideas flow through our minds.[150]

The most important unity, the unity of action, is also given new and different stress. In the epic, writes Kames, the episodes must be limited because they can "break" the unity of action.[151] In the drama, the double plot has a bad effect upon simplicity, "a chief property" in tragedy during which the mind and attention must be totally occupied by one object or concern. In comedy, however, more variety of feeling is allowable; and therefore the double plot may be justified. The tone of the underplot, however, says the neoclassic critic, must not

[149] I, 335, 336-7.

[150] Kames gives another reason for retaining the unities of time and place. They prevent breaks in the continuity of the action (II, 416): "An unbounded license with relation to place and time, is faulty for a reason that seems to have been overlooked, that it seldom fails to break in upon the unity of action."

[151] II, 394-5.

vary greatly from that of the major plot, "for discordant passions are unpleasant when jumbled together; which, by the way, is an insuperable objection to tragi-comedy". These remarks apply to the defective plot of the *Provok'd Husband*. "The same objection touches not the double plot of the *Careless Husband*; the different subjects *being sweetly connected*, and having only so much variety as to resemble shades of colours harmoniously mixed". [152]

Through this concept of close connection, he finally develops the classic idea of a streamlined drama, formerly explained by Corneille as *liaison des scènes*, continuity of scenes. To make certain that we follow his argument, Kames refers us to his first chapter which "accounts for the pleasure we have in a chain of connected facts". He mentions the same law of association that Hume considers to be of prime importance for art, the law of causality. In a single event, writes Kames, "the facts and circumstances are connected with the strongest of all relations, that of cause and effect: a number of facts that give birth to each other form a delightful train; and we have great mental enjoyment in our progress from the beginning to the end".[153] Aristotle has showed that unity of action consists in a beginning, middle, and end. While it is true that unity may be contrived in accordance with this formula, yet the unity may not be thought entirely effective. For example, the *Aeneid* and the *Iliad* possess unity; but that of the *Iliad* is inferior, because in the formation of any chain of associations the mind receives more pleasure from progression than from retrogression.

The mind hath a propensity to go forward in the chain of history: it keeps always in view the expected event; and when the incidents or underparts are connected together by their relation to the event, the mind runs sweetly and easily along them. This pleasure we have in the *Aeneid*. It is not altogether so pleasant, as in the *Iliad*, to connect effects by their common cause; for such connection forces

[152] II, 397-8.
[153] II, 403.

the mind to a continual retrospect: looking backward is like walking backward.[154]

In the drama the best way to attain unity of progression is through scene-links. These links prevent anything unconnected, anything that does not directly retard or further the action, from breaking the chain of causation.

A play analyzed, is a chain of connected facts, of which each scene makes a link. Each scene, accordingly, ought to produce some incident relative to the catastrophe or ultimate event, by advancing or retarding it. A scene that produceth no incident, and for that reason may be termed barren, ought not to be indulged, because it breaks the unity of action.[155]

Unlike Alison, Kames criticizes Corneille for this fault; but for Shakespeare he has only praise: "How successfully is this done by Shakespeare! In whose works there is not to be found a single barren scene".[156] The concept of scene-links strengthens his opposition to double-action. To Kames, then, dramatic unity of action means simply the strict neoclassic ideal, single action.

It would be a gross breach of the unity of action, to exhibit upon the stage two separate actions at the same time; and therefore, to preserve that unity, it is necessary that each personage introduced during an act, be linked to those in possession of the stage, so as to join all in one action.[157]

Furthermore, as mentioned above, in order to preserve the effect of unity, the act must be considered and felt as a unit. In the act, therefore, the unities of time and place must be strictly followed, so that the destruction of the "waking dream" of reality will be prevented and the imagination will

[154] II, 405-6.
[155] II, 408.
[156] *Ibid.* Shakespeare and Corneille are, he believes, the two greatest dramatic geniuses in the world; but he consistently favors Shakespeare: cf. I, 454-6, 501-2.
[157] II, 427.

not be compelled to readapt itself to new conditions. [158]

Kames's approach to the problem of unity in art is thus clearly independent of all previous classical authority. Nevertheless, his psychological method carries him to critical deductions not unlike those of the classic and neoclassic critics. Basically, his critical theory rests on the assumptions that the principles of human nature require order and regularity and that unity is understood as the natural order in a sequence or scenes. It is this natural order, presented through the mental machinery known as the association or connection of ideas, that is the source of the new psychological criticism.

In fine, Kames is a neoclassic associationist. Like Hume, Hurd, and Gerard, he uses the associationist psychology to explain the ways in which human nature operates and then uses this understanding of nature as a norm for art and criticism. His belief that "we are framed by nature to relish proportion as well as regularity",[159] is strongly buttressed by the conception of human nature acting not by chance but by regular and orderly laws of association. From these laws Kames derives many critical rules and doctrines, the chief of which is obviously unity. By unity Kames means simply close association or connection among the parts of a work of art. This broad doctrine of unity props three important neoclassic doctrines, the distinction among the genres, verisimilitude, and decorum. And also like Hume, Kames gives a strictly neoclassic interpretation to Aristotle's most significant literary rule, unity of action. His acceptance of utility, however, appears to conflict with his generally held neoclassicism.

Furthermore, Kames's neoclassic preference for closeness of connection, especially in the drama, causes him to admire over-simple effects and to be intolerant of complexity. Paralleling this preference for simplicity are an approval of uni-

[158] II, 428. Kames also suggests (II, 421) that the unity of tone or passion may be maintained throughout the drama by appropriate music, "vocal and instrumental", between the acts instead of by the obsolete choral links.
[159] I, 462.

formity and an opposition to diversity of taste. Kames conceives of the standard of taste as being founded on "a conviction common to the species of the perfection of common nature", and seriously believes that "individuals ought to be made conformable to it".[160] Unlike the general run of associationists, he does not in any way suggest how the connection or association of ideas may favor diversity. Far from disturbing the uniformitarian nature of his critical thought, his understanding and application of the theory of association sustain it. Like Gerard who follows him closely, he limits "common nature" to the standards maintained by an aristocratic elite:

> To ascertain the rules of morality, we appeal not to the common sense of savages, but of men in their more perfect state: and we make the same appeal in forming the rules that ought to govern the fine arts: in neither can we safely rely on a local or transitory taste; but on what is the most universal and the most lasting among polite nations. . . . Those who depend for food on bodily labour, are totally void of taste.[161]

From Burke's *Sublime* (1757) to Gerard's *Genius* (1774), the theory of association is found in unvarying prominence as the solution of many problems of art and criticism. In this brief period of time, associationism illuminates all the important features of eighteenth-century critical theory: it is used in the traditional fashion as an explanation of diversity or relativity of taste and, also, of uniformity of taste; it is used as a basis of the various critical norms, genius, the sublime, beautiful, and picturesque, and unity of action; furthermore, and what is very significant, it is used as an explanation of the regular and orderly flights of the imagination and of Shakespeare's dramatic techniques. It can be justly asserted that in the third quarter of the century the prevailing philosophy of human nature merges most successfully with critical theory. Evidently there is hardly any important work devoted to the theory of

[160] II, 490-1. Cf. above, p. 182.

[161] II, 498-9. Cf. Helen W. Randall, *op. cit.*, p. 83: Kames "had not seen that this single principle [of association] might be made the basis for a theory of art which would account for the differences in individual taste".

criticism in this period that is unaffected by the associationist conception of human nature.

In Burke's abstract work, an association of ideas of danger and terror is at the core of the sublime. But unlike Gerard and Kames, Burke does not on the whole favor association as a critical standard. His theory of the origin of taste more or less resembles that of Shaftesbury and Hutcheson. Believing that accessory or secondary associations are the sources of diversity, Burke claims the immediate reactions of the senses, uniform in all men, as the standards of taste. That Burke is well aware of the strength of the associationist approach is proved by his running commentary on its weakness and, paradoxically, by his inevitable recourse to its principles when explaining the theories of the sublime and imitation.

Burke's philosophical discussion of the sublime proved to be very popular and influential despite his failure to make any concrete literary or artistic applications. The publication of the *Enquiry* fortunately coincided with the fashionable cult of terror and the search for deeper emotions in nature, gardening, descriptive verse. Shenstone and Reynolds make explicit the relation between associationism and these romantic trends; thus they give vitality to associationism by taking it from the realm of abstract philosophy to that of practical criticism. Both are aware of the psychology as an explanation of the delightful melancholy emotions produced by ruins and gothic architecture. And Reynolds, in the late seventies, partially attempts to explain the cult of the picturesque, which Gilpin was advancing in his published tours, by means of a melancholy but delightful association with the past. In Reynolds, moreover, associationism is employed from the neoclassic as well as the romantic point of view. As we have seen, in Reynolds's thought the psychology explains the delightful emotional excitement produced by gothic architecture and the formation of different tastes, and, lastly, also furnishes the explanation of the taste for classic drapes in statuary. From the observation of the widespread and enduring association of dignity with classic clothing, Reynolds deduces that painters should use similar drapery for their portraits.

The most complete and therefore the most satisfactory associationist critical systems are not constructed by Burke or Reynolds or Shenstone, but by Kames and Gerard. Borrowing Hume's conception of the regular laws of association, these Scottish critics reinterpret and reinforce the generally accepted neoclassic approach to art. The imagination is regularized, for it is described as operating through uniform and orderly laws of association; versimilitude, decorum, unity (especially of action) are all supported by the new associationism; and, finally, contrary to Edward Young's notion, the free faculty, genius, is brought within the neoclassic fold, being placed almost entirely under the control of regular principles of association. All art, these critics imply, can be judged as it does or does not conform to the associationist principles of human nature; and they are both significant in the history of associationist criticism for their concrete applications of the psychological standard to an understanding and appreciation of Shakespeare's dramaturgy. Finally, Gerard and Kames are equally important for contributing to the continuity and popularity of the tradition and for paving the way for many of the associationist ideas in the criticism of Priestley and Beattie and for many of the ideas in the crowning achievement of eighteenth-century associationist critical theory, the *Essay on Taste* by Archibald Alison.

VI

AT THE TURN OF THE CENTURY

The extent to which the psychology of association had become intellectually fashionable in the eighties is suggested by "Sylvander" Burns's semi-serious use of the theory in a platonic love-letter (1788): "I have just been before the throne of my God, Clarinda. According to my association of ideas, my sentiments of love and friendship, I next devote myself to you".[1] But in the last twenty years of the eighteenth century, the strength of the associationist concept is better indicated by the many serious discussions of the associationist basis of the necessitarian philosophy and the utilitarian doctrine, of moral education and perfectibility. Hartley and Priestley had carried associationism into these related fields, with what results in the intellectual history of Godwin, Bentham, Wordsworth, Coleridge, and John Stuart Mill, we are already familiar. And it was in great measure owing to these moral, pedagogical, and political applications of Hartlean theory, by such significant English thinkers as Priestley, Godwin, and Bentham, that associationism became so firmly rooted in the culture at the turn of the century. Representative of the associationists who were attracted to Hartley's mechanical theory for educative and moral reasons is the historian William Belsham:

Who can contemplate [he asks,] the amazing extent and flexibility of the power of association, as explained and illustrated by Locke

[1] *The Letters of Robert Burns,* ed. Francis H. Allen (Boston and New York, 1927), IV, 78.

and Hartley, or the mechanical operation of motives in producing all our volitions, without being sensible of the unspeakable importance of attending to the early cultivation of the mind, and of inculcating, with all possible diligence, those laudable and virtuous principles, which, so far as they are not counteracted by opposite influences, must operate upon the minds in a regular and definite manner?

As Belsham implies, this theory can give great comfort to the optimistic utilitarian moralists and believers in perfectibility:

I am sensible, that the faculty of association is of a nature at once so powerful and so flexible, that by an early and skilful direction of it, it is very possible such an ardent and disinterested love of Virtue, such a noble and animating principle of benevolence, may be generated in the soul, that, leaving the very idea of a future state out of the question, all the allurements of vice united would, to a man actuated by such exalted sentiments, appear contemptible in comparison of the pleasures to be derived from Virtue.[2]

It must be remembered, then, that the associationist psychology, with its unlimited possibilities, contributed no little share to the tremendous latter-century social and political ferment.[3] And among the relatively new associationist theories there were the traditional but now vitalized associationist theories of criticism. It is, therefore, against the perspective of intense intellectual excitement, of social and political associationism, during and after the French Revolution, that the associationist interpretations of critical theory and taste must be placed.

The significant figures in this period of the history of associationist critical theory are Joseph Priestley, James Beattie, and Archibald Alison. The opposition is expressed in the pleasantly superficial and feeble protests of Vicesimus Knox and the mighty philosophic blasts of Thomas Reid. Hugh Blair, however, is generally neutral; he does not care to weight

[2] *Essays, Philosophical, Historical, and Literary* (London, 1789), I, 188, 136.

[3] Cf. Elie Halévy, *The Growth of Philosophical Radicalism* (New York, 1928), and Basil Willey, *The Eighteenth Century Background* (London, 1940).

his wholly derivative thought with the critical apparatus supplied by the modern philosophy.

The views expressed by the major figures, Priestley and Alison, do not differ considerably from those presented in the preceding period. Even though Priestley applies Hartley's theory to criticism more intensively than ever before, he comes out with the same subjectivism – that is to say, he uses human nature, the "natural" or associational effects on the mind, as the standard for judgment – and, to a certain extent, the same diversitarianism tempered by the ideal of "good" taste. Alison is obviously subjective; but, unlike Priestley, he accepts diversity in the standards of taste and believes that taste should by means of extensive associations of ideas gradually become comprehensive and mature. Priestley and Alison hold in common the Hartlean belief that taste is formed by a complex of subjective associations of ideas operating mechanically and in spite of the determinations of the will. Both these important and influential critics are equally significant for the fact that no one before them had applied associationism so extensively and so persuasively to critical theory or had studied its effects so intensively. Beattie, the third important figure of this period, generally follows his Scottish mentors, Gerard, Kames, and Hume, for his analysis of the associational psychology of the imagination, which he applies to Shakespeare's art and to standards of taste. In his discussion of the formation of taste, however, there is a suggestion of his reading of Hartley.

Though the ideas of these critics all have their roots in previously published works, it will be quickly noticed that some change in spirit and in method has taken place. In particular, Alison's development of the subjective esthetic response from a notion of Kames carries the theory of association forward into the romantic movement of the nineteenth century and testifies to the smooth continuity of thought from one century to the next. Alison's belief that taste depends only on the imagination and his description of imaginative response as ecstatic associations of ideas prepare the psychological ground for the romantic experience, the passionate abandonment to a world of emotions, the *O altitudo* of an inwardly exciting reverie or meditation in solitude.

Evidence of the strength of the psychological approach in criticism in the last quarter of the century, appears in a few essays by the genial and scholarly Vicesimus Knox. Pleasantly conservative in the manner of the adherents to Shaftesbury's school of taste, Knox declares mere sensibility and delicacy of taste – "the genuine feelings of improved or cultivated nature" or "the feelings of the majority of men coinciding for a number of years in the same object" – to be a sufficiently uniform and certain standard of taste. He does not believe it right that metaphysical subtlety should be substituted for his conception of criticism. Thus, although he has "been delighted with the philosophical criticism of many writers of North Britain", (meaning the psychological criticism of Kames and Gerard), he feels that this criticism is decidedly wrong in its method.[4]

Yet, despite his opposition to the method of "the philosophical criticism", he cannot help using it as the explanation of the favorable contemporary taste for Gothic architecture. As we should expect, Knox himself favors the "simple magnificence" of Grecian architecture over the profusion of ornament and "complicated vastness" of Gothic structures. "The Grecian manner", he asserts, "will ever retain its intrinsic beauty". But what of the Gothic manner? The answer to this question is evidence of Knox's debt to the philisophical critics and is, at the same time, suggestive of the way in which the middle ages made their appeal to the eighteenth-century imagination. Gothic works never produce a unified impression, he says; and then he adds significantly, they would never strike the mind with "ideas of solemnity" if they were viewed "merely as a work of Architecture, without admitting religious or historical associations". The awkward design of the pointed arch, for

[4] *Essays Moral and Literary*, No. 27, "On Modern Criticism" (London, 1787), I, 252, 253, 254. See also No. 84, "On Philosophical Criticism, and on the little Assistance it gives to Genius", II, 230-8.

example, is "certainly in itself unpleasing and improper". It pleases, however, by means of several associations of ideas:

for pleasing ideas, associated with objects unpleasing, will often communicate their agreeable tinge by approximation, and render even deformity no longer ungraceful. A view of the Gothic arch, in the antique pile raised by our progenitors, calls to remembrance the generations that have preceded us, renews the idea of some historical fact or celebrated personage, or suggests reflections on the piety, the zeal, the comparative ingenuity of our forefathers; and, on the whole, raises thoughts pleasingly awful on the sanctity of the time-honoured edifice. All, or any of these arbitrary associations, will give an agreeable air to an object, which might otherwise be contemplated with indifference or disgust.[5]

The psychological point of view appears only occasionally in Hugh Blair's conservative *Lectures on Rhetoric and Belles Lettres* (1783). Because Blair directed these lectures to youthful minds, they contain little that is profound and little that is original. Rarely indulging in new or daring speculation, Blair is careful to follow conventional trends of thought. He does note, however, the power of associations in creating the sublime, although he is unwilling to expand this associationism into a general theory.

I am inclined to think, that mighty force or power, whether accompanied with terror or not, whether employed in protecting, or in alarming us, has a better title, than any thing that has yet been mentioned, to be the fundamental quality of the sublime; as, after the review which we have taken, there does not occur to me any sublime object, into the idea of which, power, strength, and force, either enter not directly, or are not at least intimately associated with the idea, by leading our thoughts to some astonishing power as concerned in the production of the object. However, I do not insist upon this as sufficient to found a general theory.[6]

Blair's caution gives way again when he admits that the association of ideas is an important source of the beauty of

[5] No. 79, "Cursory Considerations on Architecture", II, 182, 184-5, 194.
[6] *Lectures on Rhetoric and Belles Lettres* (Philadelphia, 1850), "Lecture III", p. 37.

colors and figures. "The foundation of beauty" in figures is, he says, in regularity and "grateful variety". But regularity pleases in large part, he adds, by its association with the ideas of fitness, propriety, and use, "which have always a greater connexion with orderly and proportioned forms, than with those which appear not constructed according to any certain rule".[7] Lastly, he conceives of the critical norm, propriety, as originating in a "natural association of ideas", means to ends or fitness:

> We cannot look upon any work whatever, without being led, by a natural association of ideas, to think of its end and design, and of course to examine the propriety of its parts, in relation to this design and end. When their propriety is clearly discerned, the work seems always to have some beauty; but when there is a total want of propriety, it never fails of appearing deformed. Our sense of fitness and design, therefore, is so powerful, and holds so high a rank among our perceptions, as to regulate, in a great measure, our other ideas of beauty. . . .[8]

From the testimony of Knox and Blair we can deduce that the "modern" philosophical criticism did not hold complete sway in English critical theory. But it cannot be denied that many important writers, excluding Johnson and Goldsmith and others, maintained from the middle of the century the associationist points of view established by Hume and Hartley. And despite the attacks by those who followed Shaftesbury's doctrine of taste and Hutcheson's doctrine of the internal sense, the theory of association flourished until it was generally accepted in the nineteenth century as the basis of critical thought. We have noticed before that Joseph Priestley is responsible for much of the respect given the psychology at the turn of the century. The most enthusiastic and most articulate associationist of the eighteenth century, and the avowed disciple

[7] "Lecture V", pp. 50, 51.

[8] *Ibid.*, p. 54. Blair also refers to the process of association when describing Ossian's use of simile. See *A Critical Dissertation on the Poems of Ossian* (1763) in *The Poems of Ossian* (London, 1803), I, 166-8.

of Hartley, Priestley considered it his duty to spread the true gospel, Hartley's associationist theory of the human mind, and to defeat all opposing theories. Believing almost fanatically that "Dr. Hartley ... has thrown more useful light upon the theory of the mind than Newton did upon the theory of the natural world",[9] Priestley attacked the common-sense philosophy urged by Reid and his followers, Oswald and Beattie. He correctly observed that the instinctive principles of common sense are the reverse of the principles of habitual association: Reid's "notions of human nature", he asserts, are "the very reverse of those which I had learned from Mr. Locke and Dr. Hartley (in which I thought I had sufficient reason to acquiesce)".[10] Moreover, he also pointed out the inaccuracies in Hume's analysis of the principles of association and defended Hartley's use of the single principle of association, contiguity.[11] Priestley thus came to feel that one of his main reasons for living was to propagate the faith, to counteract the effect on the public of "such an incoherent scheme as that of Reid, and to establish the true science of human nature".[12]

The chief of his attempts to make Hartley available to a wider public and to establish his ideas was his useful abridgment of the *Observations on Man* in 1775 together with three essays explaining and illustrating the theory of association.[13] Another publication that contributed to the promotion campaign was, he intimates, his *Course of Lectures on Oratory and Criticism*

[9] *An Examination of Dr. Reid's Inquiry into the Human Mind* .... (London, 1775), p. 2. The first edition of this polemic was published in 1774. For other panegyrics of Hartley, see pp. 170-1, 176.

[10] P. vii.

[11] *Letters to a Philosophical Unbeliever* (Birmingham, 1787), I, 205-7, 223-4.

[12] *An Examination,* p. xi.

[13] *Hartley's Theory of the Human Mind on the Principle of the Association of Ideas* (London, 1775). A second edition was issued in 1790. In an essay prefixed to the *Examination,* Priestley applies the theory to syllogisms, inductions, and the rational processes. The three essays in the abridged *Observations* explain the doctrine of vibrations and apply the doctrine of association to memory, judgment, and complex and abstract ideas. In the *Letters to a Philosophical Unbeliever* he proves that the theory is not contrary to religion.

(1777); in this volume Priestley further explained and illustrated Hartley's ideas, but with special reference to critical theory.

Also, to show the great importance and extensive use of this excellent theory of the mind, I thought it might be of service to give some specimens of the application of Dr. Hartley's doctrine to such subjects of inquiry as it had a near relation to, and to which I had, on other accounts, been frequently requested to publish the *Lectures on Philosophical Criticism,* which I composed when I was tutor in the Belles Lettres at the academy of Warrington, this was another inducement to the publication. For it appears to me that the subjects of criticism admit of the happiest illustration from Dr. Hartley's principles; and accordingly, in the composition of those lectures, I kept them continually in view.[14]

Although Priestley frankly admits that "the most important application of Dr. Hartley's doctrine of the association of ideas is the conduct of human life, and especially the business of education", like others compelled by the associationist tradition in criticism, he does not neglect the extension of the psychology to the more frivolous realm of criticism.

In the Preface to the *Lectures*, we are informed that Priestley's theory of criticism was first expounded in 1762, when he was tutor in the Languages and Belles Lettres at the Warrington Academy. And one of his main reasons for publishing the lectures on criticism in 1777 was, he says, the necessity of illustrating Hartley's theory of the mind which he had edited only two years before. The *Lectures*, therefore, contributes to Priestley's plan of advancing Hartley in all philosophical thought, and it may be considered as an attempt to answer the need of those adherents to Hartley's system who may have wished to see an extension of this system to a traditional field of speculation and controversy.

I have been induced to do it [i.e., to publish the lectures, Priestley writes,] at this time, partly with a view to the illustration of the doctrine of the association of ideas, to which there is a constant reference through the whole work (in order to explain facts relating

14 *An Examination,* p. xii.

to the influence of Oratory, and the striking effect of Excellencies in Composition, upon the genuine principles of human nature) in consequence of having of late endeavoured to draw some degree of attention to those principles, as advanced by Dr. Hartley.[15]

Because of his fervent partisanship of Hartley, Priestley does not attempt to be so much original as inclusive. He begs his readers to "consider this work as a succinct and systematic view of the observations of others, interspersed with original ones of my own".[16] He aims only to convince his readers of the truth and adequacy of Hartley's associationism as the explanation of esthetic effects and norms. How well he succeeds can be judged by the extent to which the doctrine is illustrated. In general, his use of this doctrine closely parallels Hartley's description of the complex formation of taste by means of the association of ideas and sensations.

All beauties and admired strokes in composition, derive their excellence and fine effect, either from drawing out and exercising our faculties, by the views they present to our minds; or else transferring from foreign objects, by the principle of association ideas which tend to improve the sense of a passage.

Every thing that hath a striking or pleasing effect in composition, must either draw out and exercise our faculties, or else, by the principle of association, must transfer from foreign objects ideas that tend to improve the sense; the principal of which are views of human sentiments, of the effects of the human genius, and of a rise and improvement in things.[17]

Since the positions that Hartley and Priestley hold are generally the same, it would be tedious to describe in detail how these complex processes of association and sensation are applied to critical theory. For in more or less the same detailed fashion as Hartley, Priestley shows how the "transfers" of ideas and feelings are produced by constant associations,

15 *A Course of Lectures on Oratory and Criticism* (London, 1777), pp. i-ii.

16 Pp. iii-iv.

17 Pp. 136, 279.

which, in turn, produce the various esthetic effects. To Priestley, practically every significant critical concept can be easily derived in whole or in part from the principle of association, "that great and universal agent in the affections of the human mind".[18] Like Hartley, he describes the way in which the esthetic pleasure in uniformity and variety is formed by associations with pleasing objects in nature and art; and he does not fail to attribute the pleasure in proportion to the associated idea of utility.[19] Likewise, he explains the formation and the effect of metaphors by means of an association and transfer of ideas from one object to another in time of profound emotion; and other figures of speech, such as metonymy and synecdoche, he also derives from associations and transfers.[20] Furthermore, he observes the extensive influence of association in producing the pleasures of contrast, the effects of burlesque and climax.[21] Finally, he discusses the associationist influence in the effects as well as the formation of hyperbole, personification, and unity or completeness.[22] All these discussions of the pleasing effects of composition revolve around a common center, the associationist conception of the mind. Let us see how Priestley applies this associationism to a few traditionally important critical problems, the structure of a work of art, Shakespeare's art, the sublime, and standards of taste.

Obviously leaving Hartley for Kames and Hume, Priestley claims the norm for the structure of narrative discourses is found in "the order of nature". This order is the way in which the mind forms a successive chain of associated ideas with the greatest facility. For example, in historical narrative, the natural "chain of events" is formed by chronological or temporal association; and in a geographical narrative, place or "proximity of situation" guides the association of ideas.

[18] P. 231.
[19] Lect. 21, pp. 165-6; Lect. 22, p. 166.
[20] Lects. 22, 23, pp. 181-7, 188-9; Lect. 27, pp. 231, 238.
[21] Lect. 24; Lect. 25, pp. 211-2; Lect. 31, pp. 275-7.
[22] Lect. 28, pp. 241-2; Lect. 29, p. 247; Lect. 30, pp. 272-3.

This is making those transitions which our minds are most accustomed to, and therefore made with the most ease. It is taking advantage of the strongest associations by which the ideas of things cohere in our minds; on account of which every particular of the narration both gains the easiest admission into our minds, and is best retained when admitted: whereas the mind is greatly disgusted with unusual, and consequently unexpected, and, to us, unnatural connexions of things.[23]

But Priestley does allow digressions to appear in a work of art: "these very same reasons, drawn from the nature of things, and the state of the human mind, to which these relations are addressed, will often dictate particular deviations from the general order of narration". Thus, the historian or biographer may justifiably use the principle of cause and effect and trace an event forwards or backwards. Similarly, by means of other principles, such as similarity and contrariety, will the mind cheerfully allow excursions off the beaten track:

In all these and the like cases, a writer can never be blamed if he dispose the materials of his composition by an attention to the strongest and most usual *association of ideas* in the human mind. We are not fond of pursuing any uniform track long without interruption: so that the natural connexions of ideas not quite foreign to the subject, with others which occur in the course of a narration, may, in the hands of a judicious historian, give occasion to digressions from his principal subject, which shall greatly relieve the attention, please the imagination, refresh and assist the memory.[24]

Therefore, Priestley sums up, the danger occurs only in the event that these digressions might make it too difficult for a writer ever to lead his reader back to the principal subject gracefully. If he fails to make a graceful transition, there will be a break in "the uniformity of the whole piece". Priestley's discussion of this unity, it will be agreed, closely resembles the analyses of structural unity presented by Hume and Kames; and like these Scottish critics, he makes the unity and regu-

[23] Lect. 6, p. 34.
[24] Pp. 34-5.

larity of art dependent upon the "natural" associations of ideas in the mind.

Moreover, like Kames, to whom he admits his indebtedness in the Preface to the *Lectures*, Priestley discusses the influence of passion upon the association of ideas in the mind.[25] Knowledge of the passions, he thus believes, "eminently contributes to form a critic in works of taste and genius".[26] But as we should suspect, Priestley also carries some of Hartley's methods into this field of criticism. Two characteristic examples will serve to illustrate Priestley's many applications of the associationism of Kames and Hartley to Shakespeare's art. The first explains in Hartley's manner the reason why the appearances of art are accepted as reality.

> Vivid ideas and strong emotions . . . having been, through life, associated with reality, it is easy to imagine that, upon the perception of the proper feelings, the associated idea of reality will likewise occur, and adhere to it as usual; unless the emotion be combined with such other ideas and circumstances as have had as strong association with fiction.[27]

"This connexion of vivid ideas and emotions with reality" furnishes Priestley with a standard of effect by which he can judge Shakespeare's art of characterization. Thus, if Shakespeare accurately delineates vivid emotion, we automatically associate reality with it and are impressed with Shakespeare's correct representation of human nature.

> An attention to these affections of our minds will show us the admirable propriety of innumerable fine touches of passion in our inimitable Shakespeare. *How naturally doth he represent Cassius,* full of envy at the greatness of Caesar, whose equal he had been, dwelling upon every little circumstance which shows the natural weakness of him whom fortune had made his master.[28]

[25] Lects. 12, 13, 14, 16.
[26] Pp. 73, 125.
[27] Lect. 13, p. 89.
[28] P. 92. Emphasis mine.

Kames, however, is the source of a different associationist approach to Shakespeare's characters. In Kames's manner (and Gerard's too), Priestley indicates how the "natural" association of ideas under the influence of passion becomes a critical standard:

It is a direct consequence of the association of ideas, that, when a person hath suffered greatly on any account, he connects the idea of the same cause with any great distress. This shews with what propriety Shakespeare makes King Lear, whose sufferings were owing to his daughters, speak to Edgar, disguised like a lunatic, in the following manner: What, have his daughters brought him to this pass? Could'st thou save nothing? Did'st thou give them all?
And MacDuff,
He hath no children.[29]

Priestley's discussion of associationist sublimity is almost wholly unoriginal. Most of his ideas concerning the sublime emotion can all be found, as Monk has noticed, in Gerard's *Essay on Taste.*[30] Pure or absolute sublimity, Priestley says, is produced by magnitude and vastness; but, he further adds, "many things which, considered in themselves, and abstracted from every thing that is foreign to them, are incapable of the sublime, inspire that sentiment by their association with others that are capable of it". For example, the ideas of wealth, honor, and power become sublime only through association: "It is the causes, the adjuncts, or the effects of these things, that are contemplated, when they fill and charm the soul". Thus, "the grandeur of a palace . . . is derived from the ideas, of the labour, expense, length of time, and number of persons necessary to the erection of it". The sublimity of the ruins of buildings and cities is increased by an association of the time elapsed since they flourished and a contrasting association with their former magnificence. He notes, finally, that mean associations weaken the sublime effect; and upon the basis of this psychological fact, he advises the use

[29] Lect. 14, p. 103.
[30] *The Sublime,* p. 118

of the simplest or "the plainest terms" because there is less danger that they may be accompanied by "low" associations.[31]

Lastly, Priestley explains how taste is formed by means of the association of ideas. In discussing the bases of taste or "the pleasures of the imagination", he clearly takes his stand with Hartley's associationism and opposes the doctrine of internal sense held by Hutcheson and Gerard. Priestley steadfastly believes that "the principles in our frame which lay the mind open" to the graces and pleasures of art are those of the associationist psychology. Here he opposes the original or innate internal senses, just as he had formerly opposed Reid's instinctive common sense in the *Examination.*

Each of these kinds of feelings [passions and pleasures of imagination] are, by some philosophers, referred to so many distinct reflex, or internal senses, as they call those faculties of the mind by which we perceive them; whereas, according to Dr. Hartley's theory, those sensations consist of nothing more than a congeries or combination of ideas and sensations, separately indistinguishable, but which were formerly associated either with the idea itself that excites them, or with some other idea, or circumstance, attending the introduction of them. It is this latter hypothesis that I adopt, and, by the help of it, I hope to be able to throw some new light on this curious subject.

All our intellectual pleasures and pains consist of nothing but the simple pleasures and pains of sense, commixed and combined together in infinitely-various degrees and proportions, so as to be separately indistinguishable, and transferred upon foreign objects, by the principle of association.

We have seen the extensive influence of association in forming all the pleasures of imagination that we have hitherto enumerated, and we have seen the probability of that opinion, which represents all our intellectual pleasures as derived originally from sensible impressions, variously mixed, combined, and transferred from one object to another, by that principle.[32]

[31] Lect. 20, pp. 157-60.
[32] Pp. 72-3, 137, 231.

Taste, "or the capacity of perceiving the pleasures of imagination", is therefore gradually or progressively acquired and is "within the reach of all persons whatsoever". Because the delicate emotions raised by works of art, he continues, are produced by certain special associations, all that need be done in order to form a taste for art is to present constantly the opportunity for esthetic ideas to be acquired and associated.

In fact, since all emotions excited by works of genius consist of such ideas and sensations as are capable of being associated with the perception of such works, nothing can be requisite to the acquisition of taste, but exposing the mind to a situation in which these associated ideas will be frequently presented to it.

Of course, he admits, much depends on other circumstances, such as time of life and texture of brain; but a dislike for esthetic studies, he maintains, can be overcome by associations: "as this dislike was produced by an early association of ideas, so it may be overcome by opposite associations".[33]

Unlike Gerard and those who believe that the internal senses are the sources of the various esthetic responses, Priestley does not think it possible to separate the various pleasures of imagination into simple and isolated senses. There are, it is true, various kinds of taste; but they are all complex and they receive their complexity from the number of ideas held in association.

Let it be noted, that when each of the pleasures of the imagination are referred to some one source, I only mean, that ideas and sensations of that kind are the principal ones that enter into its composition. For, in fact, none of our intellectual pleasures are so simple as to be derived from one single source only. They are all of so complex a nature, are so connected with one another, that it is probable, there is not one sentiment of pleasure or pain that can be called intellectual . . . but what is more or less compounded of almost all the other intellectual pleasures and pains too. The principle of association is predominant in everything relating to our intellectual faculties.[34]

[33] Pp. 74, 75.

[34] Lect. 17, p. 129. Cf. Belsham, *Essays,* I, 16-7: "I am of opinion that it

As an example of "the complex pleasures of taste", Priestley refers to the pleasure "we receive from the prospect of a fine country landscape". This pleasure, Priestley assures us, is produced by a variety of associated ideas that affect the mind. It illustrates, therefore, "the doctrine of Association, and the very probable opinion of Dr. Hartley, who supposed that it is the only mental principle employed in the formation, growth and declension of all our intellectual pleasures and pains". And, as a matter of fact, Priestley's explanation of the complex taste for natural scenery, as well as for uniformity, variety, and proportion, is taken from a section in Proposition 94 of Hartley's *Observations*, "Of the Pleasures arising from the Beauty of the Natural World".[35] Therefore, it need not be repeated here.

The associations of ideas are the sources not only of the complex pleasures of imagination but also of their diversity.

> Whether it will be allowed that the principle of association is the source of *all* the pleasures which are suggested by objects of taste, or not, it is manifest that it must have a very considerable influence in this affair, and will help us to account for much, if not all, of the variety that is observable in the tastes of different persons.

Were we equally sensitive and were we exposed to the same influences and ideas, Priestley continues,

> there would be no room for the least diversity of taste among mankind. For, in those circumstances, we should all have associated precisely the same ideas and sensations with the same objects; and we should feel those sentiments in the same degree.[36]

---

will ever remain in some degree a mystery, why one writer pleases above another, and consequently why Shakespeare pleases above all others. I believe it requires a much more intimate acquaintance with the human mind than the acutest philosopher can boast, to be able to trace the origin and progress of all those associations which contribute to the formation of pleasurable ideas."

[35] Priestley, pp. 130-3; cf. Hartley, above, pp. 123-5.

[36] Pp. 133-4.

However, Priestley agrees, the reality markedly differs from this uniformitarian hypothesis. Because of the variety of events and circumstances of life, "different persons will have associated different ideas and sensations with the same objects; and, consequently, they will be differently affected upon the perception of them".[37]

Yet, despite his acceptance of the necessary diversity in taste, Priestley cannot help admitting parenthetically that a uniform standard of taste can be possible among people of similar background, "education and manner of life". This is the hope of the uniformitarians who base the standard of good taste on their favorite idea, universal or general associations. Priestley apparently gives voice to their point of view: "There seems, however, to be so great a similarity in our situations, as is sufficient to afford a foundation for a considerable similarity in taste; particularly in persons whose education and manner of life have been nearly the same". In the next breath, however, Priestley suggests how narrow the scope of this uniformity must really be: "But a standard of taste, founded upon the similar influences which persons so situated have been subject to, cannot be applied to those persons whose education and manner of life have been very different". For these differences in ideas necessarily produce a variety of associations and, consequently, a variety of tastes – modern and ancient, European and Oriental, English and French.

Notwithstanding all this liberalism, at the conclusion of these remarks on diversity Priestley seems to favor as a standard Kames's neoclassic and uniformitarian "general taste", the taste of an aristocratic elite, that is to say, the taste of those who have acquired the most and the best ideas on art. Although, therefore, it is difficult to say which of the two points of view receives Priestley's full approval, it must be remembered that an association of ideas furnishes the ground for both.

Justness of taste will be determined by appealing to the general sense of those who have been the most conversant with the subjects

[37] P. 134.

of it. A deviation from this general taste will be reckoned a fault, and a coincidence with it an excellence. . . . Persons who have not been conversant with the subjects of taste are excluded from having any vote in this case, because their minds have not been in a proper situation for receiving the ideas and sensations which are requisite to form a just taste.[38]

In his critical theory, Priestley deliberately expounds Hartley's associationist method; and since he does not hesitate to rely on Kames and Gerard as well as Hartley, he succeeds in extending the illustrations of associational influences to the structure of art, the sublime, Shakespeare's characterization, diversity and uniformity as standards of taste, and a host of other subjects. In truth, his *Lectures on Criticism* brings, as he himself says, "into an easy and comprehensive view whatever has been observed by others".[39] But his attempt to explain practically all the significant terms in the critical vocabulary in accordance with associationist principles is his own original contribution to this psychological tradition in critical thought. Moreover, as he uses it, the theory of association becomes the means by which the forms and objects of art no longer will be studied for faults or beauties in themselves or in relation to ancient models; on the contrary, they will be analyzed, and approved or disapproved only with respect to their effect on the mind. Like Hume and Kames, Priestley is fully aware of the significance that this psychology has for criticism. With him, the psychological effect, that is, the way in which ideas are associated in the mind, supplies the norms for critical judgment. His thorough-going associationist approach, patent everywhere in the lectures, is a sure sign of the increasing tendency in the later eighteenth century to examine critical problems by looking into the mind and by considering the subjective effect as of far more significance than the object. No one has been so explicit as Priestley in

[38] P. 135.

[39] P. ii.

making the individual response the basis of taste. This alone certainly betrays a romantic attitude. But, on the other hand, although emphasis is placed on subjective effects, it must be admitted that the theory, even in the liberal Priestley, is used to maintain a uniform standard of "good taste", the standard of taste that was so much respected by the conservative neoclassicists.

Priestley's contribution and influence cannot be considered apart from Hartley's. It is Priestley, Hartley's most articulate and persuasive Huxley, who carried the associationist ideas forward by the untiring persistence and the sheer weight of his propaganda. Undoubtedly, therefore, he alone is largely responsible for the accolades accorded Hartley at the turn of the century. How well he succeeded in getting Hartley known is proved by the fact that in the nineteenth century Hartley's psychology was of paramount significance, despite the favorable stress given to Humean associationism in the third quarter of the century.

Although the associationists formed a powerful faction in critical circles, they did not have everything their own way. As we have noticed, Burke and Usher had raised their voices in protest; and Knox, taking the viewpoint of the man of taste, argued against weighting down criticism with philosophy. Further, but heavier, opposition to the theory of association than that presented by such amateurs as Burke and Usher is continued in the works of the leading British philosopher in the later eighteenth century, Thomas Reid. Unlike Burke, Reid is thoroughly consistent and puts up a strong case for his anti-associationism. The refutation of Hume's sceptical theory is the professed object of Reid's first published work, *An Inquiry into the Human Mind* (1764); it is natural, therefore, for Hume's central thought, the association of ideas, to receive Reid's most cutting thrusts. Using reason and common sense to ridicule what he considers to be an irrational belief, Reid unequivocally opposes Hume's "mechanical" and associationist conception of man. Again, in his later *Essays on the Intellectual Powers of Man* (1785), he attacks the associationist notions of Hume and Hartley.[40] In these essays he is of the firm belief that the regularity – order, connection, and unity of parts – in the arrangement of a spontaneous train of thoughts in the mind cannot be adequately explained by mechanical associations of ideas: "To account for the regularity of our first thoughts, from motions of animal spirits, vibrations of nerves, attractions of ideas, or from any other unthinking cause, whether mechanical or contingent, seems ... irrational." The cause of the regularity, he asserts, is not any mechanical process but a rational process of judgment: the regular train of thought "is a copy of what had been before composed by his own rational powers, or those of some other person".[41] In addition to reason, "the effect of practice and habits" also contributes to this operation of fancy in producing regular trains of thought. All these causes, he sums up, "seem to me sufficiently to account for this phaenomenon, without supposing any unaccountable attractions of ideas by which they arrange themselves".[42] Reid thus lays great stress on the direction by judgment and reason in his analysis of the way in which a train of ideas in a regular work of art is formed. With this philosopher, art, like science, bespeaks a deliberately rational process of thought.

Granting that the fertility of the poet's imagination suggested a variety of rich materials, was not judgment necessary to select what was proper, to reject what was improper, to arrange the materials into a just composition, and to adapt them to each other, and to the design of the whole? No man can believe that Homer's

[40] *The Works of Thomas Reid,* ed. Sir William Hamilton (Edinburgh, 1872), I, 103a. Reid attacks Hume's use of the association of ideas on many grounds: he points out (I, 386b) that Hume's causality is, by his own admission, merely constant contiguity; he turns (I, 199) Hume's causality into the inductive principle; he argues (I, 399-400) against Hume's conception of complex ideas formed by association; and lastly, he believes (I, 386) that there are certainly many more principles of association than the two or three given by Hume, such as end to means, truth to evidence, consequences and uses, part to whole, subject to qualities, etc. His criticism of Hartley is mainly directed against the hypothesis on vibrations. (I, 249-52)

[41] I, 382b.

[42] I, 385a.

ideas, merely by certain sympathies and antipathies, by certain attractions and repulsions inherent in their natures, [as Hume would have insisted] arranged themselves according to the most perfect rules of epic poetry; and Newton's, according to the rules of mathematical composition.[43]

His conclusion is no less emphatic; he rejects the unconscious association of ideas as the guide of the artistic imagination.

The conclusion I would draw from all that has been said upon this subject is, That everything that is regular in that train of thought which we call fancy or imagination, from the little designs and reveries of children to the grandest productions of human genius, was originally the offspring of judgment or taste, applied with some effort greater or less. . . . If the attractions of ideas are the sole causes of the regular arrangement of thought in the fancy, there is no use for judgment or taste in any composition, nor indeed any room for their operation.[44]

But, as we have noticed, Reid does admit other influences than reason upon the train of ideas. Habit, passion, and experience are, he believes, additional influences that are equally important in suggesting trains of ideas; and they may, he intimates, be used in criticism instead of the few Humean principles of association:

A good writer of comedy or romance can feign a train of thinking for any of the persons of his fable, which appears very natural, and is approved by the best judges. Now, what is it that entitles such a fiction to approbation? Is it that the author has given a nice attention to the relations of causation, contiguity, and similitude [resemblance] in the ideas? [laws of association] This surely is the least part of its merit. But the chief part consists in this, that it corresponds perfectly with the general character, the rank, the habits, the present situation and passions of the person. If this be a just way of judging in criticism, it follows necessarily, that the circumstances last mentioned have the chief influence in suggesting our train of thought.[45]

When he examines taste and beauty, Reid clearly betrays his esthetic conservatism. He certainly combats, as Monk has

43 I, 385b.
44 I, 386a, 388a.
45 I, 387a.

said, the increasing subjectivism in critical theory after the mid-century by favoring "common principles", uniformity, objectivity, and reason.[46] But in accordance with the psychological tradition begun by Hutcheson, he agrees that taste "is considerably influenced by habit, by associations, and by opinion".[47] Already familiar with his attitude towards associationism, we should suspect that this acknowledgment of the power of association is merely verbal. That it is only superficial is proved by the fact that nowhere in his chapters on grandeur and beauty does Reid discuss the important subjective influence of associations. On the contrary, the internal taste for the arts, he reiterates, should be an intellectual power based on the operations of reason and judgment:

There is therefore a just and rational taste, and there is a depraved and corrupted taste. For it is too evident, that, by bad education, bad habits, and wrong associations, men may acquire a relish for nastiness, for rudeness, and ill-breeding, and for many other deformities.

Reid has apparently accepted the Hutchesonian analysis of associations. He uses the theory to explain the exception, but

[46] Monk, *The Sublime,* p. 145; Reid, I, 453a: "Homer and Virgil, and Shakespeare and Milton, had the same taste; and all men who have been acquainted with their writings, and agree in the admiration of them, must have the same taste. The fundamental rules of poetry and music, and painting, and dramatic action and eloquence, have been always the same, and will be so to the end of the world.... In those operations of taste which are rational, we judge of the real worth and excellence of the object, and our love or admiration is guided by that judgment as well as feeling, and the feeling depends upon the judgment we form of the object." See also, I, 492ab. Henry Laurie has commented on Reid's objection to associationism [*Scottish Philosophy, in its National Development* (Glasgow, 1902), p. 324]: "Reid maintained, as Alison did not, that 'things intellectual,' from which the beauty of objects of sense is derived, have an original beauty of their own. The belief of Reid that beauty has an objective reality, while he also held – to use the words of Coleridge – that 'we receive but what we give, and in our life alone does nature live,' is far removed from a theory which would reduce the beautiful to a subjective emotion, arising in some mysterious way from the mere association of ideas which possess no beauty of their own."

[47] I, 490a.

never the rule; that is to say, he stresses it whenever he wishes to describe the way in which taste falls away from ideal or objective perfection, from what he describes, in Aristotelian fashion, "things that are most excellent in their kind". Thus, custom, fancy, and "casual associations" have a great influence in producing a diversity in the external tastes as well as in the internal taste for beauty:

When we see such varieties in the taste of the palate produced by custom and associations, and some, perhaps, by constitution, we may be the less surprised that the same causes should produce like varieties in the taste of beauty; that the African should esteem thick lips and a flat nose; that other nations should draw out their ears, till they hang over their shoulders. . .[48]

Although there is such diversity in taste, Reid is unwilling to surrender the single standard of good taste and excellence in beauty because he fears similar diversitarian arguments may "be used with equal force against any standard of truth".[49] He evades this difficulty raised by diversity, however, by again observing that taste, like judgment, can be perverted and is, moreover, "more liable" to corruption than judgment. If these facts are considered, "it is easy", he concludes, "to account for the variety of taste, though there be in nature a standard of true beauty, and consequently of good taste, as it is to account for the variety and contrariety of opinions, though there be in nature a standard of truth, and, consequently, of right judgment".

James Beattie studied philosophy under Professor Gerard in Marischal College, Aberdeen ("he was my master in philosophy"), and there is no doubt that his teacher transmitted to him Hutcheson's ideas about the formation of taste in the "Secondary" or internal senses. Gerard's own ideas about genius and its dependence upon the inventive or combining imagination are also adapted by Beattie.[50] Lastly, Beattie leans heavily

48 I, 491b.
49 I, 492a.
50 *Dissertations Moral and Critical* (Dublin, 1783), "Of Imagination", I,

upon Gerard, as well as Hume, for his associationist conception of the way in which the imagination functions. Although, therefore, little originality can be found in Beattie's lectures and works, as the author himself modestly admits in his prefaces and advertisements, they do serve to summarize previous thought competently and to convey the associationist psychology of the imagination to the new Alisonian generation.

Beattie's psychology of the imagination, as described in his dissertation "Of Imagination" (1783) and the equivalent sections of *Elements of Moral Science* (1790), is drawn almost entirely from Hume's *Treatise of Human Nature* and Gerard's *Essay on Taste* and *Essay on Genius*. There may be some irony, therefore, in the fact that in his *Essay on Truth* (1770) Beattie viciously demolishes Hume's scepticism and atheism with the help of Reid's principles of common sense, but is at the same time greatly indebted to Hume for much of his associationism. Undoubtedly, Beattie is less consistent than Reid in his opposition to Hume, for he does nothing but repeat Hume's analysis and explanation of the laws of association governing the succession and the combination of ideas in the imagination and Gerard's application of these laws to genius, taste, beauty, and sublimity.

Beattie reduces the principles regulating the association of ideas in the imagination to five: resemblance, contrariety, nearness of situation (contiguity of time and place), cause and effect, and custom (repeated, habitual contiguity). "The relations, or bonds of union, which thus determine the mind to associate ideas, are various".[51] His analyses, so similar to those in Hume

178-99, 200-10. This edition is the Dublin reprint of the original edition (London, 1783). See also *Elements of Moral Science* (Edinburgh, 1790), I, 126-70. The latter publication is an abridgment of Beattie's lectures and of his previously published works.

[51] *Moral Science,* I, 107. For analyses of the principles, see *Dissertations,* I, 95-133; *Moral Science,* I, 106-12. Like Hume, he agrees [*Dissertations,* I, 175-6] that custom and causality "may very well be referred to that one which Aristotle calls *Contiguity* . . . . In its influence a Cause may be said to be, because it really is, *contiguous* to its Effect. And two things or ideas cannot be associated by Custom, so as that the one shall introduce the other into the mind; unless they have, once and again, or once at least, been in company together, or thought of at the same time."

and Gerard, require no repetition here. Of special significance, however, is his application of the associationist psychology to critical thought.

In an early work read and recommended by Alison, *An Essay on Poetry and Music as they Affect the Mind* (1762, 1776), Beattie falls back on the theory of association in a discussion of music.[52] Possibly anticipating the associationism of Thomas Brown, whose *Dissertation on Music and Poetry* appeared in 1763, Beattie states that sounds imitative of nature can be pleasing only if they are "*connected with agreeable or sublime affections*, and reconcilable both with melody and harmony". The extent and merit of imitative music extends, he writes, "to those natural sounds and motions only which are agreeable in themselves, consistent with melody and harmony, and associated with agreeable affections and sentiments".[53] Often, he continues, the unimitative music of certain instruments raises certain ideas and passions by accidental or customary associations: the flute suggests a pastoral scene, the organ brings to mind a church, etc. And he suggests that all instrumental music becomes expressive or significant by associations of ideas.[54] Compromising between the theories of Brown and Webb, Beattie concedes on the one hand that sounds may be esthetically pleasing only to the ear, while he insists on the other that they may as well produce their effects by subjective associations. For example, "loud and mellow sounds" may produce the sublime directly by their impact on the aural sense or indirectly by an association of ideas:

By suggesting the idea of a great power, and sometimes of great expansion too, they excite a pleasing admiration, and seem to accord with the lofty genius of that soul whose chief desire is for

[52] Alison, *Essays on Taste* (Edinburgh, 1790), pp. 82, 186-7. Beattie's essay is, however, almost entirely Aristotelian in its ideas and methods; the emphasis falls on imitation, verisimilitude, etc. Beattie says this essay was written in 1762.

[53] *The Works of James Beattie* (Philadelphia, 1809), V, 299, 305 (Pt. I, ch. vi of the essay).

[54] *Works,* V, 311-2, 327-8, 330-1, 342.

truth, virtue, and immortality, and the object of whose most delightful meditation is the greatest and best of beings.[55]

Finally, he declares, "association contributes greatly to heighten their [musical compositions] effect". It is not necessary, Beattie observes of the subjective effects of association, "that such melodies or harmonies should have much intrinsick merit, or that they should call up any distinct remembrances of the agreeable ideas associated with them". Even a faint suggestion will do: "If a song, or piece of music, should call up only a faint remembrance, that we were happy, the last time we heard it, nothing more would be needful to make us listen to it again with peculiar satisfaction".[56] National music is included in this category; for when pleasing patriotic associations are recalled, they greatly augment the listener's pleasure.[57] In connection with this subject, Beattie also mentions in another essay, "On Laughter and Ludicrous Composition" (1776), that "an object not absolutely mean is rendered sublime in some degree, by association with a sublime idea", and cites as an example a Scottish tune called a Pibroch, which conveys to a highlander's mind "the elevating ideas of danger, and courage, and armies, and military service".[58]

In the dissertation "Of Imagination" (1783), Beattie presents his best and most complete analysis of the influence of association on taste and criticism. In Chapter II, "Of the Association of Ideas", he discusses and illustrates all the principles of association and then shows, in Hartley's manner, how custom is the source of the standard of taste and of many of our ideas of beauty.

In the usual manner Beattie notes that "Resemblance, ... one of those associating principles, that lead our thoughts from one object to another", is the source of the figures founded on similarity, metaphor and simile. Following Kames and Gerard, he also notes how this principle enables poets

[55] *Works,* V, 318-9.
[56] *Works,* V, 342-3.
[57] *Works,* V, 343-5; *Moral Science,* I, 157.
[58] *Works,* VI, 254-5.

to preserve decorum of character. "When the soul is occupied by any powerful passion, the thoughts that arise in it are generally similar to that passion, and tend to encourage it".

> So that, if we know a person's character, or the passions that habitually prevail in him, we may guess, with no little assurance, in regard to the thoughts that would arise in his mind on any given occasion, that they would bear a resemblance to his predominant temper. *And thus it is, that poets are enabled to preserve the decorum of characters;* and to assign to every person, whom they may introduce as an agent in their fable, those sentiments, and that conduct, which we should expect from such a person, if he were to make his appearance in real life.[59]

He observes, like Kames, that contrast, "a natural bond of union among ideas", is often found in "works of fancy". Homer studiously employs this natural association both to diversify the events in the fable and to please the reader: "On all these occasions we are pleased with the variety; and we are also pleased with the opposition, because it makes the variety more observable and surprising, and suits that propensity of the human mind, of associating contraries, or passing from one extreme to another". The naturalness in the association of contrary ideas also contributes to our appreciation of Shakespeare's characterization. Take, for example, the words of King John upon being tortured with the heat of a mortal poison:

> Shakespeare does not make him think of coolness, for that was not the proper contrast to his feelings, but puts in his mouth the following exclamation:
>
> Poison'd, ill fare! dead, and forsook, cast off,
> And none of you will bid the winter come,
> To thrust his icy fingers in my maw;
> Nor let my kingdom's rivers take their course
> Through my burn'd bosom; nor entreat the North
> To make his bleak winds kiss my parched lips,
> And comfort me with cold.

[59] *Dissertations,* I, 99-101; *Moral Science,* I, 107-8.

"Nothing", Beattie comments, "can be more natural than the direction here given to the imagination of the sufferer".[60]

Neither vicinity (nearness of situation) nor causality is given a critical or literary application; but custom receives an extensive application to taste. Unlike Reynolds, Beattie believes that habit and custom are developed from accidental but persistent and quasi-permanent associations of ideas. Here is a clue that leads us to suspect Beattie's sympathetic reading of the *Observations on Man*, for this is precisely the position taken by Hartley.[61] According to Beattie, custom as an associating principle explains the prevalence of fashion and the differences of taste, and, moreover, "has, indeed, a very powerful influence, in determining our notions of beauty".[62] In Chapter II, Section iv, in part entitled "Origin of our Ideas of Beauty, – Colour, – in Figure, – in Attitude, – in Motion, – partly accounted for, from the Influence of Custom, as an Associating Principle", – this subject is elaborated with respect to critical theory. The enquiry is begun by a statement on the general principle:

> from associations founded in habit, many, or perhaps most, of those pleasing emotions are derived, which accompany the perception of what in things visible is called Beauty: those Colours, Figures, Gestures, and Motions, being for the most part accounted Beautiful, which convey to the mind pleasurable ideas; and those ugly, or not beautiful, which impart suggestions of an opposite or different nature.[63]

Like Gerard, he admits other and intrinsic sources of beauty; but he allows his stress to fall upon the influence of associations. Certain delicate colors, for example, have intrinsic beauty; the green of the fields, however, is beautiful, "because it conveys to the beholder many sweet ideas of fragrance, and plenty, and happy seasons". Indeed, he implies,

[60] *Dissertations,* I, 102-4; *Moral Science,* I, 108.

[61] Cf. above, p. 129.

[62] *Dissertations,* I, 116-32; *Moral Science,* I, 110-2.

[63] *Dissertations,* I, 133.

there can rarely be an objective type of beauty in colors because of the influences of subjective associations:

the beauty of colors depends so much on the ideas with which they may happen to have been associated by custom, that the same colour shall be beautiful in one object, and in another ugly, for no other reason, but because in the one, it brings along with it some pleasing, and in the other some painful, recollection.[64]

The shapes of things are also beautiful when they suggest the agreeable ideas of perfection, skill, convenience, and utility. And Hogarth's beautiful and waving serpentine is esthetically pleasing, he seriously believes, because it suggests the agreeable idea of the prime of life!

This shape, therefore, is by custom, associated in our minds with the idea of that period, when the bodily powers are most compleat, and equally remote from infirmity on the one hand, and imperfection on the other. Surely it is not wonderful, that a form, which conveys the notion of youth, and consequently of joy and hope, of health, strength, and activity, and of generous and warm affections, should please more, and for that reason be accounted more beautiful, than those other forms that convey ideas of insufficiency, and feebleness, or of decay, despondence, and melancholy.[65]

Similarly, Beattie applies this principle of association to gesture or attitude and to motion and arrives at identical conclusions – that our admiration of and pleasure in beautiful objects and motions are produced in great measure by the various delightful ideas "with which they are associated in our Imagination".[66] The beautiful movement of the sea and its effect on the mind are explained in terms of this romantic subjectivism:

The heaving of unbroken waves in the sea is beautiful; perhaps on account of their smoothness, uniformity, and easy curvature, suggesting the idea of vast agitation without difficulty; which for obvious reasons must be more agreeable, than a sluggish or weak exertion with turbulence.

[64] *Dissertations,* I, 135. These and the following ideas are repeated in *Moral Science,* I, 139-46.

[65] *Dissertations,* I, 142-3.

[66] *Dissertations,* I, 148; *Moral Science,* I, 145-6.

And the wild and turbulent ocean is *not* beautiful because it is associated with ideas of danger. Such a notion resembles faintly Burke's associationist conception of the terrible sublime.

The enraged Atlantick, rising in mountains is sublime, in the highest degree, and would yield a pleasing astonishment to one who could see it without fear; but conveys too many ideas of danger and difficulty, to produce that soothing and chearful delight, which attends the contemplation of what is beautiful.[67]

In the last dissertation, "Illustrations on Sublimity", Beattie again borrows from Gerard and therefore, as Monk has noticed, says little that is new. Like Gerard, he asserts that an association of a great idea augments the pleasure taken in a sublime object. "A fleet, or army, makes us think of power, and courage, and danger, and presents a variety of brilliant images". Long time is succeeded by many connected ideas, the uncertainty of life, death, eternity, immortality, and finally, it "is connected with an idea still more sublime", God. Thunder, tempest, and cannon give "a dreadful delight" partly by aural sensation and "partly by the ideas of power and danger, triumph and fortitude, which . . . [they] convey to the fancy".[68] Unlike Gerard, however, he does not say that poetry and painting produce their sublime effects only by an association of ideas. Nor does he say much more about the influence of associations upon the sublime, except to note in passing that Chinese architecture "has no pretensions to sublimity; its decorations being still more trivial than the Gothick; and because it derives no dignity from associated ideas, and has no vastness of magnitude to raise admiration".[69]

Beattie does not fail to discuss standards of taste. Although he agrees with the relativists in his assertion that "men may differ in their notions of beauty ... as long as they differ in customs, prejudices, passions, and capacities", Beattie positively believes "a standard there is, notwithstanding". Like

[67] *Dissertations,* I, 152, 153.

[68] *Dissertations,* II, 365-6; *Moral Science,* I, 132-3.

[69] *Dissertations,* II, 376.

Reynolds, who bases the standard of taste on general habits and permanent associations, Beattie also bases the standard on "general taste" which is opposed to the "various humours and fancies of individuals". The latter are caused by unique associations in few individuals; the former, on the other hand, are produced by associations in most men. For example, certain forms of the human body please everyone.

All this it is easy to explain upon the principles of association. What is, or appears to be perfect, in the human body, must please, as long as bodily perfection is more useful and more agreeable, than the want of it. And, while virtue and good understanding are held in any esteem among men, every look of the eye, and turn of the countenance, must give delight, which conveys the idea of acuteness, good humor, modesty, gentleness, affability, generosity, and good nature.[70]

Finally, as in Gerard, he employs the various principles of association (together with constitution, passions, and early habits) as the sources of the variety of genius. When the imagination is subject to the influence of one or another of the principles, a philosopher, poet, wit, or historian is generated. This idea is taken directly from Gerard's *Essay on Genius*.

Whatever diversifies imagination, must give variety to genius. If the fancy have acquired by nature or by habit, a tendency to pass from causes to effects, and from effects to causes, it may be presumed, that the genius, aided by accurate observation, will be philosophical. If there be a propensity to trace out resemblances, and to bring those ideas together which are *like* one another, the genius may possibly exert itself in some imitative art, as painting, or poetry; especially if there be superadded a taste for the beauties of nature, with great sensibility of temper, and a contemplative mind: but in persons less romantic, and much engaged in the business of society, or who have not in early life been accustomed to survey the grand phaenomena of creation, if the same associating principle of resemblance predominate, it may perhaps give rise to Wit; which consists, for the most part, in the unexpected discovery of similitude between things apparently unlike. A tenacious memory, with a disposition

70 *Dissertations*, I, 167, 169.

to associate those ideas that are related in time and place, seems likely to produce a genius for historical narrative.[71]

Beattie, in sum, presents a fairly complete associationist esthetics. Early in his career as author and critic the theory of association appears but spasmodically and has no organic part in his critical works. We may include in this generalization his associationist remarks on music, which may possibly have anticipated those in Brown's *Dissertation on Poetry and Music* (1763). But in his *Dissertations*, Beattie's associationism is more systematically analyzed and applied. His concept of the imagination is thoroughly permeated with the theory of association. Beauty, sublimity, genius, and the standard of taste – all receive an associationist explanation. Beattie does not employ this psychology with the consistency, completeness, or originality of Gerard or Hartley; there is, however, enough of the psychology present in his works to make him a fitting precursor of Alison's associationist critical theories.

A most appropriate finale to the tradition of associationist critical theory in the eighteenth century is Archibald Alison's *Essays on the Nature and Principles of Taste* (1790). The associationist critical theory in Archibald Alison's detailed essays is far more thoroughly employed and certainly far more sweeping in scope than that in any other treatise on taste or criticism throughout the century. Moreover, in influence, it also equals and possibly surpasses Joseph Priestley's *Lectures on Criticism* (1777), and is among the important few eighteenth-century critical works that made a noticeable impression on early nineteenth-century critical thought. The popularity in the nineteenth century of the *Essays on Taste* is not only attested to by the remarks of a dutiful son about his father's "well-known" essays "which have long taken a high place in British literature", but also by external evidence that may be more reliable and explicit.[72] The work was published first in Edin-

[71] *Dissertations,* I, 188.

[72] Sir Archibald Alison, *Some Account of My Life and Writings* (Edinburgh and London, 1883), pp. 2, 8. Abraham Mills places Alison's *Essays*

burgh in 1790; and although it was highly recommended by the *New Annual Register* (1790) and favorably reviewed with copious extracts in the *Monthly Review,* yet it did not sell rapidly.[73] In 1810, however, Alison's booksellers told him there was need of a second edition. This edition was issued in 1811 with additions and was commended by Lord Jeffrey in the *Edinburgh Review* of that year.[74] Jeffrey's approving review apparently insured its popularity with British readers, since four more Edinburgh editions were required by 1825 to satisfy the esthetic needs of the intellectual public. Other literary centers in England and America issued many cheap reprints until 1879.[75] Therefore, it may be said without exaggeration that Alison's *Essays on Taste* is, historically speaking, a minor classic. Alison's ideas, given such a wide circulation by publications and reviews of his book, accordingly become a serious concern for students of critical theory at the turn of the eighteenth century. In this essay, the psychological ground for a few typical eighteenth-century concepts and the romantic and neoclassic elements in Alison's esthetics will be discussed.

The associationist approach to criticism receives its finishing touches in Alison; his essays are solely dedicated to the task of persuading his readers that the associationist psychology

---

on the same level with Blair's *Lectures* and Burke's *Inquiry,* – "works of so much importance and so deservedly popular". See the Preface to his edition of Alison's *Essays on Taste* (New York, 1830), p. iii. See also C. M. Gayley and F. N. Scott, *An Introduction to the Methods and Materials of Literary Criticism* (Boston, 1899), pp. 87-8.

[73] *New Annual Register* (1790), p. 203; *Monthly Review,* III (1790), 361-73; IV (1791), 8-19.

[74] XVIII (1811), 1-45.

[75] The editions printed in Edinburgh number six: 1790, 1811, 1812, 1815, 1817, 1825. There are nine other editions and reprints: Dublin, 1790; Boston, 1812; Hartford, 1821; New York, 1830, 1844, 1854; London, 1853 ("Universal Library"); 1871, 1879 ("World Library of Standard Works"). In the three New York editions, Abraham Mills prepared Alison as a standard school text "with corrections and improvements" in the same manner as he prepared Burke and Blair. C. Fedeles, [*Versuch über Alisons Asthetik, Darstellung und Kritik* (Munchen, 1911), p. 8] notes a reprint which I have been unable to trace: London, 1842 ("Smith's Standard Library").

is the *only* source of taste. The signifiance of Alison's work is therefore twofold: it is the fullest expression of associationist methods in the critical theory of the eighteenth century and is, at the same time, the critical associationism that provoked the greatest discussion and that had, through Lord Jeffrey, Richard Payne Knight, Dugald Stewart, Thomas Brown, James Mill, Sydney Smith, Edward Mangin, and Sir Thomas Dick Lauder, an important influence on early nineteenth-century critical thought.[76]

Alison makes taste entirely dependent upon the imagination, to the exclusion of judgment and reason. His definition of taste is very simple. Following Burke on the *Sublime*, he limits it only to those subjective effects on the mind which are produced by beautiful and sublime objects.[77] However, taste, the ability to react to beautiful or sublime effects, is not simple; the reaction of this faculty is unlike that of the instinctive "internal senses", as described by Francis Hutcheson, Edmund Burke, or Alexander Gerard. On the contrary, this effect is complex, characterized by an emotion first raised by an association of ideas and then followed by a regular train of associated ideas in the imagination. Like Joseph Priestley, in his *Lectures on Oratory and Rhetoric* (1777), Alison follows the Hartlean psychology and specifically opposes the doctrine of the internal senses: the pleasures of taste, he claims, "may be considered not as a simple, but as a complex pleasure; and as arising not from any separate and peculiar Sense".[78]

In the second and longer essay, the essay which really lays the foundation of his critical theory, Alison describes the manner in which material objects affect the mind and produce those

[76] Cf. Sir Thomas Dick Lauder, *Sir Uvedale Price on the Picturesque* (London, 1842), p. 4: "Mr. Alison's essays on the Principles of Taste, first published in 1790, afforded the earliest complete promulgation of the Theory of Association. He was followed by Knight and Professors Dugald Stewart and Thomas Brown . . . . Lord Jeffrey's eloquent and perspicuous article in the Encyclopedia Britannica is the last treatise on the subject of which I have any knowledge."

[77] *Essays on the Nature and Principles of Taste* (Edinburgh, 1790), p. vii.

[78] P. 120.

emotions that are essential for taste. Objects become esthetically affecting when our minds associate "ideas of Emotion" with them or when these ideas are associated with other qualities that already affect us. For example, in works of art, the associated ideas of dexterity, taste, convenience, utility; and in nature, those of peace, danger, plenty, desolation – all produce an emotion in us:

In such cases, the constant connection we discover between the sign and the thing signified, between the material quality and the quality productive of emotion, renders at last the one [the sign, or the object] expressive to us of the other [the thing signified, or the emotion], and very often disposes us to attribute to the sign, that effect which is produced only by the quality signified.

This association of expressive or significant ideas is the source of the effect that material objects have upon the mind:

By means of the Connection, or Resemblance, which subsists between the qualities of Matter, and qualities capable of producing Emotion, the perception of the one immediately, and very often irresistibly suggests the idea of the other; and so early are these Associations formed, that it requires afterwards some pains to separate this connection, and to prevent us from attributing to the Sign, that effect which is produced alone by the Quality signified.[79]

Throughout this second essay, which we shall only briefly summarize here, Alison presents in great detail arguments and illustrations as proof and evidence of his contention that the only way in which objects do move us and do arouse our esthetic interest is by means of this process of subjective association. He makes it clear that ideas cannot be beautiful or sublime absolutely in themselves or independent of their effect on the mind. And he describes in detail how, in accordance with this process of association, sounds, colors, forms, and motions all derive their beautiful and sublime effects from the several kinds of associations of ideas in the mind. In Hartlean fashion [80] he lists the many sources of the various associations which

[79] Pp. 127, 128, 133.
[80] David Hartley, *Observations on Man* (1749), Prop. 94, I, 421 ff.

we might have with these "objects" of the "material world" and which are responsible for their beauty and sublimity. The sublimity of sounds, for example, is owing to associations with ideas of danger, power or might, majesty or solemnity, deep melancholy, or any other strong emotion. But the beauty of sounds is produced by associations of tranquillity, peace, light melancholy, joy, cheerfulness, gentleness, and delicacy. If these associations are dissolved, Alison argues by appealing to experience, the emotions are then no longer produced. Other arguments that he generally draws upon in order to support his subjective associationism are also taken from experience: the diversity of effects that one object may have upon many people proves that the object itself is really indifferent; one idea has never been permanently or constantly beautiful or sublime; and various circumstances contribute to our conception of beauty and sublimity.[81] That is to say, the mind, by means of the associated ideas that it supplies, is the source of all beauty and all sublimity.

But although this subjective association of ideas produces the emotion that is the foundation of the esthetic effect, it alone is not sufficient to evoke the full effect of taste. It is only the union of this association with the imagination that can produce real esthetic "delight".[82] Unless, therefore, the imagination is also excited by pursuing a train of emotions "allied" to this original emotion, there can be no esthetic response. This second characteristic of taste is the subject of the first essay. The succession of ideas in the imagination is not haphazard; on the contrary, it is regular, because it is guided by a principle of association, the principle of resemblance. And the intensity of esthetic response depends directly upon the uniformity of the associated ideas in a train.

The principal relation, which seems to take place in those trains of thought, that are produced by objects of taste, is that of resem-

[81] Cf., e.g., *Essays on Taste,* pp. 225-31.
[82] Pp. 120-1.

blance; the relation, of all others, the most loose and general, and which affords the greatest range of thought, for our imagination to pursue. Wherever, accordingly, these emotions [of taste] are felt, it will be found, not only that this is the relation which principally prevails among our ideas, but that the emotion itself is proportioned to the degree in which it prevails.[83]

In this process, the imagination is entirely passive: ideas spontaneously and mechanically pass through it guided by the principle of resemblance; and they have no definite aim or purpose but that of producing an emotional condition closely resembling romantic ecstasy. This development of Lord Kames's "waking dream" of the imagination lays the psychological groundwork of the most characteristic feature of romanticism – the ecstatic reverie. Like Alison, Kames had used the romantic experience, that experience which gives the liveliest impression of reality, as a touchstone for the success of art:

... the pleasure of a reverie, where a man, losing sight of himself, is totally occupied with the ideas passing in his mind, the objects of which he conceives to be really existing in his presence. The power of language to raise emotions, depends entirely on the raising of such lively and distinct images as here described: the reader's passions are never sensibly moved, till he be thrown into a kind of reverie; in which state, forgetting himself, and forgetting that he is reading, he conceives every incident as passing in his presence, precisely as if he were an eyewitness.[84]

Alison also believes that art is best measured by this romantic trance-like effect which occurs only when the imagination is so excited, so rapt in soothing inward associations that it fades away from the realities of life.

In such trains of imagery, no labour of thought, or habits of attention, are required; they rise spontaneously in the mind, upon the prospect of any object, to which they bear the slightest resemblance, and they lead it almost insensibly along, in a kind of bewitching reverie, through all its store of pleasing or interesting conceptions.

83 Pp. 9-10.

84 Kames, *Elements of Criticism* (Edinburgh, 1769), I, 93. Other *loci* on the reverie are in I, 172, 312; II, 329.

It is, then, indeed, in this powerless state of reverie, when we are carried on by our conceptions, not guiding them, that the deepest emotions of beauty or sublimity are felt, that our hearts swell with feelings which language is too weak to express, and that in the depth of silence and astonishment we pay to the charm that enthrals us, the most flattering mark of our applause.[85]

Alison here looks forward to the practices and experiences of some romantic writers. He has certainly brought to light the psychological basis of the romantic experience which gripped Wordsworth, as it is described in the "Lines Composed a Few Miles above Tintern Abbey" (1798), – "that serene and blessed mood, In which the affections gently lead us on". This ecstatic experience, perhaps the most characteristic of romantic traits, is described in treatises on art and in novels of the early nineteenth century. It is easy to detect the kinship between Alison's interpretation of the esthetic response and the following selections taken at random from the works of John Claudius Loudon, the well-known author of books on gardening, and Thomas Love Peacock:

A single idea of excellence presented to the fertile imagination rouses a long train of corresponding sensations, which often carry us, as it were, beyond ourselves into the regions of romance and enthusiasm.

Anthelia rested awhile in this delightful solitude.... She felt the presence of the genius of the scene. She sat absorbed in a train of contemplations, dimly defined, but infinitely delightful: emotions rather than thoughts, which attention would have utterly dissipated, if it had paused to seize their images.[86]

[85] *Essays on Taste,* pp. 14, 42.

[86] Loudon, *Treatise on ... Country Residences* (London, 1806), p. 48; Peacock, *Melincourt* (1817), Ch. x. Marianne Dashwood is a good example of the romantic tintype. She suffers from an excess of sensibility: "Marianne was afraid of offending, and said no more on the subject; but the kind of approbation which Elinor described as excited in him by the drawings of other people, was very far from *that rapturous delight, which, in her opinion, could alone be called taste.*" Cf. Jane Austen, *Sense and Sensibility* (1811), Ch. iv. My emphasis.

The beauty and sublimity of both nature and art, Alison declares, depend upon these "trains of pleasing or solemn thought" that "arise spontaneously within our minds". If our attention is confined closely to the object, whether it be Claude's landscapes, Handel's music, or Milton's poetry, our response can only be feeble, and, consequently, we shall not feel the beauty or sublimity of these works. But, on the other hand, when our imagination is given the freedom to form these trains of associated ideas, the emotions of taste are strongly roused:

It is then, only, we feel the sublimity or beauty of their productions, when our imaginations are kindled by their power, when we lose ourselves amid the number of images that pass before our minds, and when we waken at last from this play of fancy, as from the charm of a romantic dream.[87]

In short, objects may not be considered sublime or beautiful, if they do not have a powerful effect on the imagination. The effect is clearly the standard of the arts, and it is characterized by these trains of resembling ideas coursing through the imagination. Thus, when anything prevents this "exercise of Imagination" or imaginative response, such as pain, grief, business, disposition, and criticism, – the flow of ideas is limited and the sense of beauty diminished. And the most favorable state of mind for the esthetic response is therefore that "in which the imagination is free and unembarrassed ... as to leave us open to all the impressions, which the objects that are before us, can create". Or, as Alison seriously states, "It is upon the vacant and unemployed, accordingly, that the objects of taste make the strongest impression".[88]

There are, Alison says, many ways to set the imagination afire and into forming these trains of images. "There is no man, who has not some interesting associations with particular scenes, or airs, or books, and who does not feel their

[87] *Essays on Taste,* p. 3.
[88] Pp. 6-7.

beauty or sublimity enhanced to him by such connections".[89] Like Hartley, he again lists and classifies many sources of ideas – historical, national, artistic, picturesque – which are linked together by association and which convert anything into an object of taste. Historical associations, for instance, make Runnymede a scene to be admired. Literary associations, those of Petrarch especially, make the valley of the Vaucluse more beautiful. Similarly, the sublime is produced by streams of associated ideas in the imagination. "The field of any celebrated battle [such as Agincourt], becomes sublime from this association . . .".

> The additional conceptions which this [literary] association produces, and which fill the mind of the spectator on the prospect of that memorable field, diffuse themselves in some measure over the scene, and give it a sublimity which does not naturally belong to it.[90]

Moreover, national associations influence emotions and taste. Thus, although certain lines of Virgil in praise of his country may strongly affect us, they "were yet undoubtedly read with a far superior emotion, by an ancient Roman". And like Beattie, Alison writes of the diversitarian effects of this association upon the taste for music.[91]

An interesting corollary of this subjective associationism is the quantitative concept, – that is, he who has the most ideas stored in his mind can supply the most associations and therefore, according to Alison, he can feel the deepest emotion and have the most satisfactory response: "No man, in general, is sensible to beauty, in those subjects with regard to which he has not previous ideas. The beauty of a theory, or of a relic of antiquity, is unintelligible to a peasant". The beauty of the country is not deeply appreciated by the urbanite; that of a painting and natural scene gives the profoundest pleasure to a painter and landscape painter or gardener. The reading of poetry also increases the store of asso-

[89] P. 15.
[90] Pp. 17-8.
[91] Pp. 24-5.

ciations and the sensibility and has, consequently, a powerful influence upon taste.[92] Finally, those who are sensitive to the picturesque have an additional source of esthetic pleasure. Influenced no doubt by the publication in the eighties of Gilpin's *Tours*, Alison describes the effect of the picturesque upon beauty and sublimity: "The effect which is thus produced, by Associations, in increasing the emotions of sublimity or beauty, is produced also, either in nature, or in description, by what are generally termed Picturesque Objects".[93] By producing surprise, these picturesque objects "suggest an additional train of conceptions, beside what the scene or description itself would have suggested". The influence of picturesque ideas upon beauty is illustrated with selections from Goldsmith, Buchanan, Beattie, Whately, and Virgil; and the influence of the picturesque on the sublime is illustrated with selections from Virgil, Lucan, Tasso, Thomson, Whately, Diderot, and Milton.[94] To a quotation from Thomson's *Seasons,* Alison adds a particularly interesting romantic gloss:

> The scene is undoubtedly beautiful of itself, without the addition of the last circumstance [a ruin]; yet how much more beautiful does it become by the new order of thought which this circumstance awakens in the mind, and which contrasting the remembrance of ancient warfare and turbulent times, with the serenity and repose of the modern scene, agitate [sic] the imagination with a variety of indistinct conceptions, which otherwise could never have arisen in it?[95]

Paralleling this romantic conception of the imaginative effect is a belief in the relativist point of view. From the time of Addison in the beginning of the eighteenth century, the association of ideas has traditionally been used to explain the wide diversity of taste. In Alison there is no divergence from tradition; he too employs the theory of association for

92 Pp. 25, 26, 44-9.
93 P. 29.
94 Pp. 35-41.
95 P. 32.

his diversitarian approach to critical problems. Even the same object, he observes, may produce completely opposite responses: "In these and similar cases of difference in our feelings, from the same objects, it will always be found, that the difference arises from the state of our imaginations; from our disposition to follow out the train of thought, which such objects naturally produce, or our incapacity to do it".[96] In other words, the differences in esthetic responses are directly proportionate to the number of appropriate ideas associated and the kind of associational principle employed. Youth is the best time of life for imaginative freedom because it is during this period of life that practical concerns interfere least with the spontaneity of the imagination, and that the imagination is more than willing to "yield to the relation of resembling thought", the principle of resemblance. Experience and progress in life soon steal from men their willingness to associate ideas freely, "that exertion upon which so much of the emotion of beauty depends". Not only are older people unlikely to exercise the imagination, he continues, but "their associations become at the same time less consistent with the employment of it". For example, the businessman and the philosopher are prevented from indulging in the freedom of the imagination because they use a type of association to which the imagination cannot easily respond: they "have both not only acquired a constitution of mind very little fitted for the indulgences of imagination, but have acquired also associations of a very different kind from those which take place, when imagination is employed". In response to the beauties of nature, the one thinks of causes, while the other thinks of utility and value: "it would thus excite ideas, which could be the foundation of no excercise of imagination, because they required thought and attention".[97]

Moreover, Alison further makes clear, accidental and personal associations of ideas, habits and occupations of life,

[96] P. 6.

[97] Pp. 11-3. Cf. also pp. 63-5, where Alison discusses the influence of disposition on taste.

and temporary states of mind all have a powerful influence upon the diversity of taste.[98] But like most of the associationists in the tradition, although he acknowledges the soundness of the diversitarian approach to criticism, he does believe in the possibility of a "good" and perhaps a single taste. Yet Alison seems to differ somewhat from his predecessors who employ the consensus of the elect as the best standard of taste. Taking what may at the present time be considered a more modern and perhaps an eclectic view, he proposes that the goal at which critics and artists should aim is *comprehensiveness* of taste, broader experiences and multitudinous associations:

It is only when we arrive at manhood, and still more, when either the liberality of our education, or the original capacity of our minds, have led us to experience or to participate in all the affections of our nature, that we acquire that comprehensive taste, which can enable us to discover, and to relish, every species of Sublimity and Beauty.[99]

Nonetheless, there are in Alison distinct echoes of an aristocratic, neoclassical past; like Kames and Gerard, he presents, it would seem, the eighteenth-century version of the ivory-tower by excluding from the domain of art or taste those soiled by labor.

It is only in the higher stations accordingly, or in the liberal professions of life, that we expect to find men either of a delicate or comprehensive taste. The inferior situations of life, by contracting the knowledge and the affections of men, within very narrow limits, produce insensibly a similar contraction in their notions of the beautiful or the sublime.[100]

We come now to the last important critical principle that Alison derives from his conception of the associationist psy-

[98] Pp. 59-66.

[99] P. 61.

[100] P. 62. Kames, *Elements,* II, 490-1, 498-9, "Those who depend for food on bodily labour, are totally void of taste." Gerard, *Essay on Taste* (1762), IV, ii, 216-9.

chology. As we have stated before, the principle of resemblance guides and unifies the train of emotions and produces one impression. From this principle, Alison deduces that the intensity of the esthetic response and the success of a work of art depend directly upon the uniformity of the ideas in the imagination. Out of this uniformity of associated ideas in a train, Alison, like Kames, derives a rule for the regulation of art.[101] In the second chapter of the first essay, Alison distinguishes between ordinary trains of thought that have no esthetic effect and other trains that are the sources of taste. The difference between these two types of thought, he declares, "consists in two things. 1st, In the Nature of the ideas or conceptions which compose such trains; and 2dly, In the Nature or Law of their succession".[102] In the first place, that is to say, the ideas must have some effect; they must be "ideas of Emotion". In the second place, every idea in the succession must resemble its fellow so that the combination of emotions can produce a single, uniform effect. A general or regular principle of connection among the emotions composing the train serves this function and gives the succession a certain and definite character, – gay, pathetic, solemn, awful, etc., according to the first emotion excited.[103] The significance of this unity of emotional succession is easy to see, for this associationist concept was previously employed in the associationist criticism of Hume, Kames, and Gerard.[104] In the *Essays on Taste* Alison follows in the associationist tradition and likewise derives the rule of unity from this psychology:

> If it is true that those trains of thought which attend the Emotions of Taste, are uniformly distinguished by some general principle of connection, it ought to be found, that no Composition of objects

[101] Kames, *Elements,* I, 18, 27.

[102] P. 51.

[103] Pp. 54-5.

[104] For Hume, see above, pp. 90-3. Gerard, *Essay on Genius* (1774), I, iii, 46ff. But Hume, Gerard, and Kames use the associationist principle of causality, not resemblance.

or qualities, in fact, produces such emotions, in which this Unity of character or of emotion is not preserved.[105]

The arts can only succeed, Alison asserts, when they preserve unity, when the parts conform to the general character of the whole. He applies this principle rigorously to gardening and to landscape painting. The standard for the latter art, Alison writes, is the simple unity of effect:

Some general principle is universally demanded, some decided expression, to which the meaning of the several parts may be referred, and which by affording us, as it were, the key of the scene, may lead us to feel from the whole of the composition, that full and undisturbed emotion which we are prepared to indulge. It is this *purity and simplicity* of composition, accordingly, which has uniformly distinguished the great master of the art, from the mere copiers of Nature.[106]

The significance of purity and simplicity of expression for literature is obvious: a rigid application of the rule of simple unity produces a severely neoclassic and hypercritical approach to art. In a manner reminiscent of the conservative Kames (in the first chapter of his *Elements*), Alison notes how trifling defects in Virgil, Homer, Horace, Lucan, Marini, and Shakespeare, spoil perfect unity of expression and adversely affect taste. How exacting and precise this criticism can be is proved by his close reading of Milton and Beattie. The beauty of a passage in *Paradise Lost* is diminished, he maintains, by "the introduction of trifling and ludicrous circumstances". He considers the italicized words to be defective.

Now Morn her rosy steps in the eastern clime
Advancing, sow's the earth with orient pearl,
When Adam wak'd: *so custom'd, for his sleep*
Was airy light from pure digestion bred
And temp'rate vapours bland, which th'only sound
Of leaves, and fuming rills, Aurora's fan

105 P. 84.
106 P. 88.

Lightly dispers'd, and the shrill matin song
Of birds on every bough.[107]

His criticism of a line in Beattie's *Minstrel* is painfully minute:

In a description of the morning, in the charming poem of the Minstrel, there is a circumstance to which the severity of Criticism might object upon the same principle.

The cottage curs at early pilgrim bark,
Crown'd with her pail, the tripping milkmaid sings,
The whistling plowman stalks a-field, and hark!
Down the rough slope the ponderous waggon rings.

The image in the last line, though undoubtedly a striking one in itself, and very beautifully described, is yet improper, as it is incoherent both with the period of society, and the scenery of the country to which the Minstrel refers.[108]

The epic is subjected to criticism and analysis by means of the same rule. From an epic "we ... demand a more uniform tone of elevation, and a purer and more dignified selection of incidents, than from the strict narrative of real history". The poet must, in short, present only those incidents that accord with great emotions and omit "whatever in the real history of the event may be mean or uninteresting".[109]

To one whose temper inclines him to neoclassicism, this principle, the unity of associated ideas, can be very helpful. Indeed, the associationist interpretation of unity had already given support to the neoclassicism of Hume, Kames, and Gerard. And in Alison, even so late as 1790, the principle of associationist unity is used to support the neoclassical opposition to mixed genres. "This unity of character", he says, "is fully as essential as any of those three unities, of which every book of Criticism is so full". There must be no mixture of the elevated and the mean, of the serious and the ludicrous, he asserts. It is here that Alison pontifically issues a reaction-

107 P. 97. The quotation is from Book V, Lines 1-8.
108 P. 100.
109 Pp. 106, 107.

ary bull about a controversial problem supposedly settled by Johnson: "It is hence that Tragi-Comedy is utterly indefensible, after all that has been said in its defence . . .".

Had the taste of Shakespeare been equal to his genius, or had his knowledge of the laws of the Drama corresponded to his knowledge of the human heart, the effect of his compositions would not only have been greater than it now is, but greater than we can well imagine; and had he attempted to produce through a whole composition, that powerful and uniform interest which he can raise in a single scene, nothing of that perfection would have been wanting, of which we may conceive this sublime art to be capable.[110]

Instead of the romantic richness and superfluity of Shakespeare's dramas, which he is, by principle, unable to appreciate, Alison admires the economy of form and content, and the narrow, streamlined regularity and purity of Corneille's plays. In Corneille's tragedies, he states, in opposition to Kames, there is no mingling of the emotions and thus no interruption of the flow of associated ideas which is so injurious to taste. Apparently aware of the necessity of unity of emotional effect, Alison concludes, Corneille has given to his dramas "an uniform character of dignity".[111]

By unity of expression, then, Alison means uniformity of associated ideas. Thus, in accordance with a modern psychology, he has followed his Scottish forebears in reinterpreting along neoclassic lines Aristotle's unity of action. By applying his version of the rule rigidly, he has been forced to condemn Shakespeare and tragicomedy. Although the subjective effect or the uninterrupted flow of associated ideas in the imagination still remains his criterion, Alison paradoxically becomes as conservative as those neoclassic critics in the later seventeenth century who uphold as the ideal of dramatic perfection the purity and the simplicity of regular forms.

The train of thought, therefore, which takes place in the mind, upon the prospect of objects of sublimity and beauty, may be con-

110 Pp. 108-9. This is a distorted echo of Kames; see *Elements* II, 397-8.
111 Pp. 109-10.

sidered as consisting in a regular or consistent train of ideas of emotion, and as distinguished from our ordinary trains of thought.

If it is true that such trains of thought are uniformly distinguished by some general principle of connection, then it ought also to be found, that no Composition of objects or qualities produce such emotions, in which this Unity of character or of emotion is not preserved.

That Composition is most excellent, in which the different parts most fully unite in the production of one unmingled Emotion.[112]

Yet, despite his neoclassic adaptation of the associationist psychology, it is not too much to say that Alison's *Essays on Taste* forms an almost perfect link between the eighteenth and the nineteenth century. True, in opposition to this statement, there is the damaging evidence of a neoclassic conservatism in his demand for strict unity of expression, and extreme simplicity and regularity, his opposition to Shakespeare's dramaturgy and to tragicomedy, and, lastly, his fondness for aristocratic taste. But it is easy to see that Alison readily allowed a personal and perhaps lagging taste as well as the logic of his argument to dominate over the truth of his imaginative experiences. And the fact remains that he does employ the romantic imaginative experience as the touchstone of art. He who has eyes can see that his emphasis upon the subjective effect, his extravagant description of the esthetic response, his implicit belief in the individualism permitted by the diversitarian approach to taste, – are not characteristic of objective classic equilibrium and the harmony of the finite, but better characterize the psychology implicit in romantic literature and art, the vague longing for unattainable perfection, the indefiniteness of the infinite.

The romantic elements in Alison's associationist critical theory cannot be overemphasized. First, it must be observed that in this theory judgment and reason are wholly ignored. In other words, Alison regards the imagination as the sole criterion in the realm of taste and believes that it alone can

[112] Pp. 55, 56, 111.

endow objects with sublimity or beauty. The effect on the imagination is his only standard. Thus, his statement, "In the Fine Arts, whose object is Beauty, it is by its effect upon our Imagination alone, that we determine the excellence of any production", has a close counterpart in Wordsworth's subjectivism, "I felt, observed, and pondered; did not judge, Yea, never thought of judging".[113] Secondly, his conception of the esthetic response or the imaginative effect is thoroughly libertine and romantic. The imagination, he conjectures, is first stimulated to activity by an association of ideas; and, then, by means of the law of resemblance, the initial emotion produced is automatically succeeded by trains of corresponding ideas and emotions. The freer and the more unhampered the imagination is, he believes, the deeper and the better will be the response. Obviously, the roots of this notion concerning the imaginative effect are present in the "Traynes of Imaginations" of Hobbes and the "waking dream" or the "Ideas and Perceptions in a Train" of Kames. But Hobbes never and Kames only rarely suggest the ecstasy and transport of the "powerless state of reverie", in which taste is formed. While it is true that Alison derives from this conception of the imagination the important rule, unity of expression, his analysis of the imaginative response is far more significant for laying the psychological groundwork of the new romantic attitude. Therefore, because his whole volume is devoted to a careful study of the associational or imaginative effects of art, it is generally significant of a changing taste and attitude, a shift from the wish to examine the externals of things to the wish to examine the internal activity of the mind and to feel deeply of "that rapturous delight", as the ridiculously romantic Marianne Dashwood opines in Jane Austen's *Sense and Sensibility*, "which could alone be called taste".

In Alison's voluminous essays the eighteenth-century associationist critical theory has received its consummate expression.

[113] *Essays on Taste,* p. 336; *The Prelude,* ed. De Selincourt, XII, 188-9 (1850).

But it must not be forgotten that Alison's work is the result of a long tradition of careful study and tentative critical applications by Hume and Hartley, and of zealous and more methodical critical extensions by Kames, Gerard, Priestley, and even Beattie.[114] The impressive bulk and the completeness of Alison's associationist approach is therefore owing in large measure to the contributions of important and fairly complete earlier analyses. Only in this sense can it be said that his essays "afforded the earliest complete promulgation of the Theory of Association".[115] This thoroughgoing critical associationism, together with the new social, political, and moral adaptations of Hartley's theory by Godwin and Bentham, and their disciples, helped form the intellectual milieu in which the psychological and critical conceptions of Wordsworth and Coleridge first took shape. It was undoubtedly influential in determining the trend of critical theory at the turn of the eighteenth century.

[114] James Beattie, *Dissertations Moral and Critical* (1783), "Of Imagination"; *Elements of Moral Science* (Edinburgh, 1790), I, 126-70.

[115] Lauder, *Sir Uvedale Price on the Picturesque*, p. 4; see above, p. 250, fn. 76.

VII

CONCLUSION

With a major portion of the evidence gathered, it can be safely said that the influence of the theory of association upon English critical opinion has been of considerable importance throughout the course of the eighteenth century. From Hobbes and Locke to Priestley and Alison, the associationist method is employed in critical theory with unflagging vigor by many significant writers. But the influence of this psychology has not always persisted on the same level of importance as that which it finally reached in the latter half of the century. To make clear the continuity and the development of this critical theory, a brief sketch may be useful.

In England the psychological theory is first promulgated by Hobbes and Locke. Hobbes, as we have noticed, has more or less clearly based his theory of the artistic and imaginative processes on the notion of a regular and guided movement of associated ideas. Apparently because he believes the imagination functions regularly and derives its ideas from the memory, where they are stocked and "registered" in accordance with the principles of association, he has been able to reinforce the neoclassic rules requiring structural uniformity and regularity. But Hobbes's critical psychology had no positive influence on eighteenth-century writers, with the possible exceptions of Addison and Hume. Addison has probably taken from Hobbes his description of the pleasures that recollected trains of associated ideas give to the imagination. There can be a justifiable suspicion that Hume, who claims originality and acknowledges no sources, owes Hobbes a great debt, and in part transmits his conception of the regularly functioning imagination to the Scottish critics.

It is Locke's theory of association, however, that was greatly influential in our century. His formulation of the theory of "unnatural" or acquired associations of ideas that have nothing in common with each other provided a good explanation of diversity in taste, and his analysis of custom and habit or second-nature provided Gay and Hartley, as we have seen, with a conception of human nature that was to be of fundamental significance for the latter-century moralists and utilitarians. As Belsham intimates, it was Locke and Hartley who were respected at the end of the century:

> I do not hesitate to assert, that a mere classical scholar, however polished his language, or refined his taste, in real elevation and comprehension of mind, is as much inferior to the man who has attained to an intimate knowledge of the writings of Locke and Hartley, who has converted the simple and admirable theory of those great philosophers to all those excellent practical purposes to which the latter, in particular, has so ably shewn they are capable of being applied....[1]

In Locke, the associations of ideas are not regulated, as they are in Hobbes, by many principles – original perception or contiguity in time and place and the "natural" relations of cause and effect and resemblance. According to Locke, the only principle that controls or governs the association of ideas in the mind is the original connection made by chance and continued by repetition until the connection between the ideas becomes habitual or customary. This theory of "unnatural" associations of ideas caused by chance contiguity has influenced Berkeley and Hutcheson. Berkeley's description of the way in which ideas are accidentally associated with words may possibly be, as Dixon Wecter conjectures, a source of Burke's theory of poetic diction. And Hutcheson uses the psychology to explain why the internal sense of beauty is not universally uniform. His allegation that the irrational and pernicious associational effects upon the imag-

[1] *Essays, Philosophical, Historical, and Literary* (London, 1789), I, 189.

ination are the sources of diversity and change in taste is constantly reiterated through the century. Hutcheson gives the clearest and most incisive expression of the associationist basis of diversity, although Addison had noted it before him. It is, therefore, the interpretation advanced by Hutcheson which was borrowed with some modification by many writers – Turnbull, Hartley, Burke, Usher, "Estimate" Brown, and Reid.

Not until Hartley and, particularly, Hume give the theory of association vigorous and lucid exposition and application is the psychology maintained with any degree of strength by the leading critics. Hume and Hartley are responsible for the chief achievement of this psychological criticism, for it was their hypotheses and their associationist conception of human nature that superseded the classic dogmas of Aristotle as the authority for critical judgment and taste.

Hume has told how the succession of ideas in the imagination is governed by the principles of regular or "natural" association – resemblance, contrariety, and causality (which, we must remember, is really constant contiguity), – and upon these regular principles bases his rules for dramatic and epic structure. Like Hobbes, he has used this psychology of the imagination to reinforce a neoclassic conception of art; but, unlike Hobbes, he does not limit the imagination to the associated ideas in the memory. Hume distinguishes the imagination from the memory, and, for the first time, explains how the principles of association themselves control the movement of ideas in the artistic imagination. Hume's influence is seen best in the criticism of Kames, Gerard, Beattie, and Alison. All these critics use the uniformity and regularity of "naturally" associated ideas in the imagination, controlled by the associational laws of causality, resemblance, or contrast, as critical aids.

Hartley, however, uses only Locke's principle of contiguity in his theory of association. Believing that the imagination functions by means of contiguous associations of ideas, Hartley finds that taste, "the pleasures of imagination", is complex and is formed or acquired gradually by multitudinous chance associations of ideas. From his observation that certain associations of ideas are formed by almost everyone, he is enabled to deduce that general or universal associations of ideas form universal habits, customs, natures, or tastes. Thus, in Hartley, associationism has become the basis of a neoclassic uniformitarian assumption, the *consensus gentium*. Hurd, however, alone has preceded him in this uniformitarian notion; but Reynolds, Smith, Priestley, Beattie, Alison, all follow him by describing or listing the general and customary associations of ideas made in the minds of men and showing how these associations may be the sources of a universally uniformitarian esthetic taste.

The associationist approach to criticism reaches the peak of its glory in the rich forty-year period past the mid-century, especially in the critical works of Gerard, Kames, Priestley, Beattie, and Alison. In this period of the history of associationist critical theory, the influence of Hume and Hartley is obviously paramount. It is only after Priestley and Alison, and such other disciples of Hartley as Bentham and Godwin, that Hume's star was eclipsed by that of Hartley.

On the basis of this brief outline of associationist criticism, a few generalizations may be hazarded. – In the early history of its development, Addison and, more particularly, Hutcheson are notable for their use of the psychology as the explanation of diversity in taste and divergencies from neoclassic ideals. But in the later period of its evolution, and with the unacknowledged example of Hobbes before them, the major figures – Hume, Hartley, Kames, Gerard, Beattie, and Alison – use it to reinforce reigning neoclassic critical theories. Finally, in Alison, at the end of the century, the subjectivism inherent in the theory also becomes dominant. In Alison's conception of the imaginative effect may be found an explanation of the romantic experience and a transition to the nineteenth century.

While the meaning of the term "association of ideas" remained constant throughout the century, evidently its critical significance varied at different stages of the changes in taste and critical theory. An attempt, therefore, to search out a single thread of development leads to one grave fallacy. However esthetically pleasing and neat these generalizations may appear, in effect they oversimplify and narrow the real complexity of this psychological criticism, and do not satisfactorily square with all the facts. For example, what may be underestimated or ignored is the fact that the psychology confirms opposing points of view and conflicting attitudes. As we have seen, even in the same writer, such as Hartley, Priestley, or Alison, uniformitarian and diversitarian, or neoclassic and romantic strains are equally maintained. It must, consequently, be always remembered that the several critical extensions given the psychology reflect the diverse personalities of writers and the constant flux of changing taste and critical theory in the century. If the pitfalls of a simple interpretation are to be avoided, associationist criticism must be seen against this background.

Omitting, however, the difficult problem of personality, we shall turn our attention to the many important concepts that formed the critical milieu. Upon résumé it is plain that the associationist approach is diffused through practically all the distinctive features and often unresolved opposites of eighteenth-century critical theory:

1. *The imagination.* The theory of imaginative invention that this psychology has evolved definitely moves away from the traditional classic ideas of imitation. The analysis of the plastic imagination upon which genius and the poetic process depend, together with that of the passive imagination upon which the esthetic response and taste depend, is a major contribution of the associationist approach. The views held by Hobbes, Addison, Hutcheson, Hume, Akenside, Hartley, Gerard, Beattie, and Alison, are the props of that strong tradition of the mechanical imagination operating by unthinking laws of association to which Coleridge objected. This associationist conception of the imagination was familiar to Coleridge as the mechanical fancy.[2]

[2] Cf. *Biographia Literaria,* ed. Shawcross (Oxford, 1907), I, 202 (Ch. xiii): "But equally with the ordinary memory the Fancy must receive all its materials ready made from the law of association."

2. *Opposition: Internal sense and reason.* But even in the eighteenth century, some writers strenuously objected to the theory of association. Burke and Usher assert that an immediate and intuitive sense of beauty reacts to objects before any associations can possibly be made. All associations, they claim, can only be secondary to this primary sense of beauty. Their point of view, derived from the theory of taste and the internal senses held by Shaftesbury and Hutcheson, certainly *resembles* the conception of the imagination broached by Coleridge. Other objections are raised by Vicesimus Knox and Thomas Reid. From the standpoint of Shaftesbury and the cultured man of taste, Knox objects to the introduction of philosophy into criticism. Reid, however, deems the mechanical and associationist conception of the mind irrational and absurd.

3. *Taste.* The psychology of association is used in a variety of ways to explain the formation of taste for beauty, sublimity, music, nature, architecture, painting, gardening, ruins, and the picturesque. Discussions of the associationist influences upon these aspects of taste may be found in Dennis, Gay, Turnbull, Akenside, Baillie, Hume, Hartley, Burke, Shenstone, Reynolds, Smith, Gerard, Kames, Knox, Blair, Priestley, Beattie, and Alison.

4. *Diversitarianism.* The germ of the diversitarian or relative point of view may be found in Locke's analysis of associations. But diverse standards of taste, founded on the diversity of associational effects and principles, are also explained by Hobbes. Addison, Hutcheson, Turnbull, Baillie, Hartley, Burke, Shenstone, Brown, Gerard, Priestley, Beattie, and Alison, – all develop more or less successfully and with varying degrees of sympathy this anti-classical principle. It would seem, then, that diversity is the necessary complement of the subjectivism inherent in the associationist approach.

5. *Uniformitarianism.* But that this is not true is indicated by the many uniformitarian theories of criticism based upon the association of ideas. The dogma that preached the similarity of human nature the world over and from the beginning

of time often turned for support to the general and usual associations of ideas joined in the minds of men. These universal, albeit subjective, associations are obviously modern adaptations of the neoclassic assumption, *consensus gentium.* This modern interpretation is given by Hurd, Hartley, Reynolds, Smith, Gerard, Kames, Priestley, and Alison.

6. *Human nature as an esthetic norm.* The associationist conception of human nature, that is to say, the way the mind "naturally" or probably associates ideas under various conditions is used as a norm for criticism by Hume, Hurd, Gerard, Kames, George Campbell, Priestley, Beattie, and Alison. Thus, as it began to be felt that the requirements of associationist human nature must never be ignored, associationism quickly invaded literary criticism: (a) *Metaphors, similes, and poetic ornaments.* The propriety and the formation of figures of speech are discussed with respect to associationist nature by Hobbes, Dennis, Hurd, Turnbull, Baillie, Blair, and Priestley. (b) *Unity of action, verisimilitude, and distinction of genres.* The unity or uniformity of associated ideas is imbedded in Hobbes's theory; but there it is undeveloped critically. The associationist approach to neoclassic structural norms is first clearly made by Hume; and his neoclassic adaptations of unity of action are followed with further extensions to verisimilitude and the doctrine of the distinction of genres by Gerard, Kames, Priestley, and Alison. (c) *Decorum and Shakespeare's characters.* The proper or "natural" course of ideas in the minds of characters during special dramatic situations also becomes a standard, especially for judging the psychological accuracy of Shakespeare's dialogue. This standard, which may be called psychological realism, makes its first appearance in literary criticism in the latter half of the century. That art must conform to this standard, that ideas must not be in incongruous association, is maintained by Gerard, Kames, Priestley, Beattie, and, in a minor degree, by William Richardson.

7. *Subjectivism.* Underlying all these critical applications of the associationist psychology is the subjective point of view, the doctrine of effects. Whether the regularity and uniformity

or the variety and diversity of associational experience are emphasized, whether a neoclassic or a romantic point of view is evolved, the experience of the imagination remains the professed standard of the arts. This empirical criterion derived from the contemporary psychology disregards all authority, especially ancient critics and models, and lays stress only on the effectiveness of a work of art. Subjectivism, the appeal to experience, may be considered as the common denominator of the associationist approach to eighteenth-century critical theory.

That the achievements of the associationist approach are complex as well as considerable can hardly be denied. In one form or another, the psychology penetrated the thought of almost every notable critic of the century. Certainly, after reckoning the weight of a hundred years' evidence, Walter Whiter's boast in 1794 can only cause a smile for its ingenuousness, vanity, or ignorance.

> In the Attempt to Explain and Illustrate Various Passages On a New Principle of Criticism; I have endeavoured to unfold the secret and subtle operations of genius from the most indubitable doctrine in the theory of metaphysics [the association of ideas]. As these powers of the imagination have never, I believe, been adequately conceived, or systematically discussed; I may perhaps be permitted, on this occasion, to adopt the language of science and to assume the merit of Discovery.[3]

There is, however, some originality in Whiter's researches, despite the fact that the principle of criticism he uses had been developed long before. Credit must be given him for being the first to attempt the examination of the way in which Shakespeare's imagination unconsciously functioned in

[3] *A Specimen of A Commentary on Shakespeare. Containing I. Notes on As You Like It. II. An Attempt to Explain and Illustrate Various Passages, On a New Principle of Criticism, Derived from Mr. Locke's Doctrine of the Association of Ideas* (London, 1794), pp. vi-vii. His assertion (p. 63) that the theory has never "been systematically discussed as a point of taste, or as a subject of criticism", obviously has no basis in fact.

Elizabethan and Stuart days and to apply the results of his researches to textual studies. In effect, he has joined Thomas Warton's historical point of view with John Locke's associationist psychology. Whiter's methods are expressive of the unmistakably modern flavor of all eighteenth-century associationist criticism. Precisely the modernity of this psychological method is so striking and so surprising to readers accustomed to think of eighteenth-century criticism in terms of simple and rigid formulas and of unsystematic provisions for such irrational exceptions as grace and sublimity. Whiter's complex psychological criticism is prophetic of John Livingston Lowes's *Road to Xanadu* (1927); it is the reverse of Charles Gildon's *Laws of Poetry* (1721). What Whiter says of himself applies as well to all associationist critics: "To the ordinary resources of the critic we have applied an additional confirmation, derived from the most indubitable principle in the doctrine of metaphysics".[4]

The prevalence of the associationist approach proves that eighteenth-century critics have formulated a theory of criticism more complex than we had been given to believe, and in its best applications a theory to which writers today may subscribe with few apologies.

[4] P. 73.

BIBLIOGRAPHY

An enquiry into the origin of the human appetites and affections, showing how each arises from association (Lincoln, 1747).

An introduction towards an essay on the origin of the passions, in which it is endeavored to be shown they are all acquired, and that they are no other than associations of ideas of our own making, or what we learn of others (London, 1741).

Encyclopaedia Britannica (Edinburgh, 1771).

The history of the works of the learned, VIII (1706); XI, (1709).

Addison, Joseph, *The spectator,* ed. G. Gregory Smith (Everyman Library, 1907).

Akenside, Mark, *The poetical works of Mark Akenside,* ed. A. Dyce (Boston, 1875). [First ed. 1845.]

Aldridge, Alfred O., "The eclecticism of Mark Akenside's 'The Pleasures of Imagination' ", *JHI,* V (1944), 292-314.

—, "Akenside and Imagination", *SP,* XLII (1945), 769-792.

Alison, Archibald, *Essays on the nature and principles of taste* (Edinburgh, 1790).

Arbuckle, James, *Hibernicus's letters* (London, 1734). [First. ed. 1729.]

Babcock, Robert W., *The genesis of Shakespeare idolatry, 1766-1799: a study of English criticism of the late eighteenth century* (Chapel Hill, 1931).

—, "The idea of taste in the eigheenth century", *PMLA,* L (1935), 922-6.

Baillie, John, *An essay on the sublime* (London, 1747).

Beattie, James *The works of James Beattie* (Philadelphia, 1809).

—, *Dissertations moral and critical* (Dublin, 1783).

—, *Elements of moral science* (Edinburgh, 1790).

Beatty, Arthur, *William Wordsworth his doctrine and art in their historical relations* (Madison, 1927). [First ed. 1922.]

Belsham, William, *Essays, philosophical, historical, and literary* (London, 1789-1791).

Berkeley, George, *The Works of George Berkeley,* ed. Alexander Fraser (Oxford, 1901).

Blair, Hugh, *A critical dissertation on the poems of Ossian,* reprinted in *The poems of Ossian* (London, 1803). [First ed. 1763.]

—, *Lectures on rhetoric and belles lettres* (Philadelphia, 1850). [First ed. 1783.]

Bond, Donald F., " 'Distrust' of the imagination in English neoclassicism", *PQ,* XIV (1935), 54-69.

—, "The neoclassic psychology of the imagination", *ELH,* IV (1937), 245-64.

Bosker, Aisso, *Literary criticism in the age of Johnson* (The Hague, 1930).

Brett, George S., *A history of psychology* (London, 1921).

Brett, R. L., "The third earl of Shaftesbury as a literary critic", *MLR,* XXXVII (1942), 131-46.

Brown, John, *A dissertation on the rise, union, and power, the progressions, separations, and corruptions of poetry and music* (London, 1763).

Burke, Edmond, *A vindication of natural society,* reprinted in *Fugitive pieces.* Ed. R. Dodsley (London, 1761). [First ed. 1756.]

—, *A philosophical enquiry into the origin of our ideas of the sublime and beautiful* (London, 1798). [First ed. 1757.]

Burns, Robert, *The letters of Robert Burns,* ed. Francis H. Allen (Boston and New York, 1927).

Campbell, George, *The philosophy of rhetoric* (New York, 1875). [First ed. 1776.]

Chambers, Ephraim, *Cyclopaedia* (London, 1741). [First ed. 1727.]

Chase, Isabel W. U., *Horace Walpole: Gardenist* (Princeton, 1943).

Cooper, Anthony Ashley, Third Earl of Shaftesbury. *Characteristicks of Men, Manners, Opinions, Times* (London, 1731). [First ed. 1711.]

Cooper, John Gilbert, *The power of harmony,* reprinted in *The works of the English poets,* ed. Alexander Chalmers (London, 1810), Vol. XV [First ed. 1745.]

Crane, Ronald, "Anglican apologetics and the idea of progress", *MP,* XXXI (1934), 273-306, 349-82.

Dennis, John, *The critical works of John Dennis,* ed. Edward N. Hooker (Baltimore, 1939-1943).

Dryden, John, *Essays of John Dryden,* ed. W. P. Ker (Oxford, 1900).

Duff, William, *An essay on original genius* (London, 1767).

Durham, Willard H., *Critical essays of the eighteenth century, 1700-1725* (New Haven, 1915).

Fordyce, David, *The elements of moral philosophy,* first published in *The preceptor,* ed. R. Dodsley (London, 1748), II, 241-379.

Gay, John, "Preliminary dissertation concerning the fundamental principle of virtue or morality", prefixed to Edward Law's translation of William King's *Origin of evil* (Cambridge, 1739) [First ed. 1731.]

Gerard, Alexander, *An essay on taste* (Edinburgh, 1780). [First ed. 1759.]

—, *An essay on genius* (London, 1774).

Gilbert, Katherine E. and Helmut Kuhn, *A history of esthetics* (New York, 1939).

Halévy, Elie, *The growth of philosophic radicalism* (New York, 1928). [First ed. 1900.]

Hamm, Victor M., "Addison and the pleasures of the imagination", *MLN,* LII (1937), 498-500.

Hammond, W. A., *Aristotle's psychology* (London, 1902).

Hartley, David, *Observations on man; his frame, his duty, and his expectations* (London, 1749).

Hobbes, Thomas, *The English works of Thomas Hobbes of Malmesbury,* ed. Sir William Molesworth (London, 1839-45).

—, *Answer to Davenant,* reprinted in *Critical essays of the seventeenth century,* ed. J. E. Spingarn (Oxford, 1908). [First. ed. 1650.]

Home, Henry, Lord Kames, *Elements of criticism* (Edinburgh, 1769). [First ed. 1762.]

Hooker, Edward N., "The discussion of taste from 1750 to 1770 and the new trends in literary criticism", *PMLA,* XLIX (1934), 577-92.

Hume, David, *The philosophical works of David Hume,* ed. T. H. Green and T. H. Grose (London, 1875).

—, *An abstract of a treatise of human nature,* ed. J. M. Keynes and P. Sraffa (London, 1938).

Hurd, Richard, *Q. Horatius Flaccus, epistolae ad Pisones et Augustum: with an English commentary and notes: to which are added critical dissertations* (London, 1766).

Hussey, Christopher, *The picturesque* (London, 1927).

Hutcheson, Francis, *An enquiry into the original of our ideas of beauty and virtue* (London, 1729). [First ed. 1725.]

—, *An essay on the nature and conduct of the passions and affections, with illustrations on the moral sense* (London, 1728).

—, *A system of moral philosophy* (London, 1755).

Kaufman, Paul, *Heralds of original genius. Essays in memory of Barrett Wendell* (Cambridge, 1926), pp. 189-217.

Knox, Vicesimus, *Essays moral and literary* (London, 1787).

Laurie, Henry, *Scottish philosophy in its national development* (Glasgow, 1902).

Locke, John, *An essay concerning human understanding,* ed. Alexander C. Fraser (Oxford, 1894). [First ed. 1690.]

Lovejoy, Arthur O., "'Nature' as aesthetic norm", *MLN,* XLII (1927), 444-50.

MacLean, Kenneth, *John Locke and English literature of the eighteenth century* (New Haven, 1936).

Mason, John, *Self-knowledge* (Glasgow, 1839). [First ed. 1745.]

McCosh, James, *The Scottish Philosophy* (London, 1875).

McKenzie, Gordon, *Lord Kames and the mechanist tradition Essays and studies, University of California publications in English* (Berkeley and Los Angeles, 1943), pp. 93-121.

Monk, Samuel H., *The sublime; a study of critical theories in eighteenth-century England* (New York, 1935).

Morgann, Maurice, *An essay on the dramatic character of Sir John Falstaff,* ed. William A. Gill (London, 1912) [First ed. 1777.]

Ogilvie, John, *Philosophical and critical observations on the nature, characters, and various species of composition* (London, 1774).

Parr, Samuel, *Metaphysical tracts of English philosophers of the eighteenth century* (London, 1837).

Paul, H. G., *John Dennis: his life and criticism* (New York, 1911).

Percival, Thomas, *Moral and literary dissertations* (Philadelphia, 1806). [First ed. 1784.]

Pope, Alexander, *The works of Alexander Pope,* ed. Whitwell Elwin and William J. Courthope (London, 1886).

Priestley, Joseph, *A course of lectures on oratory and criticism* (London, 1777).

—, *An examination of Dr. Reid's inquiry* (London, 1775). [First ed. 1774.]

—, *Hartley's theory of the human mind* (London, 1790). [First ed. 1775.]

—, *Letters to a philosophical unbeliever* (Birmingham, 1787).

Rand, Benjamin, "The early development of Hartley's doctrine of association", *Psychological Review,* XXX (1923), 306-20.

Randall, Helen W., *The critical theory of Lord Kames* (Northampton, Mass., 1944).

Reid, Thomas, *The works of Thomas Reid,* ed. Sir William Hamilton (Edinburgh, 1872).

Reynolds, Joshua, *The literary works of Sir Joshua Reynolds* (London, 1851).

—, *Letters of Sir Joshua Reynolds,* ed. F. W. Hilles (Cambridge, Mass., 1929).

Richardson, William, *Essays on some of Shakespeare's dramatic characters* (London, 1797). [First ed. under different title: *A philosophical analysis and illustration of some of Shakespeare's dramatic characters,* 1774.]

Robbins, David O., "The aesthetics of Thomas Reid", *Journal of aesthetics and art criticism,* No. 5 (1942), 30-41.

Ruffhead, Owen, *The life of Alexander Pope* (London, 1769).

St. John, Henry, Lord Bolingbroke, *The works of the late honorable Henry St. John, Lord Viscount Bolingbroke* (Dublin, 1793). [First ed. 1754.]

Saintsbury, George, *A history of criticism and literary taste in Europe* (Edinburgh and London, 1900-1904).

Sharpe, William, *A dissertation upon genius* (London, 1755).

Shenstone, William, *The works, in verse and prose, of William Shenstone* (London, 1773). [First ed. 1764.]

—, *Letters of William Shenstone,* ed. Duncan Mallam (Minneapolis, 1939).

Smith, Adam, *The theory of moral sentiments* (London, 1892). [First ed. 1759.]

Smith, Andrew Cannon, *Theories of the nature and standard of taste in England, 1700-1790* (Chicago, 1937).

Spence, Joseph, *Crito: or a dialogue on beauty.* Reprinted in *Fugitive pieces,* ed. R. Dodsley (London, 1761). [First ed. 1752.]

Sperry, Willard L., *Wordsworth's anti-climax* (Cambridge, Mass., 1935).

Spingarn, Joel E., *Critical essays of the seventeenth century* (Oxford, 1908).

Taylor, Harold, "Hume's theory of imagination", *University of Toronto Quarterly,* XII (1942-3), 180-90.

Taylor, Tom and C. R. Leslie, *The life and times of Sir Joshua Reynolds* (London, 1865).

Thorpe, Clarence De Witt, "Addison and Hutcheson on the imagination", *ELH,* II (1935), 215-34.

—, *The aesthetic theory of Thomas Hobbes* (Ann Arbor, Mich., 1940).

Tucker, Abraham, *The light of nature pursued* (London, 1805). [First ed. 1768.]

Turnbull, George, *The principles of moral philosophy* (London, 1740).

Usher, James, *Clio: or a discourse on taste* (London, 1769). [First ed. 1767.]

Warren, Howard C., *A history of the association psychology from Hartley to Lewes* (Baltimore, 1921).

—, "Mental association from Plato to Hume", *Psychological Review*, XXIII (1916), 208-30.

Watts, Isaac, *Logick: or the right use of reason* (London, 1772). [First ed. 1725.]

—, *Philosophical Essays* (London, 1742). [First ed. 1733.]

—, *The works of Isaac Watts* (London, 1813).

Webb, Daniel, *Observations on the correspondence between poetry and music* (London, 1769).

Wecter, Dixon, "Burke's theory of words, images, and emotion", *PMLA*, LV (1940), 167-81.

Whiter, Walter, *A specimen of a commentary on Shakespeare* (London, 1794).

Whitney, Lois, *Primitivism and the idea of progress in English popular literature of the eighteenth century* (Baltimore, 1934).

Willey, Basil, *The eighteenth century background* (London, 1940).

INDEX OF NAMES

INDEX